Vocabulary Plus K-8

A Source-Based Approach

ALLEEN PACE NILSEN

DON L. F. NILSEN

Arizona State University

PEARSON

Boston   New York   San Francisco
Mexico City   Montreal   Toronto   London   Madrid   Munich   Paris
Hong Kong   Singapore   Tokyo   Cape Town   Sydney

*To our grandchildren who constantly remind us
of the richness of language play:*

*Taryn, Britton, Kami, and Erich
David, Lauren, Michael, and Jenna
Jim and Luke*

Series Editor: *Aurora Martínez Ramos*
Series Editorial Assistant: *Katie Freddoso*
Senior Marketing Manager: *Elizabeth Fogarty*
Composition Buyer: *Linda Cox*
Manufacturing Buyer: *Andrew Turso*
Editorial-Production Administrator: *Karen Mason*
Editorial-Production Services: *Walsh & Associates, Inc.*
Cover Administrator: *Joel Gendron*
Electronic Composition: *Ellen Pettengell*
Cover Designer: *Jenny Hart*

For related titles and support materials, visit our online catalog at www.ablongman.com

Library of Congress Cataloging-in-Publication Data

Nilsen, Alleen Pace.
    Vocabulary plus K-8 : a source-based approach / Alleen Pace Nilsen, Don L. F. Nilsen.
      p. cm.
    Includes bibliographical references and index.
    ISBN 0-205-39318-7
    1. Vocabulary–Study and teaching (Elementary)–United States. 2. Reading comprehension (Elementary)–United States. 3. Semantics. I. Nilsen, Don Lee Fred. II. Title.

LB1574.5.N55 2004
372.44–dc21

    2003043650

Printed in the United States of America

10 9 8 7 6 5 4 3 2 1   09 08 07 06 05 04 03

Photo credits: p. 16 by Candelyn McCall; all others by A. P. Nilsen.

Contents

Preface ix

CHAPTER ONE

Introduction 1

What Is a Source-Based Approach? 1
A Process or Generative Approach 1
An Emphasis on Real-World Relationships 2
An Explanation of Morphology 2
A Broad Definition of Metaphor 3

Distinguishing between Puns and Metaphors and Why It Matters 5

Pedagogical Principles 9
Children Need Time to Absorb the Meanings 9
Right Answers Are Better Than Wrong Answers 9
Children Learn Best When They Can Make Connections and Learn Things in Sets 10
Speaking Is More Basic Than Writing 10
Children Are Social Animals Who Teach Each Other 11
Multisensory Experiences Are Valuable 11
Many Children Enjoy Making Lists Whereas They Hate Writing Full Sentences 12

A Note to College Instructors and Leaders of Workshops 13

A Note to Teachers of Primary-Grade Children 15

CHAPTER TWO

Plants and Animals 16

Background Reading for the Teacher 16

Notes to Help Teachers Elicit Ideas from Students 17

Workshops
2.1 Straws and Sticks 19
2.2 The Language of Farming 21
2.3 Actions of Plants 23
2.4 Shape versus Action 25
2.5 Features of Animal Words 26
2.6 Heads You Win, Tails You Lose 29

2.7 Animal Metaphors 30

2.8 An Animal Crossword Puzzle 31

End-of-Chapter Activities 32

CHAPTER THREE

Human Body Parts and Actions 33

Background Reading for the Teacher 33

Notes to Help Teachers Elicit Ideas from Students 34

Workshops

3.1 Animal versus Human Heads 37

3.2 Hand It Over 38

3.3 From Metaphorical to Literal 41

3.4 A Leg Up 42

3.5 Exploring Analogies 44

3.6 Moving Our Bodies 45

3.7 Hostile Actions 48

3.8 Survival Actions 50

3.9 An Action-Packed Crossword Puzzle 51

End-of-Chapter Activities 52

CHAPTER FOUR

Letters, Shapes, and Numbers 54

Background Reading for the Teacher 54

Notes to Help Teachers Elicit Ideas from Students 55

Workshops

4.1 Fill in the Letter Blanks 57

4.2 Letters—Shapes versus Initials or Rankings 59

4.3 Circles, Rings, Rounds, and Loops 60

4.4 Lines and Angles 62

4.5 As Easy as One, Two, Three 64

4.6 Foreign Number Words 67

4.7 Approximate versus Exact 70

4.8 Unusual Uses of Number Words 71

End-of-Chapter Activities 73

CHAPTER FIVE

Food 74

Background Reading for the Teacher 74

Notes to Help Teachers Elicit Ideas from Students 76

Workshops

5.1 Fruits and Vegetables 77

5.2 Baked and Cooked Food 80

5.3 Eggs, Meat, and Milk 83

5.4 Literal versus Metaphorical 85

5.5 What's Cooking? 86

5.6 Make a Metaphor Sandwich 87

5.7 Food as Sources and Targets of Metaphors 89

5.8 Illustrate the Menus 90

End-of-Chapter Activities 91

CHAPTER SIX

Containers and Shelters 93

Background Reading for the Teacher 93

Notes to Help Teachers Elicit Ideas from Students 94

Workshops

6.1 Holding the Bag—from Literal to Metaphorical 96

6.2 From Literal to Metaphorical 99

6.3 Containers in the Home 100

6.4 The Relative Sizes of Food 102

6.5 Shelters 104

6.6 Human versus Animal Shelters 108

6.7 A Container Crossword Puzzle 109

End-of-Chapter Activities 110

CHAPTER SEVEN

Clothing 111

Background Reading for the Teacher 111

Notes to Help Teachers Elicit Ideas from Students 112

Workshops

7.1 Clothing as Metaphorical Targets 113

7.2 Hats Off 115

7.3 From Rags to Riches 117

7.4 To Sew a Fine Seam 119

7.5 A Sewing-Related Crossword Puzzle 124

End-of-Chapter Activities 125

CHAPTER EIGHT

Earth and Sky, Water and Fire 126

Background Reading for the Teacher 126

Notes to Help Teachers Elicit Ideas from Students 126

Workshops

8.1 Down to Earth 129

8.12 Geological Formations 131

8.3 Words from the Sky 135

8.4 Weather-Related Words 137

8.5 Two Kinds of Light 139

8.6 Water Words 140

8.7 More Water-Related Words 141

8.8 Fire-Related Words 145

8.9 A Fiery Crossword Puzzle 148

End-of-Chapter Activities 149

CHAPTER NINE

Tools, Jobs, and Equipment 151

Background Reading for the Teacher 151

Notes to Help Teachers Elicit Ideas from Children 152

Workshops

9.1 Hammers as Sources and Targets of Metaphors 154
9.2 Tools from Basic to Metaphorical 156
9.3 On the Cutting Edge with *s, c, sh,* and *ch* 159
9.4 Bigger and Stronger 161
9.5 Job-Related Surnames 165
9.6 Jobs with Expanded Names 166
9.7 A Tool Crossword Puzzle 169

End-of-Chapter Activities 170

CHAPTER TEN

Sports, Games, and Travel 171

Background Reading for the Teacher 171

Notes to Help Teachers Elicit Ideas from Students 173

Workshops

10.1 Play Ball 175
10.2 A Variety of Sports and Games 176
10.3 *Check, Game,* and *Play* 178
10.4 Earth, Water, or Air 180
10.5 Drivers, Pilots, Helmsmen, and Engineers 181
10.6 The Paths You Take 183
10.7 The Conveyances You Use 185
10.8 The Long Reach of *Tele* 187
10.9 A Sports-Related Crossword Puzzle 189

End-of-Chapter Activities 190

CHAPTER ELEVEN

Sounds and Music 192

Background Reading for the Teacher 192

Notes to Help Teachers Elicit Ideas from Students 194

Workshops

11.1 Bells 195
11.2 Whistles 197
11.3 The Human Voice 198
11.4 Bands and Orchestras 201
11.5 A Musical Crossword Puzzle 205

End-of-Chapter Activities 206

www.ablongman.com/nilsen

CHAPTER TWELVE

Mythology and Names 208

Background Reading for the Teacher 208

Notes to Help Teachers Elicit Ideas from Students 210

Workshops

12.1 Words from the Myths 212

12.2 Multiple Words 215

12.3 Eponyms from Real People 218

12.4 Eponyms from Places 219

12.5 A Mythological Crossword Puzzle 221

End-of-Chapter Activities 222

Bibliography 223

Index 226

Preface

Both of us have been working on the concept of metaphors and language throughout our careers at Arizona State University—Don with his students in linguistics and Alleen with her students in English Education. We decided to do some serious work with the teaching of vocabulary when Alleen had the opportunity to take a sabbatical leave in the spring and summer of 2001. We thank ASU for providing this opportunity for uninterrupted work, and we also thank ASU colleagues for their help: James Blasingame, Marysia Johnson, Mary Jones, and Kristen La Rue.

We offer a special thanks to teachers in the Phoenix area who let us come and work in their classes. These include Diana Dwyer, Janis Huerbsch, and Nicole Ainsworth at McClintock High School in Tempe; Andrea Low and Gail Spiegel in Pueblo Middle School in Scottsdale; and Micaela Muñoz at Fees Intermediate School in Tempe. Others who assisted us in working with younger children include Laurie Brown and Marilyn Brown, and family members: Rayna Larson, Nikki Wickman, Candelyn McCall, and Britton Nilsen. We also thank our ASU students who over three semesters helped us find information and polish our presentation. Lastly, we thank our editor Aurora Martínez Ramos and the reviewers: Leif Fearn, San Diego State University; Eileen E. Moore, Birmingham-Southern College; and Mary-Catherine Sableski, University of Dayton/Kettering City Schools. We are grateful to all these people for the helpful suggestions they made, and we humbly take blame for any errors that remain.

Alleen Pace Nilsen
Don L. F. Nilsen

CHAPTER ONE

Introduction

What Is a Source-Based Approach?

A source-based approach starts with basic words that have been part of English for as long as anyone can remember. These are the words that speakers created to talk about their own bodies, the plants and animals they interacted with, the food they ate, the clothes they wore, the containers and other tools they made, and the many different aspects of the earth and the sky as they were observed. We take the words that have long been used for these basic concepts and work with students to explore them to see how they have evolved and changed. We will start by describing some of the characteristics and benefits of a source-based approach.

A PROCESS OR GENERATIVE APPROACH

A source-based approach follows the ways that both individuals and cultures develop language in moving from the known to the unknown, from the simple to the complex, and from the literal to the metaphorical. This approach taps into the collective unconscious, because it starts with the concepts that have served as the foundations on which many other words have been built. As students and teachers work with variations of words, they will become adept at figuring out the meanings of words they have not seen before, a skill that in today's fast-moving and high-tech "global village" is increasingly important. We hope that users of this book will inductively learn:

- How English is enriched by words from other languages.
- How basic words carry dozens of meanings.
- How the meanings of words move from literal to figurative.
- How words follow regular patterns as they acquire new meanings.

We are quick to caution students that tracing the histories of words and their connections will not "prove" the meaning of any particular word as it is used today. However, knowing earlier meanings of words can provide valuable insights. For example, when a sixth grader told us that *managers* are supposed to be men because "it says *man* right in the word," we were happy to lead the class, over two or three days, on a search for words that have come into English from the Latin *manus*, meaning hand.

We were probably more surprised than were the students at how many direct connections we found. Our biggest surprise was discovering that the word *emancipate* means something like "being freed from the hands of someone else." Clearer examples include the way that *manuals* are also called *handbooks;* a *manuscript* is prepared by *hand* as opposed to being published or printed on a press; to *manacle* prisoners is to *handcuff* them, a *manicurist* takes care of people's *hands*, while the *manual alphabet* allows people who are deaf to communicate through fingerspelling. After hearing these examples, the class was more willing to believe that *manual training*, the *manual arts*, and *manual labor* all relate to people's—either male or female's—developing skills with their hands and that a *manager* is someone who *handles* the affairs of a business.

The students were also interested to learn how words change meanings based on different conditions. In the 1500s, when the term *manufacture* came into the language, it meant *made by hand* as opposed to something grown or made by nature. But then the industrial revolution brought about the building of factories, and the term *manufacture* developed the new meaning of something made in a factory, most likely by a machine rather than *by hand*.

AN EMPHASIS ON REAL-WORLD RELATIONSHIPS

The words we teach have natural relationships, so that rather than teaching one word at a time, we are teaching sets of words. Because these words have grown out of basic concepts, even young children have a place to start in unlocking and learning the new concepts. Because the words are related, they can be taught in what are variously called *webs, gestalts,* or *ladders.*

These real-world relationships make it unnecessary to create the kind of mnemonic devices or "memory hooks" that frequently appear in vocabulary lessons where children are given alphabetical lists of words to "look up and memorize." Memory hooks that work for only a single word are inefficient, and they may actually be counterproductive if they are based on a coincidental surface structure (a pun) rather than on a metaphor that illustrates deep-structure meaning.

Another way that teachers try to help students learn meanings of words is to teach them in the context of whatever literature the class is reading. This is a distinct improvement over teaching random lists of words, but it too has problems. One is that the teacher focuses on the one meaning within the story, which leaves children unprepared the next time they meet the word in a different context. A source-based approach vividly illustrates the fact that most words have several meanings. Children need to know this if they are going to be able to follow their teachers' admonition "to use the context to figure out the meaning." In reality, context clues seldom provide a meaning; instead, these grammatical and semantic clues serve to exclude incompatible meanings. Children need at least some idea about the general meaning of a word before they can make use of what their teachers call *context clues*.

The second problem with this approach is that the one use of a particular word in a story probably does not provide students with enough varied experiences to motivate them to think about the word. In today's fast-paced world, students (just like their teachers) are accustomed to skimming and skipping over words they do not know. When they hear an explanation of a word's meaning, they think the purpose is just to help them get through the reading assignment. They need a variety of experiences with a word before their minds can absorb it and make it part of their own vocabulary. We hope that by the time teachers have finished studying and experiencing the activities in this book, they will be able to create their own source-based lessons for whatever words they need to teach.

AN EXPLANATION OF MORPHOLOGY

Thanks to computer graphics, students already know that to *morph* is to change. By bringing the language-related concept of *morphemes* and *morphology* to students, we will encourage them to look at words as a detective might. Even one or two familiar morphemes in a word can serve as the key that will unlock the meaning of an unfamiliar word. Morphemes are the smallest units of language that carry meaning, and the mixing and matching of morphemes is a key component of our approach.

In English, bound morphemes include such prefixes as *anti-, ambi-, co-, dis-, mal-, non-, pre-,* and *un-* and such suffixes as *-ed, -er, -ess, -ful, -ing, -s,* and *-y.* Free morphemes are those than can either stand alone or be used in combinations; for example, *any, berry, child, man, room,* and *way.* They are what are commonly called root words.

J. K. Rowling's *Harry Potter* books are a wonderful place to gain an appreciation of the power of mixing and matching morphemes. One reason that Rowling does not have to include a glossary of the many new words that she uses is that she creates them from morphemes familiar to readers. For example, the *portkey* that takes whoever is holding it to a specified place is made from the morphemes *port* and *key. Port* is seen in such nouns as *airport* and *seaport* and in such verbs as *import, export,* and *transport. Key* communicates the magic and the restrictive nature of the item as in a *key* that opens a door, a *keystone* that holds up an archway, and, more metaphorically, the Rosetta Stone, which served as the *key* to unlocking the Egyptian hieroglyphics.

The names Rowling gives to her charms are equally easy to figure out and remember. For example, *Lumos!,* a charm for bringing light, uses the same light-related morphemes as in *luminous, illuminate, luminary,* and *luminescence,* while *Impedimenta!* shares morphemes with *impediment* and *impede.* The *ped* morpheme comes from the Latin word for *foot,* so the literal meaning is similar to that in "tripping someone up" or "tying their feet."

A BROAD DEFINITION OF METAPHOR

We need to clarify that our definition of metaphor is broader than that used by many of our colleagues. We see metaphor as such a productive part of language change that we originally planned to use *metaphor* as part of this book's title. However, we found that the term made people think we were teaching poetry instead of the hard-working, everyday language that is the focus of our lessons.

Because children have smaller vocabularies than adults, they often resort to metaphorical inventions. The little girl who reports that her grandmother has "a map on her legs" (she has varicose veins) as well as the little boy who brings his mother a big weed and brags, "The whole earth had ahold of it!" were not purposely making metaphors. They were simply telling something new in relation to something old. This is what all of us do both as we create our own individual language and as we contribute to the language of whatever communities of speakers we belong to. Metaphors give us the ability to use a finite number of sounds and words to communicate about a nonfinite world. More than a hundred years ago, Ralph Waldo Emerson explained in his "Nature" essay:

> Every word, which is used to express a moral or intellectual fact, if traced to its root, is found to be borrowed from some material appearance. *Right* means *straight, wrong* means *twisted. Spirit* primarily means *wind; transgression,* the crossing of a line, *supercilious,* the raising of the eyebrow.... As we go back in history, language becomes more picturesque, until in its infancy, when it is all poetry.

Emerson's idea is a key to much of what this book is about, but we nevertheless decided to use the term *source-based* rather than *metaphor* because, contrary to popular opinion, it is not easy to determine the point at which a particular usage leaves the literal and becomes metaphorical.

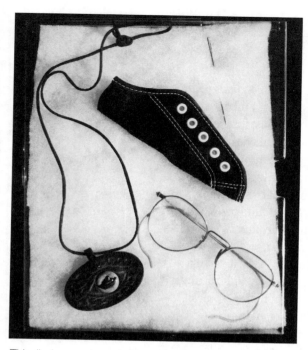

This display case is made from a heavy-duty acrylic box that started life as a cover on a computer manual. A thick piece of quilt batting keeps the items from falling out.

For example, a standard desk dictionary includes four columns of *water* words. We consider most of these to be lexical extensions because they are connected in some way to water as in *water meter, water bottle, water lily, water ski,* and *water tight.* The animal identified as a *water rat* is a lexical extension, but when *water rat* or *wharf rat* is applied to a person who hangs around beaches and wharves engaging in petty thievery, we identify the term as a metaphor. The word *watermelon* comes somewhere in between a lexical extension and a metaphor because, while a watermelon is juicy, it did not grow in water like a *water lily* nor is it filled with actual water like a *water bottle.*

As students will learn in Workshop 8.7, *watered stock* is another example of a phrase that comes somewhere between literal and metaphorical. In the days of the great western cattle drives, it referred to the common practice of taking herds of cattle to rivers or ponds just before they got to the stockyards. The thirsty cows would drink and absorb pounds of water and hence bring more money when they were weighed in. Today *watered stock* is more likely to be company shares whose worth has been artificially inflated when sold on the stock market. The meaning is similar to that in such a metaphorical phrase as *a watered-down* course. Because of such instances, we usually hedge by asking students to rank terms from more literal to more metaphorical.

The items in the acrylic box that we use to demonstrate *eye* words are fairly typical in demonstrating different degrees of metaphor. We say that the *eyeglasses* are clearly a lexical extension in being something connected to or used by the human eye. We say that the *eye of a needle* and the *eyelets* in the sneaker come closer to being metaphorical. They are like *windows* (wind-eyes), based on the common feature of a hole. The necklace is tooled leather that we bought at the House of Humour and Satire in Bulgaria. The eye on it is clearly meant to be metaphorical or even symbolic. It is similar to the *all-seeing eye* that appears at the top of the pyramid on U.S. dollar bills.

We treat all of these, except for the *eyeglasses*, as metaphors. However, other linguists might prefer to talk about the difference between these two uses as a matter of *polysemy* (many senses). They would say that the two uses are simply focusing on a different sense of the same word. We agree, but given the problems we have had in convincing people that we need to teach the concepts of morphemes and metaphors to children, we decided to simplify matters by including polysemy as a subcategory of metaphor.

We also include *similes* as a subcategory of metaphors. As we approached different teachers to see if we could come and try out our lessons in their classrooms, more than one asked us to refresh their memories over the difference between metaphors and similes. For the record, a simile is softened a bit because the speaker uses *like* or *as* to make sure the listener understands that the message is metaphorical rather than literal. The distinction between sentences that include *like* or *as* and those that do not is a surface-structure distinction. Our focus is more on the deep structure of language. Linguistics (the study of language) can be divided into five overlapping, but in ways discrete, categories:

1. Phonology (the sounds of a language and how they are put together).

2. Morphology (the way words are made).

3. Syntax (the way sentences are put together).

4. Semantics (the way meanings are communicated).

5. Pragmatics (the practical, common-sense aspects, which are what teachers usually work with).

In this book, we are working mainly with morphology, semantics, and pragmatics. The importance that some people have attached to teaching children to distinguish between surface structures that contain *like* or *as* and those that do not come from a syntactic approach to language. From a semantic and pragmatic approach, the difference is less important.

Our informal observation from working with thousands of metaphors is that speakers are inclined to use *like* or *as* when they want to be sure that the listener recognizes the metaphorical nature of what they are saying, as in the commercial, "Cleans like a white tornado." People do not want a real tornado in their home, so the advertisers are careful to include a clue that the statement is metaphorical.

Whether a particular comparison will be stated as a metaphor or as a simile is in some way similar to the question of whether an *eponym* (a word taken from someone's name) will be capitalized. In the beginning, speakers capitalize the person's name and everyone recognizes the usage as "honoring" an individual. But as shown in Chapter 12, as eponyms become part of everyday speech, the capital letter often disappears and people forget how the word started. Something similar happens with similes, which gradually move over to become what some people call *idioms* or *dead metaphors*, a term we are not fond of, because as you will see throughout this book, such metaphors are very much alive.

Someone who noticed that a friend who had not had much sleep was puffy-eyed might have said, "You look as though you have bags under your eyes," or "It looks like you've got bags under your eyes." However, the comparison is so obvious that speakers, who are always looking for quicker and easier ways to say things, soon shortened the message to something like, "You've got *bags* under your eyes." In a similar way, people began saying things like, "His clothes are *baggy*," "She *let the cat out of the bag*," "When they all ran, I was *left holding the bag*," or even, "That soldier's *sandbagging*!" Although these are variously removed from the concept of *a bag*, they are each making a comparison and so, in our broad definition, they are included as metaphors.

Distinguishing between Puns and Metaphors and Why It Matters

Alvin Schwartz starts his book *Unriddling* (Lippincott, 1983) with a classic story about a girl imprisoned in a metal room with no windows or other openings. There was a locked door but no key. The furniture consisted of only a piano and a wooden table, along with a saw and a baseball bat that happened to be left in the room. The question is, How does the girl get out of the room?

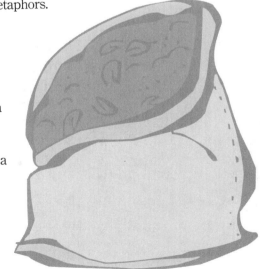

Schwartz explains that she is so smart that she figures out four different ways; readers can take their choice.

1. She uses the saw to cut the table in half. Since two halves make a whole, she crawls out through the hole.

2. She plays the piano until she finds the right key. Then she unlocks the door and lets herself out.

3. She swings the baseball bat three times. It's three strikes and she's out.

4. She runs around and around the room until she wears herself out.

As a bonanza to the joke, Schwartz says that when the girl is finally free, she shouts for joy so long and so hard that her voice becomes a little hoarse. So "she gets on the horse and rides away."

For the most part, the humor in this clever story is based on puns, words that sound the same but have different meanings. In at least two cases (*whole/hole* and *hoarse/horse*), the words are also spelled differently. English is filled with possibilities for puns because the language has something like 45 sounds and 26 letters, from which speakers have created a language that can refer to anything in the real world (past, present, or future) and anything in people's imaginations. This means that the same sounds have to do double duty. Because children like to play with language and with riddles, they are probably more aware of puns than are many adults. It is fine to encourage such language play, but we do a disservice to children if we do not help them learn to distinguish between puns, in which words accidentally sound alike, and metaphors, in which similar-sounding words have semantic or meaning relationships.

A few pages later in Schwartz's *Unriddling* book, he asks two other riddles. Notice how they differ from the one above in that they are based on metaphors.

Q I dig out tiny caves and store gold and silver in them. I also build bridges of silver and make crowns of gold. They are the smallest you could imagine. Sooner or later, everybody needs my help. Yet many people are afraid to let me help them. Who am I?

A A dentist.

Q I have a head, but I do not have eyes or ears. I foam at the mouth, but I never bite. I roar, but I have no tongue. I lie in a bed, but I have no back. I rise, I fall, I rush and run, but I have neither legs nor feet. I was born in the mountains, but I go down to the ocean whenever I can. I cannot keep still for a moment. I am restless as can be. What am I?

A A river.

Throughout this book, we work with metaphors rather than puns because we want to encourage children to use their brains to figure out true relationships. You can use these two sets of riddles with children to explore the difference between puns and metaphors. Encourage them to identify and to explain what is being alluded to in the riddles about the dentist and the river. What are the similarities between *caves* and *cavities*, between a *crown* on a king's head and a *crown on a tooth*, and between *bridges* that hold false teeth in place and the *bridges* that cross over canyons and rivers? The point to make about puns is that they are the exception rather than the rule. People laugh when they hear a pun because the coincidence of the similar sound surprises them. Two sets of children's picture books helped us get students to think about the differences

Students from first grade through college have fun looking at the puns and the metaphors in these books by Fred Gwynne and Peggy Parish.

between semantically and historically related words as opposed to those that sound alike just from coincidence. One is the *Amelia Bedelia* books (HarperCollins, beginning in 1963) by Peggy Parish, and the other is Fred Gwynne's books on word play (*A Chocolate Moose for Dinner, The King Who Rained,* and *A Little Pigeon Toad,* all distributed by Aladdin Paperbacks). Amelia Bedelia is a housemaid who always misinterprets Mrs. Rogers' directions, but no matter what mistakes she makes, her job is saved through her wonderful cooking. Fred Gwynne's books feature a little girl and the pictures she sees in her head when she hears adults talking.

We brought both sets to class thinking that Parish and Gwynne used a similar kind of wordplay. However, as we worked with the books and listened to students trying to explain the jokes to each other, we realized that Gwynne relies more heavily on puns or homonyms—words that are unrelated but happen to sound the same—while Parrish relies more heavily on polysemy—words that have different but related senses.

The *Amelia Bedelia* books gave students a new appreciation for how much speakers have to know about the real world as they interpret even such basic directions as "stamp these envelopes," "shorten these dresses," "pick up the conductor at the train station," and "practice a few numbers." In the first book of the series, *Amelia Bedelia*, Amelia tries valiantly to follow the directions left for her by her new employer. She "changes the towels" by cutting holes in them; she "dusts the furniture" by putting body powder all over the living room; she "draws the drapes" with a pencil and a sketch pad, she "puts out the lights" by hanging all the bulbs on the clothesline, she "trims the fat" from the steak by putting lace and bits of ribbon on it, and she "dresses the chicken" in baby clothes. Amelia makes her mistakes because she interprets statements literally instead of considering their extended or metaphorical meanings.

The humor in Fred Gwynne's books comes from his illustrations of what a little girl imagines when she hears about *fairy tails*, *boars* coming to dinner, the *foot prince* in the snow, children with *bear feet*, and the *train* that she is to carry at her sister's wedding.

However, some of Gwynne's puns are based on semantic relationships, and we were pleasantly surprised to find that young students were often more able than our college students to see the metaphorical relationships between a house getting *a coat of paint* and a person putting on a *coat*, between the shape of a swimming *pool* and the shape of a *pool table*, and between the actions of *pitching* a tent and *pitching* a ball. In Gwynne's *A Little Pigeon Toad*, at least one-fourth of the 21 puns included a semantic relationship:

- Mommy says trees have knots. (*Knots* in trees look as if they have been tied.)
- Daddy says city streets have manholes. (*Manholes* are made for men to climb into underground tunnels.)
- Daddy knows a man who fished for a giant hammerhead. (*Hammerhead sharks* are named because their heads resemble the shape of a hammer.)
- After dinner Mommy and Daddy are going to show their *slides*. (Photographic *slides* are named because of the way they slide into the projection slot.)
- Yarns like these are hard to swallow! (Stories, especially tall tales, are called *yarns* because of the way they *unravel* and *string listeners along*.)

Notice how often the different spellings are a clue that the words probably have no historical or semantic relationship as shown by the puns that Gwynne makes with such words as *moose/mousse, air/heir, sew/sow, pennants/penance, piers/peers, heal/heel,* and so on. The reason we want children to be able to distinguish between metaphors and puns is that with a metaphor they need to figure out the feature that is being highlighted so that they can understand the new meaning. The purpose of a pun is simply to surprise people with the coincidence of a word sounding as though it makes sense, when actually it doesn't, as with these three riddles:

Q What do you get when you cross a bee with a bell?

A A humdinger.

Q Why is it wrong to whisper?

A Because it isn't aloud.

Q How do you get down off an elephant?

A You don't. You get down off a goose or a duck.

Marilyn Bogusch Pryle, writing in the May 2000 *Voices from the Middle,* made a good point about how studying homonyms helps with reading because in most sets of two or three homonyms students already know one of the words. When they see the other words, they are pleased to realize that they know the pronunciation of such different looking words as *I'll, isle,* and *aisle; rot* and *wrought; chic* and *sheik; cache* and *cash;* and *offal* and *awful.* Having that head start, they are willing to go on and learn the pronunciations and the meanings of the other words in the sets. We agree with Pryle's idea, and also with the idea of bringing such games to class as Homonym Rummy, Concentration, and Go Fish Homonyms. But in relation to the vocabulary approach we take throughout this book, our main reason for wanting students to recognize homonyms is so that they will not confuse accidental puns with meaning-related metaphors.

Pedagogical Principles

CHILDREN NEED TIME TO ABSORB THE MEANINGS

Children need multiple exposures to new words through a variety of media. Our biggest challenge as teachers is to hold children's interest long enough that their minds have a chance to acquire (absorb rather than just memorize) the meanings of words. Because different children respond to different kinds of activities, we have used a variety of formats and activities in the workshops, and we encourage you to add your own creative ideas and interpretations.

Seeing words at the same time as hearing them is an extra help for students. One of our biggest successes was the word strips we made by typing key words and phrases on our computer in 36-point boldface capital letters, which we photocopied on card stock at twice their size. This gave us word strips large enough that they could be read from anywhere in a room. These word strips were such good teaching aids that we have included typed copies for Chapters 2 through 12 on our website for you to download and use as you wish.

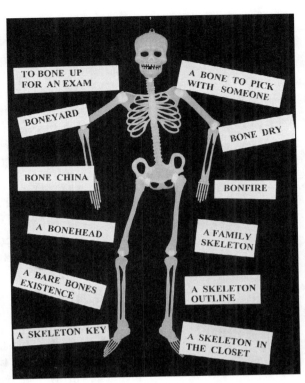

Bulletin boards are just one place to use printed word strips. See our website (www.ablongman.com/nilsen) for typed word strips that can be downloaded and enlarged for use with each chapter.

We could enter a room with nothing but a stack of word strips and succeed in teaching an interesting lesson. One technique is to let students choose one of the strips to illustrate and/or teach to the rest of the class. Another is to use the strips for bulletin boards and other kinds of postings to remind students of the topic of the week. These strips can also be photocopied in different sizes and different positions on paper to serve as inspiration for small-sized illustrations (see photos on pages 16, 55, and 127).

The workshop pages are prepared for teaching rather than for testing. Students who want to get through in a hurry will prefer to draw lines from the correct words to the spaces rather than to write in the words. Explain to students that vocabulary study differs from some kinds of problem solving because people not only have to figure out particular meanings, they have to impress them on their minds so they will remember what they learned. Writing answers, as well as saying them, will help with memory. One of the ways we make this point with our students is to tell them that when we make a list of items we want from the grocery store, we usually remember to buy everything on the list—even if we forget to take the list with us. The items were impressed on our minds through the act of writing them down.

Saying the answers out loud, and hearing other people say them, will also help students' memories. Some of the worksheet problems are identfied so that you can check answers aloud by saying things like *1b, 2d, 3g,* and so on, but we think it will be a better learning experience for your students if you call on them to read the whole sentences with the right words included.

RIGHT ANSWERS ARE BETTER THAN WRONG ANSWERS

In an attempt to provide students with multiple experiences centered on the words that are being taught, teachers and textbook writers have adopted a practice that is more appropriate for testing than for teaching. They make up four sentences using the word being taught. In three out of the four sentences, the word is used incorrectly. Children are to decide which sentence makes the best use of the word. The problem with this common exercise is that as children read the sentences over and over, they all begin to sound reasonable. Even if children are able to choose the "best" usage, three-fourths of their brainpower and time have been spent absorbing incorrect usages. This is an inefficient—if not counterproductive—way to use the limited time that teachers have to spend on vocabulary. As you will see in the workshops, a source-based approach provides teachers with materials for many different kinds of exercises, all designed to point children toward correct, rather than incorrect, answers.

CHILDREN LEARN BEST WHEN THEY CAN MAKE CONNECTIONS AND LEARN THINGS IN SETS

Thanks to various grandchildren and to a research project we did studying children's acquisition of pronoun usage, we spent almost a year immersed in the game of Pokémon. By now the game has mostly gone the way of the Hula Hoop, but when we embarked on our vocabulary project, we kept coming back to what we learned from studying how more than 100 children (ages 6 to 12) interacted with the Japanese pocket monsters.

Our observation most relevant to the teaching of vocabulary is that the children invariably talked about the Pokémon characters in sets. All but twenty of the 150 characters evolve into bigger or more advanced creatures. If children could think of the name of one of the members of a set, then they could usually think of the other one or two because of the similarities in their characteristics and their names. *Mankey*, who looks like a monkey, evolves into *Primeape*, while the sleepy-looking *Drowzee* evolves into *Hypno*, and a friendly, egg-like creature named *Exeggcute* evolves into a more vicious-looking creature named *Exeggutor*. The few single-named Pokémon (those that do not evolve) that children talked about were the ones whose names were the easiest to connect with their characteristics. For example, *Tangela* has a head of tangled (Medusa-like) hair, while *Pinsir* is a mean-looking insect with curved antennae that look like ice tongs, and *Lickitung* has a tongue that looks as if it is longer than its body. Seeing how skilled children were at making these connections reinforced an idea that we, along with other educators, have long endorsed: It is much easier to learn words in relation to each other rather than as single items.

SPEAKING IS MORE BASIC THAN WRITING

A contributing factor to the unusual popularity of the Pokémon game and the characters was that children met them first on television, where they were given "tutorials," which were lessons in how to pronounce the characters' names and on what abilities they had and how and when they would evolve. Children too young to know how to read were nevertheless matching up trading cards and talking fluently about the characters whose names and faces they connected. The game spread by word of mouth. It was only after a great deal of talk that children put forth the effort to read printed directions on their Nintendo Game Boys and to want to buy guidebooks and play the associated board games. We should not have needed Pokémon to teach us this, because linguists have always said that speech comes first and is more basic. However, our Pokémon experiences were a reminder that children need many opportunities to talk both with adults and with each other. They won't be enthused about learning words that they haven't heard over and over again in a variety of contexts and from a variety of speakers, including their peers. This is why in our lessons we put a premium on opportunities for both small- and large-group discussions.

We also put a premium on the reading aloud of good books, even for older students. Literature is a tried-and-true way of making children feel comfortable with new words, so we frequently suggest books to go along with particular topics. Ask colleagues, including your school librarian, for other suggestions appropriate to your grade level and the focus topics in the chapters.

CHILDREN ARE SOCIAL ANIMALS WHO TEACH EACH OTHER

While parents were the ones who owned the television sets that showed the Pokémon cartoons and who furnished the money to buy the Nintendo Game Boys (along with all the paraphernalia that followed), children were the ones who taught the game and the names to each other. At a family reunion, we saw a 10-year-old giving a "tutorial" to an 8-year-old, while a 5-year-old stood nearby, hanging on every word. The way children taught each other reinforces the whole concept of cooperative learning and of the value of letting children talk to each other rather than sit quietly and listen to the teacher explain the meanings of the week's vocabulary words. Assigning children to work with partners or in groups of three or four to make posters or to draw on white boards is a good way to increase worthwhile talk (see the photo on p. 152). Another good idea is to make cooperative displays as with the Palm Tree on page 34 and the Metaphorical Sandwich on page 74. We had some leftover acetate pages and so worked with one class to help each child fill nine slots with animal metaphors (see the photo on p. 17). We also encouraged children to follow our lead and bring in items for displays, demonstrations, and bulletin boards.

MULTISENSORY EXPERIENCES ARE VALUABLE

Use your own and your students' creativity and take advantage of whatever serendipitous opportunities come your way; for example, being allowed to put on a program, decorate an all-school bulletin board, make a videotape, or work with leftover craft items. When providing students with performance opportunities related to words, you might increase their comfort by letting them work in pairs when, for example, they present riddles and jokes. Help them explore whether the wordplay is based on a metaphor or a pun.

When we first thought of doing this book, we worried about how to get all the wonderful pictures that could illustrate the concepts we were discussing. Then, from our reading about the teaching of vocabulary and from our own experience, we decided that a much better idea would be for students to either draw or find pictures to make their own illustrated pages and books. In both elementary and high schools, we found it to be a great time-saver if we provided a plastic tub filled with pictures we had clipped from whatever magazines, brochures, leftover book jackets, posters, and so on that were available. Book catalogues provide wonderful pictures as do advertising brochures, because they are usually printed on sturdy paper that won't get crumpled up when stored in a tub. If we just arrived at a classroom with magazines, students were tempted to spend all their time looking through the magazines rather than focusing on the topic at hand. We also found that students got more done if we took a few minutes to go through our picture tub and pull out those pictures that included the topic at hand, such as plants, animals, human body parts, or nature.

Another good idea is to bring in a digital camera or a recyclable camera for students to take photos. Students can work in pairs or in small groups and take turns being the photographer and the model. The goal is for students to take pictures that will demonstrate the metaphorical underpinnings of words (see photos on pp. 54, 93, 112, 127, 192, and 193). They might demonstrate something like *on the seamy side* by

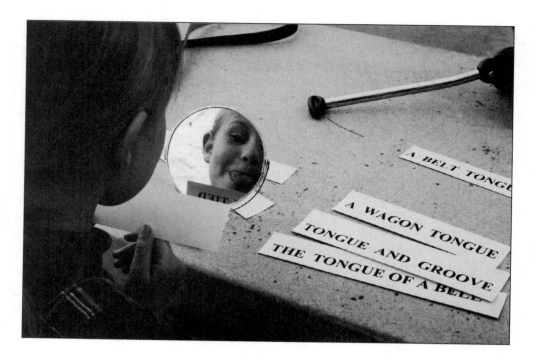

On the right, a first grader tries to look *tongue-tied* in a mirror, while below, older children pose with their *tongue* lists.

turning their clothes inside out or *climbing the wall* by imitating Spider Man. After the pictures are taken, children mount them on a page and write an explanation. The pages can be used for a class bulletin board and then after a few days added to students' vocabulary folders or notebooks.

MANY CHILDREN ENJOY MAKING LISTS WHEREAS THEY HATE WRITING FULL SENTENCES

We first thought about this one Thanksgiving while Don was washing the dinner dishes and an 8-year-old grandson was waiting to play Pokémon. This is a boy who feels tortured when his mother makes him write a one-line thank-you note, but he happily filled a whole page with a list of the places he wanted to go and the things he wanted to trade as soon as he and his grandfather could hook up their respective Game Boys.

We know that one of the "rules" of teaching vocabulary is to have children use the words they are learning in a context. We agree, but "contexts" can be created in many ways, and the whole idea of our source-based approach is to create a context through teaching words that are related to each other. To add interest to the making of lists, let students choose the words they find most interesting. If you post word strips around the room, they can get help with spelling from those. But also let students ask you, as well as neighboring children, for help with spelling.

Studies show that children remember words they have illustrated, so at least in relation to learning the meanings of words, doing an illustrated list may be a better learning experience than writing complete sentences. Young children have so many things to concentrate on when writing complete sentences that their attention may be diverted away from the meanings of the words, which should be the focus of vocabulary lessons. Providing shaped paper will put the words "in context." It is easy to cut a sheet of paper (or old file folders) into the shape of a foot for such metaphors as *foothills, footlights, foothold,* and *footnotes* and pink paper into the shape of a tongue for listing such metaphors as *tongue and groove joint,* the *tongue of a shoe,* the *tongue of a wagon,* and *mother tongue.* If computers are readily available, older students could have fun by illustrating their lists through finding appropriate computer images.

You might also watch the sale tables at copy centers and office supply stores for fancy paper that will fit one of your upcoming subjects. It is easy to find flowers (for the chapter on plants) and seaside paper or fish (for the chapter on animals). If you have lots of students, you can slice the paper crosswise into four sections so that each child gets a piece $8\frac{1}{2}$ by $2\frac{3}{4}$ inches. Children are sometimes more enthused about a task if it looks smaller.

A Note to College Instructors and Leaders of Workshops

When we were doing trial teaching at various schools, the classroom teachers liked what we were doing and how their students responded; however, they did not feel confident enough to continue with the lessons on their own. This is why we decided to direct *Vocabulary Plus* towards pre-service and in-service teachers, with elementary students being a second-level audience. We are asking for a paradigm shift in the teaching of vocabulary, and such shifts do not come easily.

For years, Alleen has observed student teachers, and she has always advocated that they supplement their explanations of a word's meaning by talking about related words and by telling stories and giving students relational hooks on which to hang the words. Only once, prior to our embarking on this concentrated study of the teaching of vocabulary, does she remember a student teacher being in control enough to do this. In principle, the student teachers agreed with the idea and the philosophy, but when they were standing in front of a class juggling three or four balls in the air (attendance, supplies, discipline, etc.) in addition to their teaching of content, they simply could not withstand the temptation to simplify matters by relying on whatever definition was printed in the teachers' guide.

One reason for using what is basically a child-centered textbook in a college classroom is that teachers need to talk about the words and the concepts until they feel comfortable with them. They need to overlearn the ideas, extend the examples, and come up with their own explanations. You and your students may not agree with our interpretations of several of the metaphors and idioms. That's fine. Even the two of us, who have lived together for over forty years, were sometimes surprised at the other person's interpretation of common terms. Alleen had always thought that *the bottom line* on something was where you sign an agreement. Don, who used to be a math major, was sure it was the *total* line drawn underneath the additions and subtractions to determine if the project would be profitable. Various dictionary editors agreed with Don, but Alleen still clings to her idea as a possible interpretation.

Language teachers need to know about such disagreements and about the miracle that so many speakers can, and do, agree on the multitude of meanings that are connected to our most basic words. A reason for using the workshops and the other materials as conversation starters, rather than as lessons to be memorized, is so that students will find out what ideas other speakers have and will realize that opinions might differ. One of the biggest stumbling blocks to communication is the false idea implied by many vocabulary lessons that words have one and only one meaning.

Another reason for using *Vocabulary Plus* as a textbook in a class or a workshop is to provide teachers with the opportunity to teach one or two lessons to supportive colleagues under favorable conditions. While they are concentrating on the matter, they need to start collecting materials for their own picture tub and to gather interesting items that they can use for *HANDS-ON* displays, for bulletin board centerpieces, and for inspiring their own students to bring in demonstration materials. Preparing word strips, visual aids, and hands-on activities to teach a lesson to supportive colleagues will give students confidence in the procedures, while also helping them to realize that even though a well-done lesson looks spontaneous and smooth, considerable pre-thinking and planning is involved.

When we guest-taught, the one question we were always asked was "How many hours did it take you to prepare all this?" We acknowledge the implication that as college teachers we had more time and support for preparing these materials than do classroom teachers. It is because we are aware of the many responsibilities teachers have that we have tried to make this a teacher-friendly book. Although the worksheets are ready to be photocopied and the answers given at the end of each chapter, we hope you will encourage teachers to use these as jumping-off points rather than as "seat-work" to keep kids busy and quiet. Toward the end of the semester, it would be good for teachers to find words that are in their curriculum or in a piece of literature they are planning to teach and prepare a source-based lesson on a few of these words. They do not need to be as thorough as we have been, but they should go through the effort as a way of internalizing the process. We hope they will be happily surprised by seeing how many relationships they can find.

Once teachers have chosen their words, they should look them up in a good dictionary and pay special attention to their histories and to their various meanings. They should look at neighboring words, which may be related, and also brainstorm with colleagues and friends because many related words will not start the same and will therefore not be neighbors in a dictionary. The more teachers work with this, the more skilled they will become. These are the guidelines that helped us find the groups of words presented in this book.

1. **Spelling** is a good clue to word relationships because it changes more slowly than does pronunciation. The repetition of letters, especially unusual clusters of letters that are not pronounced, serve as relational clues: For example, *kn* is a tell-tale sign of a relationship between *know* and *acknowledge,* while *gn* shows a relationship between *sign* and *signature, mn* between *mnemonic* and *amnesia,* and *prehen* between *apprehend* and *prehensile.*

2. **Semantics, or meaning,** is another good clue. As shown throughout this book, new meanings often develop through metaphors. And even though some of these metaphors can be far-fetched, it is important to look for and teach metaphorical extensions because they are the clues to a similarity in meaning. By working with many metaphorically related words, students will begin to understand that most metaphors focus on only one or two features. For example, the pages in students' *looseleaf* notebooks are not green, nor are they shaped like leaves. However, they are thin like leaves and they can be separated from their books as easily as leaves can fall from a tree.

3. **Historical relationships** provide clues to similarities in meanings that many students find memorable. For example, when students understand how the eleventh-century French conquerors of England considered it gross to talk about

table meats with the same terms that they used to talk about animals on the hoof, they will be ready to connect such French terms as *beef, mutton, venison,* and *pork* to the old Anglo-Saxon terms of *cattle, sheep, deer,* and *pigs.* And when students hear the story about sailors standing on deck around the *scuttle bucket* (a water barrel with a hole to dip out drinking water), then they will probably remember that today's *scuttlebutt* is the kind of gossip that workers share when they gather around the office water cooler.

4. **Pragmatics** is related to *practical* and is another way of alluding to *common sense.* Teachers need to apply both their life experience and everything they know about the world to their teaching of vocabulary. It is not always possible to devise or trace connections among words, and we should not try to force such connections. Instead, we should give our students a head start by focusing their attention on the thousands of useful words that have clear and true relationships.

A Note to Teachers of Primary-Grade Children

We realize there are tremendous differences in the reading and writing abilities of 6- and 7-year-olds as compared to 12- and 13-year-olds. We apologize that the workshops are written at a reading and writing level far above that of first and second graders. In having to make a choice, we decided that it would be possible for teachers of young children to adapt the material by teaching it orally and letting their students provide the artwork and displays. Their biggest help will be the word strips from each chapter, which can be downloaded from our website.

In our guest teaching, we had the most fun with young children. Over and over again we found that their lesser abilities in reading and writing were compensated for by their strong interest in, and fascination with, language. We loved the way their eyes would light up when they made a connection and the way they would come and tell us about some "original" discovery they had made from the material we brought for our *HANDS-ON* table. Their enthusiasm reminded us of something we read in Walter Redfern's 1984 book, *Puns,* where he noted that naturalists who observe animals in the wild regularly point out that while the young of various species are obviously having fun as they engage in rough-and-tumble play with each other and with their parents, they are also learning the skills they will need for survival. Redfern compares this to the way children play with words much like they do with toys. Without this kind of language play, he says children will lack practice in the art of thinking, which is the most complex and powerful survival tool that humans have.

As teachers, we need to encourage the playful and uninhibited attitudes that enabled our students to learn to speak when they were toddlers. This means having fun with language and appreciating how skilled children are at connecting old information (words they already know) with new information (words they want to learn). We hope the following chapters will make it easier for you and your students to have fun while you learn. We devised the Workshops for your convenience and help in teaching these concepts, but please do not think that you need to use all of them with any particular class. In the interest of saving paper, you can probably teach many of the concepts on an overhead or a chalkboard. The end-of-chapter activities can usually be done orally with help from printed word strips. However, it may be easier to get children involved if you photocopy and distribute the fables for reading at the ends of Chapters 5 and 11 and the suggested activities at the end of Chapter 8. Use only as many of the workshops as your students seem to benefit from. As a general rule, the more difficult concepts are placed toward the ends of the chapters.

CHAPTER TWO

Plants and Animals

Background Reading for the Teacher

Jack Rosenthal, editor of the *New York Times Magazine,* wrote one of his columns "On Language Fossilizing" (September 10, 1995), in which he talked about the usefulness of such dated idioms as *dialing* a phone and how people who have never seen a piece of carbon paper still put *cc:* and *bcc:* (*carbon copy* and *blind carbon copy*) at the bottom of correspondence. His main area of focus was the idioms from farm language. He explained that between 1910 and 1920, when farm population peaked, one-third of all Americans lived on farms. By 1950, the number was 15 percent, while today it is less than 2 percent. "If people know how high the corn will get, they probably got their information from musical comedy rather than rural reality."

This chapter is about the language of farming in relation to both plants and animals. We are starting with this area because it is so rich in lexical extensions and metaphors. Most children feel a relationship with both plants and animals, either through actual experience or through various media. We will work first with plants and then move on to animals. Because these are both such rich areas and pictures are plentiful, a good project for this chapter would be to let children do a page of trading cards.

Such terms as *plant, grow, sow, reap,* and *harvest* illustrate the concept of linguistic generalization because their meanings have expanded to cover a wide range of human activities. Another interesting thing about plants is the way their names serve as both the sources and targets of metaphors. Big, generic concepts (*grass, trees, trunks, branches, roots,* etc.) are sources from which other things are named, while smaller, individual plants (*foxtail, cattail, morning glories,* etc.) are metaphorical targets, that have received their names from better known concepts.

Because his little sister had to bring the family dog from home for his report on dog metaphors, 12-year-old Christian enlisted her ponytails as part of his *Dog and Pony Show*. Other metaphors on the bulletin board posters made by his classmates include *In the Doghouse, A Dog-Eared Book, A Dogleg Road, A Lucky Dog, Puppy Love, Hot Dogging, Dog Tired, Hush Puppies for Tired Dogs,* and *Dogged Determination*.

Notes to Help Teachers Elicit Ideas from Students

Depending on where you live, what time of year it is, and the level of your ambition, you might want to bring in a bundle of straw to provide students with several hands-on experiences.

Here are some of the insights that today's urban children can get from interacting with something that for earlier generations was simply a part of everyday life.

- If you bring in a big enough bundle (or a bale) so that it is heavy, children who try to lift it will begin to understand the old proverb about "the straw that broke the camel's back."
- Students who look through empty straws will see how *soda straws* were invented. (We do not suggest drinking through real straws because of pesticides and other contaminants.)
- Those who try to weave even a miniature place mat will gain new appreciation for *straw hats, straw baskets,* and *straw mats.* They will also gain new appreciation for the story of the princess whose foolish father bragged that she could spin straw into gold. There are many versions of *Rumpelstiltskin* to read aloud, including Paul O. Zelinsky's Caldecott Honor Book (Dutton, 1986).
- Those who try to build a house using straw will see why the house built by the first little pig collapsed when the wolf came and "huffed and puffed" and blew the house down. (Actually, experimental houses are currently being made from straw packed between more solid concrete or adobe walls. Promoters point to its low cost combined with its qualities of insulation because of the air stored in individual straws.)
- Those who make a *strawman* (a miniature scarecrow or a doll) will see why in an argument people would rather attack *strawmen* than real issues. It is very easy to topple a strawman.
- If you *draw straws* for particular classroom duties or privileges, children will understand what is now done with slips of paper but is still called *drawing straws.* They will also see why it has to be the longest, rather than the shortest straw, that is considered the winner. (If the shortest straw was the winner, people would be too tempted to break little pieces off.)
- If a presidential election is coming up, you could conduct a *straw poll* or a *straw vote.* Give each student a piece of straw to place in front of a picture of the candidate he or she prefers. Talk about why *straw votes* are not considered official. (They are too unreliable because people could break their straws in two or provide extra straws on their own, thereby voting more than once.) Also make the comparison to a *straw boss,* a person who has informally been given the role of a boss without having the real authority.
- Children who drop a handful of straw on the classroom floor or who spread it outside to help people walk through mud or muck without sinking in and getting dirty will learn the meaning of the word *strewn* to describe a haphazard and random pattern of things that are scattered around.
- With your help, they can also learn that *strawberries* were named from the way the plant branches out to resemble scattered straw.

We had leftover acetate sheets from Pokémon, which children enjoyed filling, but later we found students had just as much fun gluing cards onto a regular sheet of paper (top). Because plants and animals are everywhere, children can easily find things at home to bring in for "show-and-tell." Ten-year-old Jim (bottom) is wearing a clown's *bulbous nose* and holding a *light bulb* and an *onion bulb.*

While we suggest bringing in a whole bundle of straw, all that we managed were these two stalks of wheat that we pulled from a florist's bouquet. They were nevertheless one of our most effective hands-on items with everyone wanting to feel the beards on the wheat and to peek through the straw.

When you finish with your word study, you can bring in scissors, black paper, and glue. Let children have an art project where they make pictures from nothing but the straw. In some parts of the world, this is a highly developed skill. If it is appropriate to the climate you live in, you might ask the custodian to let your children pack the leftover straw around the roots of fragile plants to protect them for the winter.

If you prefer a simpler way to get children thinking about plants and what they stand for, you might read Shel Silverstein's book *The Giving Tree* (HarperCollins, 1964), which is a good example of how a tree can serve as a symbol. Another suggestion is Shirley Ann Williams's *Working Cotton* (illustrated by Carole Byard; Harcourt, 1992). It is the story of a young girl whose family are migrant farm workers. Students who are good readers might appreciate reading Frances Hodgson Burnett's now classic *The Secret Garden* (Heinemann, 1911).

You might introduce the animal part of the chapter by reading an old folk tale such as *Goldilocks and the Three Bears, The Billy Goats Gruff, The Three Little Pigs;* such newer books as Arnold Lobel's *Fables* or one of his *Frog and Toad* books; one of H. A. Rey's *Curious George* books; or Dr. Seuss's *Cat in the Hat* stories. Talk about the characteristics the author assigns to the animals. Depending on your students' ages and interests, you might talk about the truthfulness of the characteristics that speakers have assigned to animals. The idea of a *wise old owl*, for example, probably comes from the fact that owl's eyes, which are unusually prominent, do not turn as do other animals' eyes. This means that owls must turn their heads to look in different directions and so they appear to be studying things intently.

Because children are familiar with animals and their characteristics, you might want to use animals to introduce children to the concept of analogies as in such a sentence as "Barking is to dogs as meowing is to cats." You could write the following words on the chalkboard or on an overhead and then orally present sentences that students could complete by choosing one of the words.

cub	hive	neighing	scales	swimming	wool

1. _____ are to fish as hairs are to horses.

2. Quacking is to ducks as _____ is to horses.

3. A _____ is to a bee as a den is to a bear.

4. A colt is to a horse as a _____ is to a bear.

5. Flying is to birds as _____ is to fish.

6. Hair is to camels as _____ is to sheep.

As the students suggest what should go in the blank spaces, talk with them about what is being compared. For example, *scales* and *hair* are skin coverings, *quacking* and *neighing* are sounds, while *hives* and *dens* are homes, etc.

Straws and Sticks

Name: _____ **Period:** _____ **Date:** _____

You probably remember how in the old story of *The Three Little Pigs*, the first little pig built his house with straw, while the second little pig built his house with sticks. Only when the third little pig built his house with bricks was it sturdy enough to last.

The reason that the storyteller used straws and sticks is that in rural farm areas both of these items were so common that they were practically free. *Straw* is the leftover stalks and hulls after such grains as wheat, barley, and oats have been threshed. Based on the fact that straw is cheap and relatively unimportant, if someone is called a *straw boss*, this means that the person is just playing the role of a boss. In a similar way, a *straw vote* is not a real vote. It is just pretending as when some schools have their own elections for president. The *last straw* is the same thing as the *straw that broke the camel's back*. The allusion comes from an old parable based on the fact that straw weighs so little that people are tempted to keep piling it on, thinking a little more will not matter.

In spite of the fact that straw is a by-product from grain, it has a surprising number of uses. *Straw hats, straw baskets,* and *straw mats* are in everyday use. We drink through a *soda straw,* which is artificially made so as to be cleaner and sturdier than a real straw. And depending on the part of the country you live in, gardeners cover newly planted lawns with straw. As winter comes, they also pack straw around the roots of plants. The reason is that the air in each straw acts as good insulation.

The verb *strewn* as in "The books were *strewn* on the floor," comes from the random or crossways appearance of straw lying on the ground. *Strawberry* plants are named because they grow with their stems reaching out and spreading across gardens in a similar random style. Speakers who have not seen strawberries growing on the ground focus more on the color of the berries. They use *strawberry* to mean red. For example, a *strawberry blond* has reddish-blond hair while a *strawberry roan* horse is a darker red.

On farms, *sticks* are almost as common as straw. Their shape is the basis for such metaphors as *lipstick, matchstick, candlestick,* a *stick of gum*, a *hockey stick,* and a *joystick* on video games. *Stick* developed in Middle English from a root word meaning *point* or *prick*. This old meaning is seen in the use of *sticker* as the name for thorns. Although these kinds of *stickers* are made by nature, they *stick* into things in a similar fashion to how we use pins and thumbtacks.

Read these sentences and choose which of the following terms to write in the blank spaces. Each one illustrates an extended or metaphorical use of either *straw* or *stick*.

stick-in-the-mud	**soda straws**	**sticking plasters**	**stickler**
strawberry marks	**straws**	**stuck**	**walking stick**

1. Because straw is hollow, it is the model for today's _____.

2. Some people call adhesive bandages _____.

3. The _____ is an insect camouflaged by nature to blend in with plants.

4. Birthmarks that are red in color and slightly elevated are called _____.

5. A person who is a _____ for details keeps getting hung up on things.

6. Someone in an argument who grasps at _____ is like a drowning person with nothing useful to grab onto.

7. A _____ is a party-pooper.

8. If you are *stuck in town*, it could be that your car really is _____ in the mud or that, metaphorically, you have a social obligation.

The Language of Farming

Name: _____   **Period:** _____   **Date:** _____

Read through these charts that illustrate various uses of language about farming. After you have read and talked about the information, complete the sentences that illustrate extensions of the words.

Term	Lexical Extensions	Sample Sentences
plow	plowing snow plowing	*Plowing* fields is hard and monotonous work. Ships *plow* through ocean waves like farm *plows* go through soil. *Snowplows* can push a larger quantity of snow than farm *plows* can push soil. A taxpayer will complain if he has to *plow through* several years of tax records to find something.
cultivate	cultural culture	To *cultivate* a garden is to give it whatever it needs for good growing conditions. The piece of gardening equipment called a *cultivator* loosens the soil and helps to remove weeds. A *cultivated* person has a good education and good taste. Parents like their children to *cultivate* friendships with people who have similar values.
plant	implant planting plants to plant	Literally, *planting* is putting seeds or seedlings into the ground. Metaphorically, *plants* can be factories designed for various kinds of production. A fighter might *plant* a hit on his opponent's chin. A dishonest person might *plant evidence* at a crime scene. Comedians sometimes *plant* stooges in the audience.
garden	gardener gardening	*Gardens* are thought to be peaceful places. *Gardens* are smaller than farms, but *truck gardens* produce vegetables to be taken into cities. Public parks, especially those with many flowers, are often called *public gardens*. Something described as *garden variety* is "good," but still of amateur quality.
weed	weeders weeding weeds	*Weeds* are any kind of plants growing where they are not wanted. It takes good eyes and careful work to *weed* a garden without damaging the good plants. Many gardeners now use chemical *weeders*. It is easier to *weed out* undesirable plants than to *weed out* out-of-date books in libraries.
prune	pruners pruning	*Pruning* trees and bushes is cutting out the dead branches or ones that are not needed. *Pruning* expenses means to cut back and be more efficient.

harvest	harvest moon harvesters harvesting	Farmers *harvest* their crops at the end of each growing season. In late September when the full moon seems extra bright, it is called a *harvest moon* because people can see well enough to keep working. Things as diverse as fish, ice, and living cells are *harvested*.
reap	reaper reaping	To *reap* is to harvest, but it sounds old fashioned because it originally meant cutting with a scythe. It also has a religious tone because of the Biblical admonition, "Whatsoever ye shall sow, that also shall ye *reap*."

Choose the most appropriate terms to write in the blank spaces of these sentences, which use the farm terms in metaphorical ways. Talk about the relationships between the metaphorical uses in these sentences and the literal uses related to farming.

> **cultivating**   **garden path**   **Grim Reaper**   **harvesting**
> **implant**   **plowed**   **pruned**   **weeds out**

I. The valedictorian _____ through his speech without ever looking up.

2. The coach says the athletic program must be _____ by 15 percent.

3. The _____ is a personification of death.

4. Suzie wants to be a model and so is _____ contacts with agencies and photographers.

5. Teachers and schools hope to _____ good attitudes in children's minds.

6. Scientists were concerned about new regulations on _____ stem cells.

7. When someone is led up the _____, that person is being fooled but in a pleasant or inconsequential way.

8. Every summer our librarian _____ old or damaged books.

Actions of Plants

Name: _____ **Period:** _____ **Date:** _____

In the process of *growing*, plants *put down roots* and *sprout, bud, flower*, and *bloom*. Children are sometimes called *sprouts* because they grow so fast. Extra smart children are referred to as *budding geniuses*, while people not so smart might be called *blooming idiots*. Either way, the term alludes to processes not yet finished.

Wallflowers lean against walls, while ivy *clings* to walls, and trees *branch out* and *spread their limbs*. Virtually all plants produce *seeds* and, after growing to maturity, will *wilt* and *die*. The dramatic picture made by falling leaves is probably the reason that most Americans talk about *fall* rather than *autumn*.

The *root* of a plant grows underground and provides the plant with nourishment while also anchoring it to the ground. When people move to a new town and *put down roots*, they do such things as find jobs, buy houses, enroll in schools, and join churches. The *root of a problem* is what keeps it a problem, while the *roots of your teeth* keep them in your mouth. Many of the words studied in these lessons are considered to be *root words* because other words grow from them.

A *windfall* occurs when the wind blows hard enough to knock fruit or nuts from a tree. Whoever comes along can easily scoop up what would have taken considerable effort to pick. Metaphorically, a *windfall* is any sudden and unexpected benefit.

Just as the branches of bushes and trees spread, people *branch out* into new fields, and *branch campuses, branch libraries,* and *branch railroads* are located at a distances from the main part. *Limb* is an alternate name for *branch*; however, *limbs* can refer to human arms and legs whereas *branches* cannot. When athletes *limber up*, their arms and legs resemble tree limbs swaying in the wind. The warning against *going out on a limb* comes from tree climbing. The further out someone goes, the greater the chance of the limb's breaking so that the climber falls.

A *stump* is the remaining trunk and roots of a tree after it has been cut or broken. When a person's arm or leg has been amputated, the remaining part is called the *stump*. If you get *stumped* while taking a test, your thinking has been cut off.

Being fruitful is a good description of trees that produce apples, pears, plums, and peaches. However, farmers also want their walnut, pecan, and almond trees, as well as their vegetable gardens and their fields to be *fruitful*. As an extension of this concept, people hope to make *fruitful investments*, have *fruitful discussions,* and spend *fruitful years* at college.

Choose the most appropriate words to go in the following blank spaces. Then talk about the connections between the plant-related meanings and their metaphorical uses.

| blossom | fruitful | root | rooting out | stump | wallflowers | wilting | windfall |

1. When you _____ for a team, you are supporting it.

2. It was a _____ when the cleaners gave her $30 for snagging her jacket.

3. Tell your mom to bring cold drinks —we're _____ fast.

4. Because of their_____ talks, there may not be a walkout.

5. It is not just at dances that people can feel like _____.

6. _____ evil is as hard as digging out a tree by the roots.

7. We enjoyed watching their romance _____.

8. Analogy questions always _____ me.

Shape versus Action

Name: _____ **Period:** _____ **Date:** _____

Garlic *bulbs*, onion *bulbs*, and tulip *bulbs* have been around much longer than light bulbs, but people think of light bulbs as the basic word because they have more association with light bulbs. Also, a picture of a light bulb being turned on has become the symbol for a bright idea, an image that fits better with the *bulb* of a syringe and the *bulb* at the bottom of a thermometer than with something buried underground.

The shapes of trees have inspired people to talk about *family trees*, while the thinness of leaves is the feature being emphasized when speakers talk about putting paper in a *looseleaf notebook* or *leafing through a book*. Neither the *leaf* of a table nor a *leaflet* is shaped like a leaf, but both are thin.

The shape of *bushes* make speakers describe people's hair as *bushy*, while the shape of small grains of rice or wheat make people describe unclear pictures as *grainy*. If speakers describe a *mushroom* cloud, they are using a shape-related metaphor, but if they say something like "Support for the idea *mushroomed*," they are using an action-related metaphor alluding to how fast mushrooms grow.

Knots form on tree trunks wherever something impedes growth, as when a branch starts to grow and then gets cut or broken off or where the tree comes up against something solid. Metaphorically, speakers use the word to describe the *knots* tied in cords or ropes. The comparison is based on a similarity in appearance rather than in action.

From what you learned by reading and talking about the material in the last two workshops, figure out whether each of the italicized metaphors alludes to the shape of a plant or to an action of the plant. Write either ACTION or SHAPE by each sentence. Talk about the connections between the actual plants and these metaphorical uses.

_____ **1.** I was disappointed that my pictures turned out to be so *grainy*.

_____ **2.** One of the trademarks of clowns is their *bulbous* noses.

_____ **3.** That *branch* of the family has never come to reunions.

_____ **4.** A child prodigy is the opposite of a *late bloomer*.

_____ **5.** The bill was *stuck* in committee so it never came to a vote.

_____ **6.** Because of an accident, traffic was routed around the *cloverleaf*.

_____ **7.** They are *branching out* into selling motorcycles as well as cars.

_____ **8.** Science fairs are a good way to encourage *budding* geniuses.

_____ **9.** The news caused his hopes to *wilt*.

_____ **10.** I hope they had a *fruitful* discussion.

Features of Animal Words

Name: _____ **Period:** _____ **Date:** _____

Here are some charts that will help you see some language processes that are similar
to the ones you just looked at with plants.

Term	Lexical Extensions	Sample Sentences
bear	bear claw pastry bear hug bear for work teddy bear	A *bear claw* probably has as many calories as two donuts. Morris is embarrassed his mother is always giving him *bear hugs*. *Teddy bears* are named after President Theodore Roosevelt, who once refused to shoot a bear that had been caught for him. Our teacher is a *bear for work*; she gives us homework even on weekends.
bee	beehive beeline quilting bee spelling bee	*Beehive* hairdos are not as fashionable as they used to be. As you might guess, the *Beeline Highway* in Arizona is relatively straight. People participating in either *quilting bees* or *spelling bees* are *busy as bees*. Someone who has a *bee in her bonnet* is all excited or bothered about something.
bug	bedbug bug-a-boo bug-eyed computer bug bug someone bug a place	One reason motels are expensive is the constant laundering to prevent *bedbugs*. A *bug-a-boo* is anything people are afraid of. Real *bugs* used to crawl into computers to get warm, but today's *computer bugs* are programming problems.
dog	dog days dog and pony show dogged dogfight dog-ear hotdog underdog	The *dog days* of summer are so tiresome that it is almost a relief when school starts. If someone describes your wonderful performance as a *dog and pony show*, they are insulting you. *Dogged determination* goes a long way toward success. Librarians do not appreciate it if you *dog-ear* (turn the corners down) the pages of the books you borrow. In tournaments, the *underdogs* often win because they get the support of the crowd. *Hotdogging* on a skateboard is dangerous.
fish	fishbowl fish-eye fishing fishtailing fishy	The family did not like living in a *fishbowl* so they moved out of the governor's mansion. That's a pretty *fishy* excuse. My uncle's van has a *fish-eye* in the back. When my aunt is disgusted, she says, "Well, that's a fine *kettle of fish*."

pig	piggish piggyback piggybank pigpen pigskin pigtails	The new school made them feel like *guinea pigs*. Her room is a *pigpen*. It's harder to carry someone in front of you than *piggyback*. My rich uncle gives new babies in our family a *piggybank* with a $50 bond tucked in the top. The boys were *piggish* about the dessert.
rat	rat fink rat tail ratty	One of the rats in *Mrs. Frisby and the Rats of NIMH* was insulted to learn about what people call the *rat race*. Frank Sinatra was part of the *Rat Pack*. A hundred years ago, women used to use bunches of discarded hair called *rats* to support their bouffant hair styles. Today, girls *rat* their hair by back-combing.

Most of these usages are easy to figure out, but some animal metaphors are harder. For example, if speakers live in parts of the country where there are no moles, they will be less likely to understand metaphors based on moles. Moles are little brownish-colored animals that tunnel underground. They are generally considered a nuisance because of the way they make holes and bumps in people's lawns. Here are three ways that their name has been extended.

- Spies who infiltrate enemy organizations are called *moles* because their work is hidden or "underground."
- The colored bumps that grow on people's skin are called *moles* because of their brown coloring and because they look like little creatures hiding under someone's skin.
- The old proverb "Don't make a mountain of a *molehill*" shows that many speakers were almost as familiar with molehills as they were with mountains.

PART I The pairs of sentences below connect the name of a common animal to something else. One sentence in each pair is based on the appearance of the animal that is mentioned, while the other sentence is based on an action of the animal. Read the sentences and talk about their meanings. Write ACT in front of the ones that are making a comparison to what an animal does. Write APPEAR in front of the ones that are making a comparison to what an animal looks like. For example, you should write APPEAR in front of such a sentence as, "In England pedestrian crosswalks are called *zebras* because they are striped." You should write ACT in front of such a sentence as "Calling someone a *chameleon* is saying that the person changes to fit the situation like chameleons change their coloring."

A. RATS

_____ **1.** *Rat-tailed* combs have long handles on them.

_____ **2.** Despicable people are sometimes called *rats*.

B. KANGAROOS

_____ **1.** In a *kangaroo court*, the justice is informal and irregular; it jumps around.

_____ **2.** The company that sells *Pocket Books* chose a picture of a kangaroo as its logo.

C. RABBITS

_____ **1.** *Rabbit ears* help portable television sets get better reception.

_____ **2.** In boxing a *rabbit punch* is to the back of the neck—when rabbits fight they grab their opponents by the backs of their necks.

D. ROBINS

_____ **1.** *Robins-egg blue* is a pretty color that symbolizes springtime.

_____ **2.** In a *round robin* tennis tournament, players move from court to court like robins move from one nest to the next.

E. SPIDERS

_____ **1.** *Spider Man* in the comics and in the movies can climb up the sides of buildings.

_____ **2.** A *spider monkey* has long legs.

F. DOVES

_____ **1.** Carpenters make *dovetail joints* when they want to firmly attach two boards together.

_____ **2.** People who are *doves*, as compared to *hawks*, are peace-loving.

PART II Talk about the animal comparisons in the following phrases. After you understand how they relate, make up a sentence showing that you understand the meaning.

1. To be happy as a *lark* _____

2. To *duck* a responsibility _____

3. To be *ant*sy _____

4. To *squirrel* something away _____

5. To deal with a loan *shark* _____

6. To be a *bully* _____

7. To drive a *caterpillar* _____

8. To *kid* around _____

9. To *crow* about winning _____

Heads You Win, Tails You Lose

Name: _____ **Period:** _____ **Date:** _____

When speakers use the concept of animal tails as a metaphorical device, they often specify the species because it helps to be more descriptive as when talking about people's hair being in *ponytails, pigtails, duck tails,* or *rooster tails.* A *rat-tail* comb has a long straight tail like a rat, while a *cattail* reed not only looks, but feels, like a cat's tail. Swallows are unusual in having forked or split tails and so their name is used in the term *swallowtail coat* for a tuxedo with tails. *Swallowtail butterflies* are also named after these birds. Doves have tails that fan out, so carpenters took their name for *dove-tail joints,* the kind where boards are sawed into matching fanned notches so that they fit together like a puzzle. *Dovetail joints* are used to join the corners of high-quality furniture.

With other uses, speakers are not so specific. They might allude to something as a tail because of its general shape, or they might base the reference on something being positioned opposite to the head.

PART I With the following allusions, figure out the basis for the comparison and in the spaces write SHAPE, POSITION, or BOTH.

1. The *tail* of a kite _____

2. *Taillights* on a car _____

3. The *tail* of a comet _____

4. A *tail* gate party _____

5. Heads or *tails* on a coin _____

PART II The following usages are more metaphorical. Talk about their meanings and then try putting the italicized words in sentences to show that you understand their meanings. Notice how number 6 is more abstract and, in that sense, more metaphorical than the others. Feel free to change grammatical details as you write your sentences.

1. The *tail of a storm* _____

2. Detectives *tailing* suspects _____

3. Being *tailgated* by another vehicle _____

4. An airplane having a *tail wind* _____

5. An airplane going into a *tailspin* _____

6. A human going into an *emotional tailspin* _____

Animal Metaphors

Name: _____ **Period:** _____ **Date:** _____

Read the following sentences and use what you know about the real world and about the characteristics of these fairly common animals to choose the appropriate term to write in the blank spaces. Talk about what the metaphors are emphasizing in relation to the particular animals.

A. DOGS	dog fight	hotdogging	doggedly

1. A _____ skateboarder is showing off.

2. Pilots in a _____ are trying to down each other.

3. She clung _____ to her hopes of winning.

B. BUGS	bugging	bug	bug-eyed

1. Sandra is _____ her parents for own TV.

2. His new glasses made him look _____.

3. Spies use little microphones to _____ rooms.

C. RATS	rat on	a rat	ratty

1. A _____ apartment is rundown.

2. To _____ someone is to be a tattletale.

3. If you smell _____, something is wrong.

D. FISH	fish	fishtailing	fishing for

1. When big trucks start _____ on the freeway, other drivers better watch out.

2. At the club, he felt like a _____ out of water.

3. Mynalee is always _____ compliments.

E. PIGS	pigskins	pigged out	pigtails

1. I can see why _____ are favorites with active little girls.

2. Footballs are called _____ even though many are made from artificial leather.

3. We _____ on pizza after the game.

An Animal Crossword Puzzle

Name: _____   **Period:** _____   **Date:** _____

Use these clues to work the crossword puzzle.

ACROSS:

3. He is such a _____ I stay away from him.

4. It is illegal to secretly _____ telephones.

6. Radio and TV antennas are called _____ ears.

8. The Chicago _____ made it into the finals.

9. Missing a _____ ball is embarrassing for big league baseball players.

12. His story was really _____.

13. Our teacher has a _____ on her forehead.

DOWN:

1. People _____ books to remember the page.

2. A _____ valve has two flat handles so it is easy to turn.

5. "Oh, _____!" is an expression of frustration.

7. A _____ is a direct route between two points.

10. A _____ fence zigzags.

11. A loan _____ takes advantage of people who borrow money.

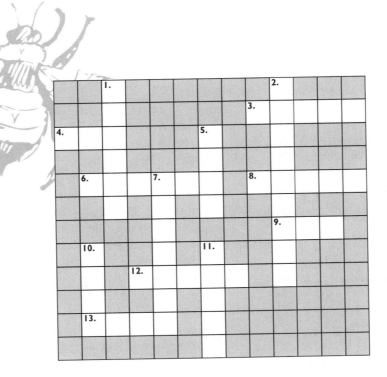

Workshop 2.1: 1. soda straws, **2.** sticking plasters, **3.** walking stick, **4.** strawberry marks, **5.** stickler, **6.** straws, **7.** stick-in-the-mud, **8.** stuck.

Workshop 2.2: 1. plowed, **2.** pruned, **3.** Grim Reaper, **4.** cultivating, **5.** implant, **6.** harvesting, **7.** garden path, **8.** weeds out.

Workshop 2.3: 1. root, **2.** windfall, **3.** wilting, **4.** fruitful, **5.** wallflowers, **6.** rooting out, **7.** blossom, **8.** stump.

Workshop 2.4: 1. shape, **2.** shape, **3.** shape, **4.** action, **5.** action, **6.** shape, **7.** action, **8.** action, **9.** action, **10.** action.

Workshop 2.5: Part I: Action = rats, kangaroo court, rabbit punch, round robin, Spider Man, doves. Appearance = rat-tailed, Pocket Books, rabbit ears, robins-egg blue, spider monkey, dovetail joints. **Part II: Possible answers: 1.** Larks appear to be happy as they fly around singing. **2.** A person ducking out on a responsibility is like a duck dipping its head in a pond. **3.** Being antsy is being as jumpy as if you are being bitten by ants. **4.** In good weather, squirrels scurry around gathering food to store in their nests for winter. **5.** Loan sharks take advantage of people who need money like real sharks hurt people in the ocean. **6.** Being a bully is to push your own weight around. **7.** Caterpillars have wheels that resemble the moving skin of real caterpillars. **8.** Baby goats were called kids before human children took their name. **9.** Crows strut and call out so self-confidently that their name has become a verb for obnoxious bragging.

Workshop 2.6: 1. both, **2.** position, **3.** both, **4.** position, **5.** position.

Workshop 2.7: A. 1. hotdogging, **2.** dogfight, **3.** doggedly. **B. 1.** bugging, **2.** bug-eyed, **3.** bug. **C. 1.** ratty, **2.** rat on, **3.** a rat. **D. 1.** fishtailing, **2.** fish, **3.** fishing. **E. 1.** pigtails, **2.** pigskins, **3.** pigged out.

Workshop 2.8: Across: 3. bully, **4.** bug, **6.** rabbit, **8.** bears, **9.** fly, **12.** fishy, **13.** mole. **Down: 1.** dogear, **2.** butterfly, **5.** rats, **7.** beeline **10.** worm, **11.** shark.

End-of-Chapter Activities

1. Choose one of these plant-related idioms to illustrate. When you show your picture to the class, be ready to tell whether you chose to draw a literal or a metaphorical interpretation.

☐ That was the straw that broke the camel's back.
☐ The grass is always greener on the other side.
☐ It is time to put down roots.
☐ She can't see the forest for the trees.
☐ He is always going out on a limb.
☐ Branching out is important for personal growth.
☐ The teacher is really good at planting an idea.

2. Proverbs are abbreviated stories based on common ideas. Because animals are more active than plants, we are more likely to have stories about them. Choose one of these animal-related proverbs to illustrate and explain. Which two say almost the same thing?

☐ You can't teach an old dog new tricks.
☐ You can lead a horse to water but you can't make it drink.
☐ Don't count your chickens before they are hatched.
☐ A bird in the hand is worth two in the bush.
☐ Little boys are made of frogs and snails and puppy dog tails.
☐ Birds of a feather flock together.
☐ Don't change horses in midstream.
☐ Don't sell the bearskin until you've caught the bear.

3. This lesson has been about how the names of well-known plants and animals have been given to other items. However, with plants and animals that are not so well known, the process also works the other way around. They are likely to be given metaphorical names based on a similarity to something people do know about. Here are some that have metaphorical names. You can probably think of others. Choose one to draw a picture of and to explain to your classmates.

Plants	Animals
Bottlebrush trees	Centipede
Cattail reeds	Ladybug
Foxtail grass	Pinto pony
Four o'clock flowers	Polar bear
Jack in the pulpit flowers	Ring-tailed raccoon
Weeping willows	Scissor-tailed flycatcher

4. An alternative would be to design your own plant or your own animal and give it a fantastically appropriate name. Plants come in such a wonderful variety that creative people like to invent their own plants, along with their own creative names. Dr. Seuss drew *Truffula Trees* in *The Lorax,* while in the *Harry Potter* books J. K. Rowling invented a *Whomping Willow* that guards the entrance to the secret passage on the Hogwarts School grounds. If you have played Pokémon, then you probably remember the combination plant and dinosaurs named *Bulbasaur, Ivysaur,* and *Venusaur.* There is also *Oddish,* which looks sort of like a *radish,* and the flowers *Bellsprout, Weepinbell,* and *Victreebel* that vaguely resemble the real plants called *Silver Bells.* You can get ideas for creating new animals from the book *Scranimals* (Greenwillow, 2002), which is made up of poems by Jack Prelutsky and pictures by Peter Sis. These two creative men have scrambled both plants and animals into such creatures as *hippopotamushrooms, bananacondas, ostricheetahs,* and *porcupineapples.* Maybe they will inspire you to create and name some animals of your own.

CHAPTER THREE

Human Body Parts and Actions

Background Reading for the Teacher

Because people naturally learn about their own bodies before they learn about anything else, the human body is an exceptionally rich source of lexical extensions and metaphors. While some metaphors are based on internal organs such as the heart, many more metaphors are based on the parts of people's bodies that are clearly seen and that people feel they have control over. An attention-getter that we used in several classes was the fact that *palm trees* are named for their leaves' resemblance to the palms of people's hands. Students in the first class liked their palm tree so much we had to leave it there. Since we had used up our old straw placemats, in the second class we made a trunk from crumpled brown paper tied with binder twine.

Throughout this chapter, use the examples and the workshops as conversation starters. This is such a rich area that you may want to take your students beyond what we have prepared. It will help students to get involved if you bring into the classroom several of the items that are mentioned—for example, a *thimble* (from *thumb bell);* a newspaper *head*line; a needle with an *eye* and a shoe with *eyelets* and a *tongue*; a bottle with a *neck, mouth*, and *shoulders*; a comb or a rake with *teeth*; a skateboard with a *lip*; a piece of *elbow* macaroni; a *navel* orange; and a *heel* of bread. Also encourage students to bring in real items as they talk about various extensions and metaphors. In three different

Eight-year-old Luke shows off his Halloween teeth and the teeth of a comb and a rake (top). He got so "into" the idea of body metaphors that when he drew his foothills he gave them toenails (bottom).

classes, students enjoyed experimenting with a hands-on table of items named for tongues. We included a mirror so they could look at their own tongues and also the *tongue of a belt*, the *tongue* on a miniature wagon, the *tongue* of a shoe, two short pieces of *tongue-and-groove* board that could be fitted together, a bell with a *tongue*, a little book identified as being written in *your native tongue*, and a drawing of the snake that speaks *parseltongue* in the *Harry Potter* books. We set out printed word strips to reinforce the names and were pleased to see that children enjoyed matching up the word strips and the items.

Depending on the interest of the class and on how much time you have, you might want to expand this chapter and work with such additional terms as *eyes, noses, arms,* and *hearts*. If you teach older students, you could engage their help in collecting terms and metaphors related to these concepts. A dictionary will give them a good start, but they can also brainstorm with each other and with their friends and parents.

Notes to Help Teachers Elicit Ideas from Students

You might begin this chapter by talking about the following sets of phrases. They are printed in enlarged type and in boldface on our website if you want to do the exercise on an overhead projector. Blink your eyes when you talk about a *blinking traffic light* and hold up your *thumb* when you talk about a *thumbnail* sketch. With students' help, circle the phrases that allude to a part of the human body. These will be the oldest words, while the newer items were given their names because of having something in common with the body part. Talk about whether the two items are similar in shape, size, or in some other way. *To toe the line* comes from sports where honest competitors keep their toes behind the line until after the starting gun has sounded. The recently named *Jaws of Life* device that emergency workers use to rescue people from wrecked cars alludes to the opening, not the closing of, jaws because the tool is used to pry open cars that have been crushed.

Literal versus Metaphorical

1. A vein of ore … A blood vein

2. A blinking traffic light … To blink your eye

3. A human nose … The nozzle at a gas pump

4. A heel of bread … A heel on your foot

5. A fat lip … The lip on a skateboard

6. Elbow macaroni … Someone's elbow

7. A person's toe … To toe the line

These fifth-graders are not likely to forget that palm trees are so named because their fronds resemble the palms and fingers of people's hands. We came to class with the trunk already made from a straw placemat cut up and glued on cardboard. The children were happy to trace their hands and cut them out to make the fronds.

8. The facing on a building … Face-to-face combat

9. Your leg … The first leg of a trip

10. A person's spine … The spine of a book

11. A tearjerker book … A tear

12. A person's jaws … The jaws of life tool that emergency workers use to pry people from wrecked cars

Another way to get children talking and thinking about body part metaphors is to use the items in the following chart as conversation starters. The words in the first two columns are also printed in heavy type on our web page so that you can download them and put them on an overhead. Either you or students in your class can probably supply sample sentences more fitting to your particular students than the ones that are given here just to get your thinking started.

Term	Lexical Extensions	Sample Sentences
hair	haircut hairsbreadth hairline hairy	For things associated with *hair*, we have such basic words as *haircut, hairpin, hairdo, hairdresser, hairpiece,* and *hairstyling.* The fineness of hair is the basis for such metaphors as *hairline crack,* a *hairline fracture,* a *hairline* spring in a watch, and a *hair trigger* in a gun. Having a *hairy* experience is a shorthand way to say you had a *hair-raising* experience, meaning you were so frightened that the hairs on your arms stood up. To come within a *hairsbreadth* of something means having had a very narrow escape. People who insist on *splitting hairs* are quibbling over little details.
ears	earache eardrop eardrum earful earlobe earring	A musical person might be described as having *an ear for music* or being able to *play by ear.* If you *have someone's ear*, the person respects what you say. If your *ears are burning*, someone is talking about you. *Ears of corn* look like donkey ears, but they were actually named from a Middle English word meaning *edge.* The *rabbit ears* on portable TV sets are a shape comparison.
brow	eyebrows	*Brows* are usually called *foreheads*, except when we talk about our *eyebrows.* If someone earns something by the *sweat of his brow*, he has worked hard. Someone who looks *browbeaten* appears humble and picked on. Speakers are being metaphorical rather than literal when they talk about *high brow* versus *low brow* taste. The *brow of a hill* is shaped like a person's forehead.
cheek	cheeky	*Cheeks* are soft and vulnerable, which is why the Biblical admonition to *turn the other cheek* was startling advice. People fighting *cheek by jowl* are in vicious and close combat. Today people are more likely to have verbal fights and to use *tongue-in-cheek* humor. Someone who is *in your face* might be described as *cheeky.*

mouth	mouthpiece mouthy	If a *cheeky* person is also talkative, she might be described as *mouthy*. Lawyers often act as the *mouthpiece* or the spokesman for their clients. Having *many mouths to feed* means being responsible for supporting several people. To *put your foot in your mouth* is to have said something embarrassing. Both bottles and rivers have *mouths*. Being *down in the mouth* means you are not smiling. We hope the phrase *smash-mouth football* is figurative rather than literal.

Humans engage in basically three kinds of actions. One kind is intellectual and involves the thinking that people do. We are not treating that kind in this chapter because it is too abstract to illustrate clearly. The other actions that people engage in are those that they consciously think about as opposed to those that the body does on its own. We talk about both of these actions.

In Workshop 3.7, where students look at the lexical extensions of *attack, fight, hit, kick,* and *strike,* they are asked to find the sentence in each set that comes closest to expressing real hostility. The ones we would choose are:

Be careful, that's an *attack shark*.

Jesse is a *fighter pilot*, so he gets called up only when there are real problems.
I think he has his own private *hit man*.

Little kids get carried out of stores *kicking and screaming* because their parents won't
    buy what they want.

It's not true that lightning never *strikes* twice in the same place.

Finding sentences that have little to do with hostility will be harder because *hostility* is an attitude, and it is not always possible to know what kinds of things have attitudes. For example, when speakers say that "the serum is *attacking* the poison," they could just as well say that the serum is *counterbalancing* or *negating* the poison. However, the word *attack* seems better. It is shorter and more dramatic, plus it gets the listener emotionally involved because people know what it means to be *attacked*. Positive uses of *hit* (*Hit Parade, hits* on Broadway, *hits* on a website, etc.) probably relate to this same kind of emotional involvement.

Animal versus Human Heads

Name: _____ **Period:** _____ **Date:** _____

Heads are obviously an important part of people's bodies. They enable people to hear through their ears, see through their eyes, smell and breathe through their noses, and eat and speak through their mouths. Medical technology has made it so that even such complex organs as the heart and the lungs can be repaired or even transplanted, but no one has been able to live without a head. The importance of heads is shown in allusions to someone as the *head* of a company, the *headmaster* of a school, the *headquarters building* of an institution, and the *headlines* on a newspaper. Other metaphors are based on a similarity in shape as when speakers talk about a *head* of lettuce or a *head* of cabbage.

   Still other head metaphors are based on a similarity in position. Human heads are at the top of our bodies, which means that when something is called a head because it is on top, the reference is to a human head. But if something is called a head because it is in the front, the allusion is to an animal's head. In the following sentences, if the allusion is to something being in the front, write ANIMAL, but if it is to something being on top, write HUMAN.

_____ **1.** The crash was in all the *headlines*.

_____ **2.** Rescuers have made little *headway* in getting to the victims.

_____ **3.** Put your *headings* in capital letters.

_____ **4.** My grandfather collects *arrowheads*.

_____ **5.** Our plane was late because of heavy *headwinds*.

_____ **6.** One of their *headlights* was out.

_____ **7.** This may have been why they had a *head-on* collision.

_____ **8.** Our candidate stood *head and shoulders* above the rest.

Hand It Over

Name: _____ **Period:** _____ **Date:** _____

PART I Many metaphors are based on people's hands and on such parts of their hands as *fingers, knuckles, thumbs,* and *palms*. This is because people do so many things with their hands, and unlike internal organs of the body that we do not see, people's hands are out in front and clearly visible. This chart illustrates some of the extended uses of the word *hand*.

Term	Lexical Extensions	Sample Sentences
hand	handicraft handle handout handshake handwrite handy	People who are *handy* are good with *handicrafts*. The *hands* of a clock could as easily be called the *arms*. *Handles* on cups, knives, pans, and suitcases are meant to connect to people's hands. When you *hand in* your homework or give someone a *handout*, you actually use your *hands*. But when you *hand* someone over to the police or win a contest *hands down*, your hands may not be involved. If a man asks for a woman's *hand* in marriage, he wants more than her hand. *Hand-to-hand* combat probably involves bayonets and rifle butts more than hands. *Hands* are such useful parts of the body that some workers are referred to simply as *ranch hands* or *deck hands*. When *the handwriting is on the wall*, something is obvious, even if nothing was actually written on a wall.

As you think about the sample sentences in the chart, decide on three in which *hand* is used to stand for something that really includes more than someone's hand. Talk about the meanings and see if you can create three additional sentences to illustrate the same principle.

A *hand* is only part of what is being talked about.

1. _____

2. _____

3. _____

Now do something similar for metaphors based on an action that hands do. You will have more to choose from in this category.

The *hand* metaphor is based on an action.

1. _____

2. _____

3. _____

PART II Now read these charts showing extensions of words that name parts of people's hands. Choose one idea from each part and write a sentence that illustrates a metaphorical use of the word on the appropriate part of the hand on the next page. Be ready to share your sentence when the class talks about fingers, knuckles, thumbs, and palms. Tell whether your metaphor is based on shape or action or on something else.

Term	Lexical Extensions	Sample Sentence
finger	to finger fingerling fingernail fingerprint fingertip ladyfingers	The *Finger Lakes* in upstate New York fan out like fingers. *Ladyfingers* are only one kind of *finger food*. Some small fish are called *fingerlings*. *Having a finger in every pie* is interfering in other people's business. Having things *at your fingertips* means being prepared. In the days of Sherlock Holmes, *fingerprinting* was a new tool for detectives.
knuckle	knuckle	*To knuckle down* to a task is to work at it earnestly. Calling someone a *knucklehead* is almost the same as saying he or she is a *bonehead*. A *knuckle sandwich* is a hit in the mouth. *To knuckle under* means to put your fists down and adopt a nonfighting stance. In baseball a *knuckler* or a *knuckle ball* is a slow pitch controlled by the way the pitcher holds the ball.
thumb	thumb thimble	It takes strong thumbs to push in *thumb tacks*. Because thumbs are good for flipping pages, dictionaries have *thumb indexes*. To *thumb a ride* is to hitchhike. *Thumbs up!* means you like something. The State of Michigan is shaped like a mitten with *the thumb* sticking out into Lake Huron. A *thumbnail* sketch is unusually small. The famous dwarf, *Tom Thumb*, was named after Hans Christian Andersen's story of *Thumbelina*. Sewing *thimbles* are literally "bells for thumbs." If you *thumb your nose* at someone or something, you are expressing disdain.

palm	palm tree palmist	*Palm trees* are named because the fronds look like people's hands turned inside out. A computer company chose *Palm* as the name for its handheld computer to emphasize how small it is. *Palm Sunday* is named after the *palm* branches laid in Christ's path when he entered Jerusalem. A *palmist* is someone who tells the future by reading the lines on people's *palms*. If someone *palms something off* on you, they have tricked you into taking it.

Figure 3.1 A handful of metaphors

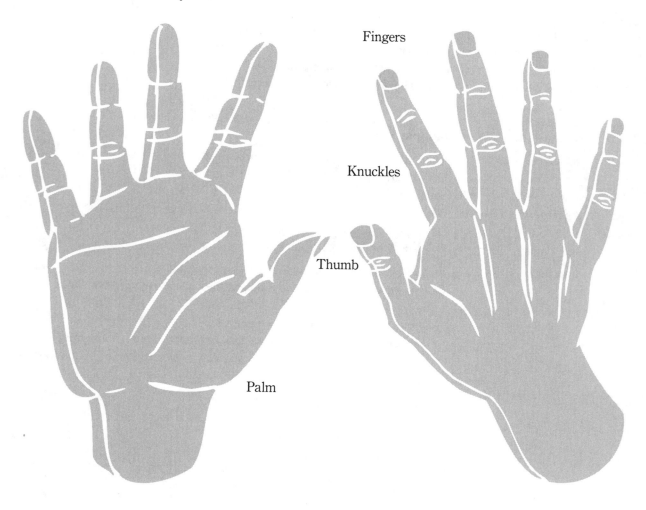

Fingers

Knuckles

Thumb

Palm

From Metaphorical to Literal

Name: _____ **Period:** _____ **Date:** _____

These sentences use body parts in a metaphorical sense. Show that you can figure out the sources of metaphors by writing a new sentence for each italicized body word in which you use it in a more literal sense. Feel free to change the endings or the part of speech of the body words. For example, with the sentence, "She *faces* a job change," you could write a sentence using *face* to refer to someone's actual face, as in "She has a round *face* like her mother's."

1. She had no idea what was in her grandmother's treasure *chest*.

_____

2. When Michael went to meet Sarah's family, he put his best *foot* forward.

_____

3. Kimberly is up to her *ears* in work.

_____

4. I've got to *hand* it to you—you wowed the judges!

_____

5. The family is into the stock market over their *heads* and will lose a lot of money.

_____

6. They like to *brain*storm before making an important decision.

_____

7. Her favorite piece of jewelry is a *tear*drop pendant.

_____

A Leg Up

Name: _____ **Period:** _____ **Date:** _____

Legs are the longest and the strongest of our limbs and, as might be expected, have provided English with many extended meanings. Some languages have different words for animal and human legs and for the legs on tables and chairs. However, English makes *leg* serve all these purposes. Even triangles are said to have *legs*, as do journeys and competitions. Things associated with human legs include *leg warmers, legroom*, and the *legs* of pants. More metaphorically, if you have *a leg up* on a project or on someone you are competing with, you have a head start or a boost of some kind. This probably relates to someone already being part way up when climbing a ladder or getting on a horse.

Knees are the main joint in the middle of humans' and some animals' legs. *Kneeling* is the act of crouching on one's knees and is sometimes used to symbolize humility. The *kneehole* in a desk is where people put their knees. *Knee socks* come up to the knees, while *knee pants* come down to the knees. *Knee-high* is a kind of measurement as in the old saying from the Midwest about corn being *knee-high* by the Fourth of July.

Feet are often referred to in the singular form of *foot* as in *footstool, footstep, footpath, footprint,* and *footrest.* Speakers were being more metaphorical when they gave the name *foot* to a measurement of 12 inches, which is about the size of a large man's foot. The *footage* in film is a second-level metaphor, perhaps inspired by the fact that film resembles a tape measure. The *foot* on a sewing machine, as well as the *foot pedals* in cars and on musical instruments, resemble the shape of a human foot.

Heels are a low and unimpressive part of the body, thus the related metaphors usually have negative connotations. To be a *heel* is to be a lowdown person, while if someone is described as *down at the heels*, the allusion is to a person's shoes being worn or shabby. However, the usual meaning is broader in implying that someone's life is not going very well.

Toes are more active parts of the body. *To be on your toes* means to be alert, while if you compete with someone *toe-to-toe*, you are considered an equal. People who are *pigeon-toed* walk with their toes pointed in. *Toeing-in* on a car is when the fronts of the forward tires are closer than the backs. When carpenters talk about *toeing* or *toe-nailing*, they are talking about driving nails in at a slant.

Read the sentences below and choose the most appropriate of these terms to write in the blank spaces. Talk about what the metaphorical meanings in these sentences have in common with the more literal meanings.

| drag their feet | foot | foothills | footlights | footnotes | head over heels |
| kneecapping | leg | leg pulled | leg work | tiptoe | toehold |

1. Doing the _____ for a political candidate is no easy task.

2. The _____ on a stage are the ones near the actors' feet.

3. In the 1970s, the word _____ came into the language to name the terrorist act of crippling people through damaging their knees, most likely by shooting.

4. If you have a _____ on getting a job, you have a slight advantage.

5. Our former governor was always putting his _____ in his mouth.

6. Families often _____ around sensitive topics.

7. To be _____ in love means the person's brain is not where it should be.

8. It is no fun to bring along people who _____ every time there's a new idea.

9. In books, _____ are at the bottom of the page.

10. We had run out of things to talk about by the second _____ of the trip.

11. Snow covers mountain tops long before it gets down to the _____.

12. To get your _____ is to have a joke played on you.

A Leg Up

Exploring Analogies

Name: _____ **Period:** _____ **Date:** _____

PART I Fill in the missing words from these paragraphs exploring connections between various parts of the human body. Choose from the following words, some of which might be used more than once.

> air   arms   blood   feet   hands   insects   legs   palms   soles   talons

As humans it is easy to recognize the similarities among different parts of our bodies. For example, we can see that our *knees* are to our **(1.)** _____ as our *elbows* are to our **(2.)** _____, and that our *toes* are to our **(3.)** _____ as our *fingers* are to our **(4.)** _____. While it may be a little harder, we can see that the fleshy part of our hands, the **(5.)** _____, are similar to the fleshy part of our feet, the **(6.)** _____, and that our lungs process **(7.)** _____ as our hearts process **(8.)** _____. These analogies are based on how parts of the body work.

Another kind of analogy could be based on similarities between humans and animals. For example, *toenails* protect humans' **(9.)** _____ as **(10.)** _____ protect birds' *feet*. And in some senses, *eyebrows* work for humans as *antennae* work for **(11.)** _____. At least they grow from similar parts of the body.

PART II Just as we can compare the various parts of human and animal bodies, we can also compare what our bodies do. Fill in the blanks to complete these analogies.

> drinking   hearing   shivering   seeing   shaving   tasting   walking

1. Sniffing is to a nose as _____ is to a tongue.

2. Sweating is to being hot as _____ is to being cold.

3. Cutting is to hair as _____ is to whiskers.

4. Hearing is to ears as _____ is to eyes.

5. Crawling is to babies as _____ is to adults.

6. Breathing is to air as _____ is to water.

7. Seeing is to eyes as _____ is to ears.

Moving Our Bodies

Name: _____ **Period:** _____ **Date:** _____

Read these paragraphs about basic movements and then choose the appropriate words to complete the sentences that are written underneath.

A. ***Crawling*** is the first way that babies get around. Because people stay low when they crawl, the space underneath some houses is described as *crawl space*. In cold climates, the *crawl space* provides a layer of air between the house and the land, which in winter is frozen. It also allows workers to *crawl* underneath a house to repair pipes. When speakers use *crawl* to refer to things other than people *crawling*, the focus might be on slowness, as in "During rush hour, the traffic on Highway 102 *crawls along*." And even when referring to people, the allusion might be metaphorical as in this sentence, "My grandmother advises patience by telling us we have to *crawl before we can walk*." In the sample sentences below, one sentence focuses on slowness, another on an action that resembles a baby crawling, and one on people being so scared that the hair stands up on their arms so that they feel like bugs are crawling over their skin. Write the appropriate phrases in the blanks and then talk about the basis for the metaphors.

Australian crawl	crawl up	skin crawl

1. Lots of people stay after movies to see the credits_____ the screen.

2. The movie was so creepy, it made my _____.

3. At swimming this week we are practicing the _____.

B. ***Stepping*** is the most common way of moving our bodies forward. All families celebrate when a baby takes its first step. We extend this feeling of congratulations when we say such things as "I'm glad he is *stepping forward* and taking responsibility" and "If you take it *step by step*, it will be easier." The *step pyramids* in Egypt look smooth from a distance, but are really made like giant *stair steps*. When people talk about *stair-step* children in a family, it means that the children are about the same age apart so that when they stand in a row, the tops of their heads are about the same distance apart as are stair steps. *Stepparents* and *stepchildren* are so named because there has been a death or a divorce and maybe a remarriage. The new families are *a step* away from the original family structure.

Figure out the basis for the comparisons in the following sentences and write the appropriate phrases in the blanks. Notice that one of them is an allusion to the way the driver of a car steps on the gas pedal to make the car go.

| step down | step on it | step up |

1. The mayor plans to _____ before his term is complete.

2. They have promised to _____ their efforts for the homeless.

3. _____ or we will be late!

C. *Walking* is the process of taking steps in a regular pattern so as to move forward. Most of the extended meanings of this word relate to actual walking, but in a special sense. For example, at a big college a football player who gets on a team without having been recruited and given a scholarship is called a *walk-on*. When people *walk away* with a prize or *walk out* on their families, there is more involved than just walking. Kids used to ask for *walkie-talkies* for their birthdays, but now that cell phones are available, they ask for *Sony Walkmans®*.

See if you can write the appropriate phrases in the following sentences and then explain the relationships to basic walking.

| a walk in the park | walk the plank | walk-through | walking stick |

1. _____ insects are hard to spot.

2. Dress rehearsal for the play is tomorrow; tonight is just a _____.

3. She claimed the achievement tests were so easy they were _____.

4. Pirates used to make their captives _____.

D. *Running* is almost like walking except that it is faster and people have to work harder at it. This means that when it is used as a metaphor it will refer to things that are harder than walking. Candidates *run* (not *walk*) for office. A patriotic motto from the 1970s, "These Colors Don't Run," was printed in red, white, and blue and was meant as a challenge. Because when people *run* they cover longer distances than when they walk, *run* sometimes indicates that something is long, as in "Their contract *runs* for 24 more months," "The rope has to be *run through* both pulleys," and "Lace *runners* are no longer fashionable on tables and dressers."

With the following sentences, write the appropriate terms in the spaces and then talk about whether the movement is happening with people's feet or with something else.

| ran up | run | run-around | runaways | running | runs | runway |

1. That truck can _____ either on gas or electricity.

2. It took two days to get the plane off the _____ after its landing gear collapsed.

3. Diabetes _____ in my family.

4. Everyone was surprised at the bill they _____.

5. She suspected that she was being given the _____.

6. My aunt is worried about Blanche _____ with a wild crowd.

7. There's a shelter for _____ in downtown Sacramento.

E. *Jumping* takes more energy than crawling, stepping, walking, and running because people have to lift their whole bodies when they jump. The action has to be quick because gravity pulls people's bodies back down. This quickness is what is implied in such sentences as, "When he sends down a request, I *jump to!*" and, "That movie director likes to make *jump-cuts* instead of fade-outs."

Write the appropriate terms in the following sentences and talk about whether the allusion is to quickness or something else.

| jump | jump rope | jumpers | jumping to |

1. We're going because it is just a hop, skip, and _____ away.

2. Some _____ rhymes are really funny.

3. It takes experience and patience to keep from _____ conclusions.

4. The school dress code requires boys to wear shirts with collars and girls to wear _____.

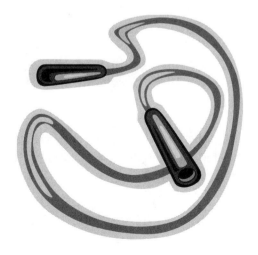

Hostile Actions

Name: _____ **Period:** _____ **Date:** _____

Because hostile actions have dire results, the terms related to *attacking, fighting, hitting, kicking,* and *striking* are important words in our language. But, as shown by the following chart, speakers adapt hostile words to many other situations. It is a way of exaggerating the importance of whatever we want to draw attention to. For example, if one of your friends responds to what you have said with, "Those are *fighting words!*" chances are that your friend does not really intend to "fight" about the matter. He is simply expressing a mild form of disagreement or disapproval of what you have said.

Read through the words and sentences on the following chart. Talk about what the sentences mean. Circle the one sentence in each group that has the closest relationship to hostility. Talk about the other sentences and why they are being compared to hostile actions. Underline any sentences you can find that express little or no hostility as with the one under *kick,* "It's fun to *kick back* on Fridays and go to the movies."

Term	Lexical Extensions	Sample Sentences
attack	attacked attackers	He didn't think it fair that she *attacked* his reputation. Be careful; that's an *attack shark.* My brain's numb; I'll *attack* the problem again in the morning when I'm fresher. It will be several hours before we know if the serum is *attacking* the poison.
fight	fighter fighting fought	The Wisconsin *fight song* has been adopted by hundreds of high schools. During holiday seasons, many people take extra steps to *fight* depression. It was a hard-*fought* campaign, but the candidates now say they will all cooperate. The x-rays show that she has a *fighting chance.* Jesse is a *fighter pilot,* so he gets called up only when there are real problems.
hit	hitter hits hitting	Songs that have once been on the *Hit Parade* seem to last forever. There is a *hit man* on "The Sopranos" TV show. Our website has had over 4,000 *hits* in its first month. He's so good they use him as a *clean-up hitter.* Much to our surprise, it was a *hit* in New York even though it failed in Boston.
kick	kick back kicker kicking	I get a *kick* out of all the excuses he makes. It's fun to *kick back* on Fridays and go to the movies. People wonder whether doctors get *kickbacks* on the medicines they prescribe. Finding out that my computer had crashed was a real *kicker.* Little kids get carried out of stores *kicking and screaming* because their parents won't buy what they want.

strike	on strike strikers striking struck	It took at least a couple of seasons for fans to forgive baseball players for *striking*. My uncle was always telling me that to get ahead I would have to *strike while the iron is hot*. She was *struck* with the idea as soon as she saw the photos. If you're going to *strike* out on a journey, you better plan ahead. When the clock *struck* midnight, the party was just getting started. It's not true that lightning never *strikes* twice in the same place.

Write three sentences here in which you use hostile words in a nonhostile or metaphorical way.

1. _____

_____

2. _____

_____

3. _____

_____

Survival Actions

Name: _____ **Period:** _____ **Date:** _____

Our bodies undertake many actions that we seldom think about because they are necessary to our survival.

PART I Actions outside of People's Conscious Control

The actions alluded to with the following terms are ones that our bodies do without conscious direction. Think about the basic meanings and then try to figure out the appropriate term to write in the blank spaces in the following sentences. Talk about the relationships between the basic actions and the more metaphorical ones illustrated in the sentences.

breath	breather	digest	growing	sweating

1. There has never been a _____ of scandal about the Wiley family.

2. Some jury members cannot _____ all the information they are given.

3. Excitement has been _____ ever since the new school programs were announced.

4. After taking a test, the hardest part is _____ out the time between finishing the test and the getting your grade.

5. Let's stop and take a _____ .

PART II Actions under People's Conscious Control

The actions alluded to in the following sentences are just as necessary to survival, but they are more under people's control. You are at least aware of what you are doing when you go to *sleep* and *wake up*; when you *bite, chew,* and *swallow* your food; when you *stand up* and *lie down*; and when you *see* or *watch* something. Write the appropriate terms in the blank spaces left in the following sentences. Then talk about the relationships between the basic meanings of such words and the more metaphorical meanings that are illustrated in the sentences.

biting	see	sleeping	stand	swallow	wake up

1. The sleet made it a _____ storm.

2. "Let _____ dogs lie" is my uncle's motto.

3. She is gullible to _____ Kerry's flattery.

4. I don't _____ how we can collect that much money.

5. I like that old saying about "_____ and smell the flowers."

6. Patrick says he will _____ tall and not let anyone change his mind.

An Action-Packed Crossword Puzzle

Name: _____ **Period:** _____ **Date:** _____

Use these clues to fill in the crossword puzzle, which uses *action* words in metaphorical ways.

ACROSS

2. Now that's over, we can _____ a sigh of relief.

3. It is really hard to _____ their story about meeting an alien.

5. She is the most _____ woman I have ever met.

6. The bill passed only because our Senator was _____ on the job.

7. We are happy about the number of _____ on our website.

9. The motor has been _____ for the last couple of hours.

DOWN

1. Halloween is a good time for decorating with creepy _____.

4. The family has been _____ prejudice for years.

5. She hopes to use this job as a _____ stone to something better.

8. Everybody has been _____ since the bomb alert yesterday.

More Basic Phrases: 1. a blood vein, **2.** to blink your eye, **3.** a human nose, **4.** a heel on your foot, **5.** a fat lip, **6.** someone's elbow, **7.** a person's toe, **8.** face-to-face combat, **9.** your leg, **10.** a person's spine, **11.** a tear, **12.** a person's jaws.

Workshop 3.1: 1. human, **2.** animal, **3.** human, **4.** animal, **5.** animal, **6.** animal, **7.** animal, **8.** human.

Workshop 3.2: Possible Answers: When the hand is only part of what is being talked about: ranch hands, deck hands, hand in marriage. When the hand metaphor refers to an action: handicrafts, a handout, hand-to-hand combat, handwriting on the wall.

Workshop 3.3: Possible Answers: 1. Human *chests* hold the treasures of our hearts and our lungs. **2.** For most people, their right *foot* is better than their left. **3.** Her mother says she can get her *ears* pierced if she gets all As and Bs. **4.** His right *hand* is in a bandage. **5.** The water was over the child's *head* when his grandfather grabbed him. **6.** They are afraid he has a tumor on his *brain*. **7.** She could not keep the *tears* back when she heard the news.

Workshop 3.4: 1. leg work, **2.** footlights, **3.** kneecapping, **4.** toehold, **5.** foot, **6.** tiptoe, **7.** head over heels, **8.** drag their feet, **9.** footnotes, **10.** leg, **11.** foothills, **12.** leg pulled.

Workshop 3.5: Part I: 1. legs, **2.** arms, **3.** feet, **4.** hands, **5.** palms, **6.** soles, **7.** air, **8.** blood, **9.** feet, **10.** talons, **11.** insects.

Part II: 1. tasting, **2.** shivering, **3.** shaving, **4.** seeing, **5.** walking, **6.** drinking, **7.** hearing.

Workshop 3.6: A. 1. crawl up, **2.** skin crawl, **3.** Australian crawl. **B. 1.** step down, **2.** step up, **3.** step on it. **C. 1.** walking stick, **2.** walk-through, **3.** a walk in the park, **4.** walk the plank. **D. 1.** run, **2.** runway, **3.** runs, **4.** ran up, **5.** run-around, **6.** running, **7.** runaways. **E. 1.** jump, **2.** jump rope, **3.** jumping to, **4.** jumpers.

Workshop 3.7: The allusions to actual hostility that should be circled are probably the references to an attack shark, a fighter pilot, a hit man, little kids kicking and screaming, and perhaps the idea of fans feeling hostile toward striking baseball players. Allusions that carry little hostility are probably those sentences related to attacking a problem in the morning; the Wisconsin fight song; the Hit Parade, a hit on Broadway, and hits on a website; getting a kick out of someone's excuses; kicking back on Fridays; and being struck with an idea, a clock striking, and striking out on a journey.

Workshop 3.8: Part I: 1. breath, **2.** digest, **3.** growing, **4.** sweating, **5.** breather. **Part II: 1.** biting, **2.** sleeping, **3.** swallow, **4.** see, **5.** wake up, **6.** stand.

Workshop 3.9: Across: 2. breathe, **3.** swallow, **5.** striking, **6.** asleep, **7.** hits, **9.** running. **Down: 1.** crawlers, **4.** fighting, **5.** stepping, **8.** jumpy.

End-of-Chapter Activities

1. An activity to help students look at less common words that are used in relation to human actions is to collect a set of pictures showing humans in action. Book jackets are a good source, and so are magazine covers, catalogues, alumni magazines, and programs from athletic and other performance events. Glue a picture to a poster board and underneath the picture tape two sheets of lined paper—one labeled ACTION WORDS and one labeled DESCRIPTION WORDS. Tape these sheets lightly so that they can be replaced for use with other classes and at other times. Make four or five of these posters (depending on how big your class is), number them, and tape them to a wall or lay them out on worktables. Spread them far enough around the room that groups can gather comfortably around each one. Divide the class into small groups. Give each group a number to match a different poster and explain that each group starts with its number and then works through the other posters in order.

The students' task is to brainstorm and make notes to themselves of words or phrases that are appropriate to each picture. With older students, you can explain that the ACTION words are some form of a verb while the DESCRIPTION words are adjectives or adverbs. When the groups settle on their "best" words, they are to write four ACTION terms and four DESCRIPTION terms underneath each picture. The trick is that they cannot use any words that have already been used. This means that they must read and think about all the words their classmates have already written. As each group gets closer to its last poster, students will probably need to exert themselves to think up new words.

After all the words are written, read them aloud and talk a little about any that need explanations or that you can build on. Also, without embarrassing anyone, correct misspellings. Leave the posters up long enough that they can be used for a writing exercise in which students choose their "favorite" picture to explain in a paragraph. These paragraphs will probably be better if you encourage, but do not force, students to use words from the lists. The lesson will be a success if students feel comfortable enough to use even one or two words that they wouldn't have used before this lesson. It takes many experiences with new words before students feel real "ownership" over them.

2. A fun group project to help younger students remember the relationship between the palms of their hands and the name of *palm trees* is for students to trace hands, cut them out, and then tape or pin one onto a bulletin board that has already been prepared with a trunk and a sign "We all have a hand in this palm tree." (See the photo on p. 34.) For the trunk in one class, we used crushed brown paper and binder twine. For another class, we cut up a straw placemat.

3. Another idea for a concluding activity is to draw a giant hand (or foot, or leg, or even a whole person). Give each student an index card on which to write a metaphorical sentence. It is a good review for the class to have students read and explain their metaphors as they post them on the appropriate part of the silhouette. If you download the word list from our website, you can perhaps adjust the size and run the words off as labels or space them out four to a page. If you photocopy them on cardstock and cut them into fourths, students will have prelabeled cards on which to work. Having such cards is an efficient way to make sure that students illustrate a variety of concepts.

4. In one of our classes, a student brought in a list of "Exercises for Lazy People" from a "Dear Abby" column. These could be made into word strips and distributed for students to illustrate. Afterwards, when students show their pictures, you can talk about whether they did a literal picture (literal pictures are much easier to draw, thus this is mostly what students will provide) or a metaphorical picture. Lead students in talking about why it is easier to draw the literal than the figurative interpretations. This should help them understand one of the reasons that speakers use concrete examples to allude to abstract ideas.

☐ Jumping to conclusions

☐ Beating around the bush
☐ Climbing the walls
☐ Passing the buck
☐ Dragging your heels
☐ Pushing your luck
☐ Making mountains out of molehills
☐ Hitting the nail on the head
☐ Running around in circles
☐ Climbing the ladder of success
☐ Opening a can of worms
☐ Starting the ball rolling
☐ Jumping on the bandwagon
☐ Picking up the pieces
☐ Going over the edge

Abby chided the contributor for not including "Putting your foot in your mouth."

Here are some additional proverbs or clichés that students might illustrate through a poster, a cartoon, or a short, short story:

☐ Lend me your ears!
☐ My lips are sealed.
☐ Two heads are better than one.
☐ She's always putting her foot in her mouth.
☐ I'm all thumbs when it comes to decorating.
☐ He's the backbone of the community.
☐ I would give my right hand for that. (A good example of this appears near the end of Book Four in the *Harry Potter* series.)

CHAPTER FOUR

Letters, Shapes, and Numbers

Background Reading for the Teacher

We start this chapter with alphabet shapes because it is the part that surprised students and convinced them these were not the same lessons they had in kindergarten about circles, triangles, and squares.

Many letters of the alphabet have come full circle in that they started out as pictograms representing objects directly and literally, as when the capital A (tilted on its side) was a picture of an ox's head with horns, while an M was a picture of waves in water, or in some systems, a mountain. As writing systems became more sophisticated, these pictograms gave way to the beginning sounds of the items they pictured so that the letters of the alphabet as now used by English speakers represent sounds rather than items.

But because virtually all English speakers are familiar with the shapes of the twenty-six letters in the alphabet, more than half of their names have been adapted to name other common items ranging from *Cheerios®* (cheery Os) to *H-gear shifts* (three forward gears plus reverse). The metaphors are mostly based on the shape of capital letters, but when talking about the *I-formation* in football, speakers say that the fullback "dots the *i.*"

As a way to illustrate the difference between a letter used as a shape and as a word, you might tell about one of our foreign students at the University of Michigan in Ann Arbor. He came to class looking frustrated. When we asked what was wrong, he told us about being stopped and scolded by a police officer. He was driving to school when he saw a sign that read "No U Turn." He thought the sign meant something like, "No—Do not enter this street. You turn," and so he immediately turned around and received a lesson in English, courtesy of the Ann Arbor Police Department.

Nine-year-old Hassan (top) poses "behind the 8-ball" (a key chain from a dollar store) while 10-year-old Jim (bottom) displays the poster he made of alphabet shapes.

The more unusual the items on our *Hands-on* table, the longer children would examine them and read and rearrange the labels. The antique block is from Don's childhood, and the miniature brass bicycle was something we plucked from a keepsakes shelf at home.

Older, more sophisticated students might be interested in talking about the relatively few cases where it is hard to tell if a name is based on a shape or something else. For example, the *V-8 engine* is based on the shape (the eight cylinders are placed so that the engine is bigger at the top than the bottom), while *V-8 juice* is a kind of pun taken from the name of the engine but with the *V* standing for *vegetables*. Even this is no longer true, in that the company is now making *V-8* fruit drinks. In *X-ray*, the *X* stands for something "unknown," as in mathematical formulas, but the *X-crossing* signs near railroad tracks are based on shape because they show a train track crossing over a highway. When *Christmas* is written *Xmas*, the *X* is a metaphor for a shape because it is a picture of the cross that Jesus carried over his shoulder on the way to the crucifixion.

Another difference that you might want to talk to older students about is how language play based on the shapes of letters differs from the language play in William Steig's book *C D B* (Windmill, 1968), where letters are used as if they were individual words, or at least syllables. This is the kind of play people are using when they sign off their e-mail with *BCNU* (be seeing you) or make jokes on their license plates as with *10SN1* (tennis, anyone?) or *IMNLUV* (I am in love).

When you work with the numbers part of this chapter, you might read aloud Jon Scieszka and Lane Smith's *Math Curse* (Viking 1995), an oversized picture book that could inspire students to look a little differently at numbers. If you can find the children's 1928 classic *Millions of Cats*, by Wanda Gag, it would also be fun to read as an illustration of Workshop 4.7 on approximate versus exact.

Notes to Help Teachers Elicit Ideas from Students

Here are the basic letter-shape metaphors we found. You will have better luck in getting the idea across to students if you look around your house (or stop at a dollar store) and bring in examples of such common tools as a *T-square,* a *C-clamp,* a *U-bolt,* and an *S-hook.* Wearing a *T-shirt* (either *V-necked* or round-necked) or a *U-necked* or an *A-line* dress would also help to stimulate students' thinking. Because the items are so easy to draw, this is a good time to use white boards and markers. After you have introduced the idea, you might encourage pairs of students to brainstorm and draw pictures of items they can then introduce to the class. Or you can lead students in a classwide brainstorming session in which you ask them to draw five or six of the items as you and your students describe them. Here are those most commonly referred to with alphabet names; you may be able to think of others.

A: A-frame house, A-ladder, A-line dress

C: C-clamp

D: D-ring

E: E-building

H: H gear shift

I: I-beam in construction, I-formation in football

J: J-bar on a ski lift, J-hook for hanging things, J-stroke in canoeing

K: K-turn in driving (for parallel parking)

L: L-shaped room, ranch-style L house

O: O-ring (the part on the Challenger Shuttle that failed), Cheerios®

S: S-curve, S-hook

T: golf tee, T-bar on a ski lift, T-ball, T-bone steak, T-dock, T-formation in football, T-intersection, T-shirt, T-strap on shoes

U: U-bolt, U-neckline, U-turn

V: V-6 or V-8 engine, V-groove in wood, V-necked shirt or sweater, V-situp exercise.

X: X-crossing, X-frame of a car, X-stretcher

Y: Y-splice, Y-intersection

Z: Z-frame of a car, Z-frame gate

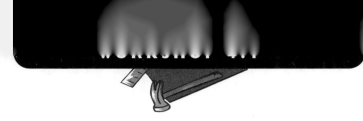

Fill in the Letter Blanks

PART I Think about the shapes of the following sets of letters and write the appropriate letters in the blank spaces.

A, C, D AND E:

1. Carpenters use _____-clamps to hold boards together until they dry.

2. It takes a lot of shingles to put the roof on an _____-frame house.

3. Some kids hang little toys or decorations from the _____- rings on their pack backs.

4. _____-ladders don't have to be leaned against a wall.

5. _____-line dresses do not have belts.

6. _____-buildings are designed so that more of the rooms can have windows.

I, J, K, AND L:

1. On steel _____-beams, the ends have little crosspieces that hold the bolts.

2. Before you can get a driver's license, you need to learn to make _____-turns so that you can parallel park.

3. The most common stroke in canoeing is the _____-stroke.

4. Apartments often have _____-shaped rooms with the smaller part being used as a dinette or breakfast nook.

5. When a football team decides on the _____-formation, the fullback "dots the I."

6. A _____-hook works well for hanging ropes or buckets.

S, T, U, V, AND X:

1. The speed limit on that _____-curve is 30 miles per hour.

2. A _____-necked sweater is easier to get over your head than one with a round neck.

3. When you see an _____-crossing sign, you need to watch for a train.

4. A _____-bolt fastens things together sort of like a padlock.

5. When we eat out, my father always orders a _____-bone steak.

6. If you need to hang a bucket on a chain, it helps to have an _____-hook.

7. On most days, at least half the kids in our class are wearing _____-shirts.

8. *Xmas* is an abbreviation for Christmas because the _____ is a picture of a tipped cross, like the one Christ carried up the hill in Jerusalem.

9. On busy streets, _____-turns are dangerous.

10. A _____-8 engine has eight cylinders and is bigger at the top than at the bottom.

11. Now that kids play _____-ball, the games are more fun to watch.

PART II T is such a basic shape that it has inspired more names than any other letter. Think about its shape and then draw a little picture of each of the following T-shaped items and see if you can figure out the advantages.

1. A T-dock on a recreational lake as compared to a dock that extends only straight out from the shoreline.

2. A T-bar on a ski lift as compared to a J-bar.

3. A carpenter's T-square as compared to a yardstick.

4. A T-formation in football as compared to an I-formation.

Letters—Shapes versus Initials or Rankings

Name: _____ **Period:** _____ **Date:** _____

Read these sentences with letters in them. In the ones where alphabet letters are being used as metaphorical names for things with similar shapes, draw a small picture of the item. By those where the alphabetical letters are used as initials to stand for words, write INITIALS and talk about what the initials stand for. Where the alphabetical letters are used to rank something as if letters in the alphabet were numbers, write RANKING.

1. Our back gate kept drooping, so my father put in a new *Z-frame gate*.

2. She's an *A student*.

3. A *Y-intersection* involves the same number of streets as a *T-intersection*.

4. My mom won't let me go to a *PG movie* until she has read a review of it.

5. I'm not sure I want to have an *X-ray*, if doctors do not know what those rays are.

6. When you play a *C-chord* on the piano, you skip *D* and *F*.

7. An *X-stretcher* provides support in the middle so that the canvas will not tear and let the patient fall.

8. I like the shows on the *WB Channel*.

Circles, Rings, Rounds, and Loops

Name: _____ **Period:** _____ **Date:** _____

What the shapes in this lesson have in common is that they are more or less *round* or *circular*. It is easy to see this in such terms as a *round steak* and a *ring around* the *bathtub*, but it's not so easy to see when speakers say something like, "I'll see you *around*," or when they talk about a *round* in a boxing match.

The *loops* that a belt goes through on a pair of pants are not exactly *round*. However, they are closed so that the belt does not fall off. This idea of an enclosure is what is communicated when people talk about a person *being in the loop* or *out of the loop*. When people say this, they are usually talking about the difference between friends (those with whom you share *inside* information) and *outsiders* (those you do not communicate with). Historically, in the City of Chicago, this had a more concrete meaning. An elevated train makes a loop around the center city. The businesses *in the loop* had a higher prestige address than those *outside of the loop*.

Circuses got their name because in Rome the chariot races were held on circular race courses. These big celebrations with lots of people watching were the first *circuses*. Today when people talk about a *three-ring circus*, it is almost as if they are repeating themselves because a *ring* and a *circle* are the same thing. The reason *circuses* have three *rings* is so that while the scenery and equipment is being changed and the animals taken out of one ring, the audience will still have something to watch. When performers are working in all three rings at the same time, the audience is dazzled and does not know what to look at. It is from this that people began referring to any confusing and noisy event as a *three-ring circus*.

Read the following sentences about *round* shapes and use what you know, along with the clues that are given, to select the appropriate terms to write in the blank spaces.

A. *Ring* has many meanings ranging from the *rings* people wear as jewelry to *boxing rings* (which aren't even round), and to the designs on *ring-tailed* animals and *ring-necked* birds.

ring	ringer	rings	ringside

1. When you _____ a telephone or a doorbell, electronic sound waves extend outward like ripples fanning out in rings on a pond.

2. Crime _____ are people who band together to keep outsiders from knowing about their activities.

3. Having a _____ seat is being close to any kind of action that is exciting to watch.

4. A _____ is a skilled person who enters a contest pretending not to be very good.

B. *Cycle* is a word related to *circle*. You are probably already familiar with many common words that include *cycle* to refer to something round.

> **bicycles**   **cyclone**   **motorcycles**   **recycle**   **tricycles**   **unicycles**

1. The message *Please* _____ is communicated by three arrows bent in a circle.

2. A kind of storm that makes a circle is called a _____.

3. When children are little, they ride three-wheeled _____.

4. When they grow up and get more skilled, they can ride two-wheeled _____.

5. Children who are really skilled and can learn to balance on just one wheel can ride _____.

6. People who ride _____ do not have to pedal because the motor makes the wheels turn around.

C. The prefix **circum** also comes from *circle*. A *circumferential* highway is one that *circles* a town. Other names for these kinds of *round* highways are *Beltway* and *Loop*.

> **circumlocution**   **circumnavigated**   **circumstantial**

1. In police work, _____ evidence is whatever happens to be "standing around" at the site of the crime.

2. To *navigate* is to travel, so someone who has _____ the globe has traveled around the world.

3. *Locution* is a word relating to talk, so _____ is "talking around" something without getting to the point.

Lines and Angles

Name: _____ **Period:** _____ **Date:** _____

English speakers show a preference for straight lines and right angles. They trust someone who is a *straight arrow* more than someone who is *crooked*. If they say someone is *loopy* or *running around in circles*, they are saying the person is foolish or out of control. The person has gotten *off the straight and narrow*.

Rect- comes from the Latin root word for *right*. Both *rectangles* and *squares* have *right angles*. Such angles are 90 degrees. Their name indicates that they are the *right* kind of angle, the kind that will help furniture and houses stand up straight. Other English words that show the connection between *rect-* and *rightness* include *rectitude* (righteousness) and the *rector* of a church (a person who represents or teaches the *right way to behave*).

If someone wins something *fair and square*, the person has won it in the *right way*. When people talk about getting three *square meals* a day, they mean three complete or good meals. A *square* person used to be considered a *right* person, but now if someone is called a *square*, the idea is probably that the person is a nerd or geek.

Line is a word with even more connections to doing things *right*. If someone is described as being *out of line*, this probably means that the person has done something more serious than when a child steps out of line while walking from one class to the next. In a similar way, when people's actions are *in line with* their religion or with greater goals, they are doing more than staying in a *line*. The following sets of *line* words are divided into categories dealing with different areas of the language. Read the sentences and write the appropriate words in the blank spaces.

A. HUMAN BEHAVIOR   deadline   draws the line   toe the line

---

1. A _____ is the time by which something should be done. It comes from a line drawn around prisons showing escapees that they would be shot if they crossed the line.

2. To _____ is to obey rules, in general. The idea is that people who obey the rules are careful not to let their toes cross the starting line of a race or the baseline in tennis.

3. When someone _____, that person is setting up the rules. The image comes from sporting officials drawing lines in the sand to establish the starting points for races or the boundaries for ball games.

B. TRAVEL a beeline   bus lines   telephone lines

1. A _____ is the shortest distance between two places.

2. Wireless communication has made _____ less important.

3. _____ are also called *bus routes*.

C. SPORTS a line drive   line of scrimmage   linesman

1. The front line in a war is similar to the _____ in a football game.

2. The _____ in tennis calls a ball out if it lands on the wrong side of the line.

3. In baseball, a _____ is a ball that is hit hard and straight (without an arc).

D. COMMUNICATION line of type   lineage   lines   outlines

1. To read between the _____ means to get more out of a story than is at first apparent.

2. When people talk about their _____, they are talking about lines on their genealogy chart.

3. Printers do not like to leave a _____ all by itself at the top of a page.

4. Teachers encourage students to make _____ to help them plan the lines of their papers.

E. BUSINESS bottom line   line of credit   line of work

1. Your _____ is what you do to earn money.

2. When people talk about the _____ on a planned project, they are talking about how all the figures add up and whether the project will be profitable.

3. People's _____ is their history of paying bills and how much they can be trusted.

F. HANGING THINGS clothesline   fishing line   line

1. To throw someone a _____ could happen near water where someone is too far from the shore, in a play where someone needs prompting, or more metaphorically, wherever someone needs help.

2. In football, a _____ tackle is when a player holds his arm straight out to the side so that another player runs into it and falls down.

3. A _____ can be as simple as a piece of string or as complicated as see-through nylon guaranteed to hold 50 pounds.

As Easy as One, Two, Three

Name: _____ **Period:** _____ **Date:** _____

Even though speakers frequently talk about *four-leaf clovers, four-lane highways, four-letter words* (swear words), and *four-eyes* (people who wear glasses), the numbers that speakers rely on the most are *one, two,* and *three*. These are examples of *cardinal* numbers. They are called cardinal because the numbers that people use for counting are the most important. *Cardinal*, in the sense of describing something as important, is also seen in the title given to high officials in the Catholic Church and in the description of some sins as *cardinal*. Such number words as *first, second,* and *third* are described as *ordinal* numbers, because they give the *order* of things. In this workshop we will look first at the cardinal forms of *one, two,* and *three* and then at their ordinal forms of *first, second*, and *third*.

A. CARDINAL NUMBERS

One is an especially powerful word when we think of all the words that it is a part of. These range from the indefinite pronouns *anyone, everyone,* and *no one* to such words as *alone, only, lonely,* and even *atonement*, which means something like "at one with God." When golf players make a *hole-in-one*, people are so impressed with their skill or luck that they sometimes use the phrase for any surprising accomplishment. *One-way streets* are designed to make traffic flow smoothly, but people's thought processes are not going to flow smoothly if they have *one-track minds* or if their thinking is *one-sided* or *one-dimensional*. While being *number one* usually means being the best, as with a city's *number one soccer team* or a radio station's *number one hit record,* movie reviewers who award one star out of a possible five to a film are saying that the film is a failure.

Two is almost as important as *one* because of how the human mind tends to think of things as opposites and to divide things into two parts. Nearly half the words in standard desk dictionaries that start with *tw-* relate in some way to the number *two*. *Twilight* is the time of day when there are two kinds of light—a combination of daytime and nighttime reflections. A *twig* is a stick that branches in two directions. *Twine* is string that has been *twisted*, and *twelve* is the number when *two* has been added to *ten*. *Twins* are two babies born on the same day from the same mother. Based on this concept, speakers have created such words as *Twin Peaks, Twin Cities,* and the now world famous *Twin Towers*, which collapsed on September 11th. When Lewis Carroll wanted to create a funny pair of twins for *Alice in Wonderland,* he named them *Tweedledum* and *Tweedledee* so as to emphasize that they were alike. *Twofer* is a new term that such businesses as restaurants and airlines use to advertise special sales when customers can buy two items for the price of one.

Three is a bigger number and so does not get quite as much attention as do *one* and *two*, but still the human mind shows a preference for things that come in *threes*. Among the earliest stories that you heard were probably *The Three Little Pigs, Three Billy Goats Gruff, Goldilocks and the Three Bears,* and the nursery rhyme about *Three*

Blind Mice. When you grew older and watched TV and movies, you probably saw *The Three Musketeers* and perhaps reruns of "The Three Stooges." Something that is *three-dimensional* is well rounded, or at least gives the impression of having depth. In a *three-legged race*, two runners act as a team with their inside legs tied together. Highway safety engineers often designate *three-way stops* at intersections where there have been accidents. These are places where one road joins another and the drivers who are looking straight ahead tend not to notice the incoming traffic. With small airplanes, *three-point landings* are considered perfect because the two main wheels and the tail wheel touch the ground at the same time.

Read these words and write the most appropriate ones in the blank spaces below. Talk about which sentences are using the terms metaphorically and which ones are alluding to actual numbers.

one-shot	one-track	one-upmanship	three-mile	three of a kind
three strikes	threesome	two-handed	two-way	twofer

1. If you miss a _____ opportunity, you are as out of luck as a duck hunter who cannot get his gun reloaded before the duck flies away.

2. My uncle won't pay for power steering, so driving his pickup is a _____ job.

3. He has a _____ mind.

4. In most card games it is good to get _____ .

5. Any close relationship has to be a _____ street.

6. It is harder to play golf as a _____ than with either two or four people.

7. "Friends Fly Free" is the slogan for Southwest Airlines when it has its _____ sale.

8. Our school is like baseball; _____ and you're out.

9. Playing _____ makes you feel smarter than your associates.

10. Historically, there has been a _____ limit on what are considered territorial waters.

B. ORDINAL NUMBERS

First is an alternate way to say that something is *number one*. We all know that a person who wins a blue ribbon for *coming in first* in a race has gotten to the finish line before the other runners. But if your mother wins a blue ribbon because her pie *comes in first* at the state fair, it is not because she brought it to the fair before the other women brought theirs. Instead, it was judged as being of the highest quality. In both of these situations, the person won a blue ribbon for being "the best." In a race, "the best" is shown in relation to time, but in other situations the best is not a matter of time but of quality. There is still another sense to ordinal numbers and that is closeness, as when you talk about a *first cousin* or about having heard something *first hand* (from the person who had the experience) rather than *second hand* (from someone who is just passing on information that he or she heard from someone else).

Ordinal numbers are comparisons and so have to be looked at in their particular contexts. For example, the violinist playing *first chair* in a high school orchestra is undoubtedly a very good musician, but still he or she is not as good as the person playing *third chair* in the Philadelphia Philharmonic. When people talk about something being *second-rate* or *third-rate*, they are usually implying that something lacks quality. The U.S. Post Office used to have *second-class* and *third-class* postage rates. People did not want to pay for something that sounded so unappealing, and so Post Office officials now identify mail with such code words as *presorted* and *nonprofit*. The travel industry had to do something similar. People are happy to be identified as *first-class* passengers, but they did not want to be considered *second-* or *third-class* passengers, so airplanes now have such categories as *First Class, Business, Tourist,* and *Economy.*

Read the following sentences, and in the space before each sentence write TIME, QUALITY, or CLOSENESS to show that you can figure out the sense in which each ordinal word is being used. Notice that CLOSENESS can refer to either physical or emotional closeness.

_____ **I.** The position of *First Lady* is an important part of U.S. politics.

_____ **2.** My aunt plays *second flute* in the Phoenix Symphony.

_____ **3.** The *first-aid* kit is to be hung where everyone can see it.

_____ **4.** In the winter, but not in the summer, it is easy to wake up at *first light.*

_____ **5.** Merrily was insulted when, in the midst of an argument, the teacher said she was using *second-rate* logic.

_____ **6.** Our house is *third* from the corner.

_____ **7.** It would be cheaper to buy two seats in tourist class than one in *first class.*

_____ **8.** The band did not collect as much money as they hoped, so they had to stay at a *third-rate* hotel.

_____ **9.** Being the *first-born* male in a family used to be more important than it is today.

_____ **10.** Even though people always talk about red, white, and blue, in contests, the red ribbon goes to the person who comes in *second*, while the blue ribbon goes to the person coming in *first.*

Foreign Number Words

Name: _____ **Period:** _____ **Date:** _____

   Visitors to foreign countries are quick to learn the names of numbers so that they can pay for things without getting cheated. For hundreds of years, traders as well as ordinary travelers have been learning each other's numbers and then bringing them home and using them in their own languages. If you live in the southwestern United States, you have probably heard about *Cinco de Mayo* (the fifth of May), which is a Mexican holiday. This expression is new enough to English speakers that most people recognize it as non-English, but in reality, all English speakers use many more foreign names for numbers than they realize. Here are explanations of some of them. Choose from the listed words the terms that best fits into the blanks. Talk about the meanings and see if you can think of additional examples.

A. *Uni* comes from Latin for one. When people join a labor *union*, they hope the group will act as *one* body. If you have something truly *unique*, it is the only *one* of its kind. A recently coined term is *unibrow* to refer to people with such thick eyebrows that they almost meet over their noses.

unicorns	unicycle	uniforms

1. When playing soccer, it helps to have _____ so you can quickly tell one team from another.

2. It takes balance to ride a _____ well.

3. In old fairy tales _____ were beautiful white horses with one horn.

B. *Mono* is Greek for one. When you play *Monopoly*, you are trying to see if someone can *monopolize* the property, that is, get it for just one person.

monogrammed	monorails	monotonous

1. At amusement parks people ride _____ that go on one track.

2. Someone with a _____ voice has only one tone.

3. A _____ uniform has the player's name sewn on.

C. *Prime* is another Latin word that means *first* or most *basic,* as when we talk about someone's *primary interest*. A *prima donna* is the lead (or first) singer in an opera. Children learn to read out of *primers*, and when people paint a room, they first put on a *primer coat*.

> | primary | primary grades | prime rib |

I. At restaurants, _____ is one of the more expensive meals because it is considered a number one cut of meat.

2. The _____ colors (red, yellow, and blue) can be mixed into orange, green, and purple.

3. At schools, the _____ are first, second, and third.

D. *Bi* comes from Latin where it means *two*. The *bicentennial* of the United States was its 200th birthday. A *bicycle* has two wheels, while if you look at a body builder flexing his upper arm, you can see that his *biceps* are two muscles that work together.

> | bifocals | bilingual | binoculars |

I. People have to focus both sides of _____.

2. A _____ person can speak two languages.

3. Older people often need _____ to focus on things both close up and far away.

E. *Duo* is another Latin word for *two*. From this, we get the word *double* and also *dozen* (*ten* plus *two*). To *dissect* something is to start by cutting it into at least *two sections*. People used to settle disagreements by having *duels* with guns.

> | on the double | doubleheader | duet | duplex |

I. A house built for two families to live in is a _____.

2. If someone wants you to move fast as you are moving, she might shout, "_____!"

3. A _____ consists of two people performing together.

4. When two baseball games are played back to back, it is called a _____.

F. *Tri* came into English from both Latin and Greek where it means *three* as in *triplets* (three babies born from the same mother on the same day), three people singing in a *trio*, a *triangle* having three sides and three corners, a *tricycle* having three wheels, and a *triple-decker sandwich* having three layers.

> | Bermuda Triangle | triathlon | triceratops | tripods |

I. A _____ is a dinosaur with three horns.

2. The _____ has a reputation for causing planes and ships to disappear.

3. In sports tournaments, a _____ includes three different activities.

4. Photographers often use _____, three-legged stands, to hold their cameras.

G. **_Quad_** is a Latin root word for _four,_ as seen in such English words as _quadruplets,_ _quarts,_ and _quartets._ While football games, dollars, and hours each contain _four quarters_, these _quarters_ are quite different things.

| quad | quarterfinals | quarterpounder |

1. One of McDonalds'® best-selling products is its _____.

2. Our soccer team has made it to the _____.

3. A _____ is a basically square area (a _quadrangle_) in the middle of a town or on a college campus.

H. **_Dec_** is a Greek and Latin root meaning _ten._ The most surprising place we see it is in the name of _December,_ which is now the twelfth month in the year. When December got its name, it really was the tenth month. Later, Julius and Augustus Caesar had months of the calendar named after them. They wanted summer months because that is when they had their military victories. This pushed the months after _July_ and _August_ out of their appropriately named places.

| decade | decimal points | decimating |

1. A _____ is a ten-year period.

2. As a way of _____ their enemies, Roman soldiers used to kill one out of every ten soldiers that they captured.

3. In math, _____ illustrate how our counting system is based on units of ten.

I. **_Centum_** is a Latin word for 100. Every time you read a price tag, you use this word as when you see that something costs one dollar and 67 _cents_. On television, you might have seen Roman soldiers called _centurions_. These were officers in charge of 100 soldiers.

| centipedes | century | percentage |

1. From 1864 to 1964 was one _____.

2. Interest on loans is reported as a _____.

3. _____ have lots of feet, but not actually 100.

4   10   100

Approximate versus Exact

Name: _____ Period: _____ Date: _____

As illustrated by the name of *centipedes*, people sometimes use number words as approximations, rather than as exact figures. Speakers were surprised to see an insect with so many legs, so they grabbed for a big number and named it a *centipede*. Later, when they ran across an animal with even more legs, they grabbed for a bigger number and named it a *millipede*, from the Latin word for *thousand*. Of course this insect does not have a thousand legs.

Most people assume that the name of *The Thousand Islands* in the St. Lawrence Seaway is a similar kind of exaggeration. But when someone took the time to actually count the islands, they were surprised to find more than a thousand. No one has ever bothered to count the bits of chopped pimentos, green peppers, and onions that float in a bottle of *Thousand Island dressing*. If you are buying something for a million dollars, you would expect to pay that actual amount, but often a *million* is just a rounded-off reference to any large number as when people refer to the *millions of cars* on the freeway. In a joke about a man offering to bet his friend a million dollars, the friend responds, "Make that $20 and I'll take you up on it!" This would not be a joke if people did not recognize the term as an exaggeration instead of a real number.

When people talk about *half* of something, it is especially hard to know whether something is truly or only approximately *half*. Read the following sentences and in the space before each sentence write EXACT if you think the number word is referring to something that has been, or can be, measured. Write APPROX if the number word is an exaggeration or a metaphor. Talk about your reasoning.

_____ **1.** In Arizona, *century* plants bloom about every 25 years.

_____ **2.** According to the calendar, we can expect a *half moon* tonight.

_____ **3.** A *decade* is ten years.

_____ **4.** The pilot took off even though *zero visibility* was predicted.

_____ **5.** It is mostly kids who are called *half-pints*.

_____ **6.** Never in a *thousand years* will I agree to that.

_____ **7.** Flags flew at *half-mast* after the accident.

_____ **8.** The *Hundred Year War* actually lasted 120 years.

_____ **9.** Sears is having a *10% off* sale this weekend.

_____ **10.** That is a *half-baked idea*.

Unusual Uses of Number Words

Name: _____   **Period:** _____   **Date:** _____

At the beginning of this chapter, we saw how English speakers use letters of the alphabet for more than writing words. As shown in these examples, English speakers also use number-related terms for more than counting. Read and talk about these examples and be ready to use them for some of the answers on the crossword puzzle on the next page.

Give me five! is a way of asking for a friendly open-handed slap. This is similar to the *high five* or the *low five* greeting that athletes give each other. These kinds of greetings have become fashionable only within the last few years. However, the idea goes back thousands of years. Holding out open palms is an expression of goodwill because it shows that someone is not carrying a weapon or making a fist for hitting.

A 180-degree *turn* means that someone has made two 90 degree turns and so is now facing in the opposite direction. When people use the term, they are usually expressing surprise because the action has been unintentional as when a car skids on the ice. Speakers also use the term metaphorically to talk about someone who has had a change of heart about something.

Dixie as the name for the Southern states and *Dixieland jazz* come from the French word *dixième*, meaning ten. Because of the influence of French on the South as still seen in New Orleans, the Confederate $10 bill was called a *Dixie*. Later, the coincidental naming of the *Mason-Dixon* line to separate slave states from free states furthered the name. *Dime* (for 10 cents) also comes from *dixième*. English speakers left out the middle three letters to make the word easier to say and to write.

Being behind the 8-ball is an expression that comes from the game of 8-ball pool. In this game, the rules are that the number 8-ball is to go into the pocket last. If a player's ball is behind the 8-ball, that player is probably going to lose because he cannot get to his ball next. Metaphorically, if you are *behind the 8-ball*, you are somehow disadvantaged.

Numero uno is Spanish for *number one*. English speakers use it for variety and to show a playful attitude.

Mega comes from Greek, where it means *more* or *large*. In English we use it in the word *megaphone*, which increases the power of someone's voice. People also use it as a playful way to exaggerate in such phrases as *megabucks* and *megatrouble*.

Pente is a Greek word for *five*. The most famous *five-sided* building in the world is the *Pentagon*, just outside of Washington, DC. This is the headquarters building for the U.S. military.

Heinz 57 is a playful way to refer to a mixed-breed dog. The idea came from the Heinz food processing company, which for nearly a hundred years used *57 Varieties* as a company slogan to advertise the fact that they canned or bottled lots of different foods. They did not really limit themselves to 57 varieties, but buyers still got the correct idea that the company made more than ketchup and mustard.

Use these clues to fill in the number-related crossword puzzle.

ACROSS:

2. The _____ grades in school are first, second, and third.

3. The South is called _____ because of the French word for *Ten*, which was printed in big letters on Confederate $10 bills.

4. If your mother has _____, your family will have to buy three baby cribs.

6. _____ is a way to refer to things that are usually big

8. A person who makes a 180-degree turn ends up going in the _____ direction.

9. A mall located between three different towns might be named _____ City Mall.

10. The Spanish way to say *Number One* is _____ *Uno*.

DOWN:

1. A _____ has four sides and is often designed as a gathering place on college campuses.

2. The five-sided _____ in Washington, DC was damaged in the September 11th attacks.

3. A _____ is a couple as when two people sing a *duet*.

5. September used to be the_____ month of the year until July and August were inserted.

6. If someone says, "I'll bet you a _____ dollars," the person is probably joking.

7. A high _____ is based on the old custom of showing people that you are not carrying a weapon or going to hit them with your fist.

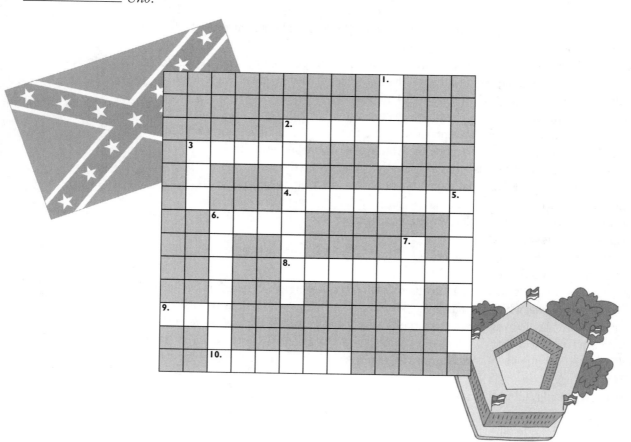

Workshop 4.1: Part I: A, C, D, and **E. 1.** C-clamps, **2.** A-frame, **3.** D-rings, **4.** A-ladders, **5.** A-line, **6.** E-buildings. **I, J, K,** and **L: 1.** I-beams, **2.** K-turns, **3.** J-stroke, **4.** L-shaped, **5.** I-formation, **6.** J-hook. **S, T, U, V,** and **X: 1.** S-curve, **2.** V-necked, **3.** X-crossing, **4.** U-bolt, **5.** T-bone, **6.** S-hook, **7.** T-shirts, **8.** X, **9.** U-turns, **10.** V-8, **11.** T-ball. **Part II: 1.** Many more boats can park around a T-shaped dock. **2.** Two people can be carried by a T-bar (they stand on the small crosspiece at the bottom and hang onto the longer cross-piece at the top), while only one goes on a J-bar. **3.** A T-square allows the carpenter to check for right angles on both sides. **4.** A T-formation spreads out the action while an I-formation concentrates it.

Workshop 4.2: 1. draw picture, **2.** RANKING, **3.** draw two pictures, **4.** INITIALS for "Parental Guidance" but also a kind of ranking, **5.** RANKING (X implies that something is beyond the ordinary or the known as in X-rated movies), **6.** RANKING, **7.** draw picture, **8.** INITIALS for Warner Brothers.

Workshop 4.3: A. 1. ring, **2.** rings, **3.** ringside, **4.** ringer. **B. 1.** recycle, **2.** cyclone, **3.** tricycles, **4.** bicycles, **5.** unicycles, **6.** motorcycles. **C. 1.** circumstantial, **2.** circumnavigated, **3.** circumlocution.

Workshop 4.4: A. 1. deadline, **2.** toe the line, **3.** draws the line. **B. 1.** beeline, **2.** telephone lines, **3.** bus lines. **C. 1.** line of scrimmage, **2.** linesman, **3.** line drive. **D. 1.** lines, **2.** lineage, **3.** line of type, **4.** outlines. **E. 1.** line of work, **2.** bottom line, **3.** line of credit. **F. 1.** a line, **2.** clothesline, **3.** fishing line.

Workshop 4.5: A. 1. one-shot (metaphorical), **2.** two-handed (literal), **3.** one-track (metaphorical), **4.** three of a kind (literal), **5.** two-way (metaphorical), **6.** threesome (literal), **7.** twofer (literal), **8.** three strikes (metaphorical), **9.** one-upmanship (metaphorical), **10.** three-mile (literal). **B: 1.** closeness, **2.** quality, **3.** time, **4.** time, **5.** quality, **6.** closeness **7.** quality, **8.** quality, **9.** time, **10.** quality.

Workshop 4.6: A. 1. uniforms, **2.** unicycle, **3.** unicorns. **B. 1.** monorails, **2.** monotone, **3.** monogram. **C. 1.** prime rib, **2.** primary, **3.** primary grades. **D. 1.** binoculars, **2.** bilingual, **3.** bifocals. **E. 1.** duplex, **2.** on the double, **3.** duet, **4.** double header. **F. 1.** triceratops, **2.** Bermuda Triangle, **3.** triathlon, **4.** tripods. **G. 1.** quarterpounder, **2.** quarterfinals, **3.** quad. **H. 1.** decade, **2.** decimating, **3.** decimal points. **I. 1.** century, **2.** percentage, **3.** centipedes.

Workshop 4.7: 1. approx, **2.** exact, **3.** exact, **4.** approx, **5.** approx, **6.** approx, **7.** exact, **8.** approx, **9.** exact, **10.** approx.

Workshop 4.8: Across: 2. primary, **3.** dixie, **4.** triplets, **8.** opposite, **9.** tri, **10.** numero. **Down: 1.** quad, **2.** pentagon, **3.** duo, **5.** seventh, **6.** million, **7.** five.

End-of-Chapter Activities

1. There are dozens of beautiful alphabet books that are fun to look at, including Bill Martin and John Archambault's *Chicka Chicka Boom Boom* (Simon & Schuster, 1989), Margaret Musgrove and Leo and Diane Dillon's *Ashanti to Zulu* (Dial, 1976), Arnold and Anita Lobel's *On Market Street* (Greenwillow, 1981), Mitsumasa Anno's *Anno's Alphabet: An Adventure in Imagination* (Crowell, 1975), Catherine Hepworth's *Antics!* (G. P. Putnam's Sons, 1992*),* and Bert Kitchen's *Animal Alphabet* (Dial Books, 1984). All of these books are organized around words that start with particular letters of the alphabet. After you have looked at these books (or others that your library has), figure out how as a class you can make a new kind of alphabet book with illustrations that represent things that are named from letters of the alphabet. Stephen T. Johnson, in his *Alphabet City* (Viking, 1996), has painted real-life things that are in the shape of letters of the alphabet. However, the items are not named for the letters. If you want to stick to things that are named for

the letters, as in this lesson, you will have to skip some letters of the alphabet because not all of them have had things named after them. However, you can probably find enough items that each student in a class will be able to make a page.

2. Choose one of these shape-related idioms to illustrate. Your picture can be either literal or metaphorical, but be ready to explain the different meanings.

- ☐ Bent out of shape
- ☐ Shape up or ship out
- ☐ A three-ring circus
- ☐ To be out of the loop
- ☐ To be loopy
- ☐ To be crooked
- ☐ Running around in circles
- ☐ To be a straight arrow
- ☐ Straighten up and fly right
- ☐ Three square meals a day

CHAPTER FIVE

Food

Background Reading for the Teacher

From birth to death, food is one of the things that gives people not only sustenance, but also pleasure. It is to be expected that anything this important in people's lives will become the source of many metaphors. Some of the most memorable scenes in classic children's books are about food; for example, the story of "The Doughnuts" and the machine that would not shut off in Robert McCloskey's *Homer Price* (Viking 1943 and 1971), the warm supper waiting for Max at the end of Maurice Sendak's *Where the Wild Things Are* (Harper and Row, 1963), and the way food influenced Templeton's crucial role in *Charlotte's Web*. The rat decides to go to the fair with Charlotte and Wilbur only after the old sheep explains to him:

A fair is a rat's paradise. Everybody spills food at a fair. A rat can creep out late at night and have a feast. In the horse barn you will find oats that the trotters and pacers have spilled. In the trampled grass of the infield you will find old discarded lunch boxes containing the foul remains of peanut butter sandwiches, hard-boiled eggs, cracker crumbs, bits of doughnuts, and particles of cheese. In the hard-packed dirt of the midway, after the glaring lights are out and the people have gone home to bed, you will find a veritable treasure of popcorn fragments, frozen custard dribblings, candied apples abandoned by tired children, sugar fluff crystals, salted almonds, popsicles, partially gnawed ice cream cones, and the wooden sticks of lollypops. Everywhere is loot for a rat—in tents, in booths, in hay lofts—why a fair has enough disgusting leftover food to satisfy a whole army of rats.

Templeton finds that the old sheep was telling the truth and when he comes back to the crate after his first night at the fair he is "swollen to twice his normal size," but he is still thinking of food. And Wilbur, who, in desperation, is begging Templeton to climb up and get Charlotte's egg sac so they can take it back to the farm, does the only thing he can think of. He makes a solemn promise to Templeton: "Get Charlotte's egg sac for me, and from now on I will let you eat

These were the first seventh graders at Fees Intermediate School in Tempe to finish their drawings for the filling of the class's metaphor sandwich. By the time the whole class had contributed drawings of such things as *a bunch of baloney, a big cheese, a cute tomato, someone in a pickle,* and *a peppy cheerleader,* hardly any of the bread was left showing.

first, when Lurvy slops me. I will let you have your choice of everything in the trough and I won't touch a thing until you're through."

Depending on the age of your students, you might want to reread and focus on the food-related parts of Dr. Seuss's *Green Eggs and Ham* or such old folktales as "The Little Red Hen," "Goldilocks and the Three Bears," "Jack and the Bean Stalk," or "Three Billy Goats Gruff." After these "old" examples, students might volunteer information about food in the *Harry Potter* books or in other stories they have recently read. A wonderful new book (that we wish we had written) is *Eat Your Words: A Fascinating Look at the Language of Food* by Charlotte Foltz Jones, illus. by John O'Brien (Delacorte, 1999). While our approach throughout this text is source-based, Jones goes the other direction and works mostly with food as the receiver or target of metaphors. This means her book can be a fun way to supplement this chapter.

Here are two different versions of traffic jams, a metaphor that most children can relate to.

For the metaphor sandwich, as suggested in Workshop 5.6, a worksheet is supplied, but it would be more fun for students if they could contribute their individual drawings to a class sandwich made to look like one of those six-foot sandwiches supplied for parties by specialty shops (see the photo on p. 74). If you provide play money for students to glue on for *lettuce*, you can be assured that they will remember at least one of the metaphors talked about in this chapter. See our website for pretyped lists of possible terms. Here are some of the less obvious background facts you might want to share with students as they choose how to illustrate their contributions for a sandwich or for some other kind of food-related bulletin board.

- *Bread* and *dough* are slang terms for money, similar to the phrase *bringing home the bacon*. Both metaphors are based on the idea that these are basic foods, which families will get in exchange for their money.
- An *upper crust* person has a high level of prestige comparable to the way the upper crust of a loaf of bread or a pie tastes better than does the soggy lower crust. A *crusty person* is one who has a hard outer shell or who is hard to get through to.
- *Bread-and-butter* notes thank a hostess for general hospitality, not actually for bread and butter. The same meaning of "basic" is seen in *bread-and-butter pickles* or when a college describes a consistently popular class as a *bread-and-butter* course for the department. *To butter someone up* is to flatter the person. It has a connotation of greasiness.
- The name for *mustard gas*, the chemical compound used in war, is based on its strength rather than its contents, while *mustard plasters*, an old-fashioned treatment for chest colds, really were made from mustard. The Biblical parable about the *mustard seed* is a based on the fact that something so tiny can have such a pungent taste. The comparison is being made to the power of even a little bit of faith.
- *Red pepper* or *cayenne pepper* is so strong that it is the actual basis of the *pepper spray* that police officers use to break up a crowd. But if police officers *pepper a crowd* with rubber bullets, the comparison is to the way pepper is sprinkled onto food. This is the same image as when baseball players *pepper* the infield with hits and when teachers *pepper* students with questions. Describing a person as *peppy* is similar to the old saying about someone being *full of ginger*. The comparison is to something *tasty* or *spicy*. A *salt-and-pepper* beard or hair is a metaphor based on color as when a dark-haired person begins to go gray.
- *Traffic jams* are one of the metaphors that young people are intimately acquainted with and enjoy drawing.

The picture on the left is from the acrylic boxes that we fixed as introductory material. The frying pan is a refrigerator magnet from a dollar store, while the other items are cutouts from magazines. On the right are four of the cards drawn by seventh graders. We went to class with lots of preprinted cards, but several students preferred to think of their own metaphors as with the *hot tamale* and the *strawberry blonde*.

- Something *cheesy* is cheap and flimsy, as is the *cheesecloth* in which curds used to be hung to drain and form solid cheese. The image of these hanging bags of curds is probably what gave rise to the old joke about the moon being made from *green cheese*.

  Food is a topic that children have had lots of experience with and so they will be able to supplement many of the words and ideas presented in this chapter.

  As an end-of-chapter activity, we present some Aesop's Fables that are related to food. Illustrating these stories would probably be fun for students. And, as suggested elsewhere, this could be a good time for two or three older children to meet with two or three younger children to tell the stories and show their pictures. In exchange, the older students could listen to the younger students read them a story.

Notes to Help Teachers Elicit Ideas from Students

A good way to move students toward thinking about language that has evolved in relation to food is to ask them to identify the common feature that relates the item of food on the left to the nonfood item or action on the right. It worked well for us to do the exercise orally, but we stood close to a chalkboard so we could draw whatever children didn't seem to know. A *pie chart* was the only puzzler in the group we worked with.

1. A head of cabbage	_____	A Cabbage Patch doll
2. A pie	_____	A pie chart
3. A restaurant menu	_____	A computer menu
4. A nut	_____	An idea expressed in a nutshell
5. Jam	_____	A traffic jam
6. Lettuce	_____	Paper money

Fruits and Vegetables

Name: _____   **Period:** _____   **Date:** _____

Read these descriptions of fruits and vegetables. Then choose the most appropriate words to write in the blank spaces of the more metaphorical sentences that follow. Talk about the food items and what they have in common with the way they are used in the metaphorical sentences.

A. *Beans* are an efficient kind of food because dried beans do not spoil and they can be carried around in buckets or gunnysacks. Cowboys in the old U.S. West used to practically live on beans flavored with bacon and salt and perhaps some chili peppers. At night they would bank their coals and put a pot of beans in the fire to cook all night so they would have food ready for the next day. Beans are so basic that cheap restaurants are sometimes referred to as *beaneries*. In modern business, it is considered an insult to call someone a *bean counter* because it means that person is concerned only with trivial details. If someone *spills the beans*, the person has given away a secret. One explanation of this metaphor (which some linguists reject) is that people used to vote with black beans and white beans. If someone accidentally tipped over the voting container, then everyone could see whether the black beans or the white beans were winning.

Beanie Babies®	beans	full of beans	jelly beans	string bean

1. Former President Ronald Reagan kept jars of _____ around for his guests.

2. Rowan Atkinson uses the stage name *Mr. Bean* to emphasize his _____ appearance.

3. If _____ were filled with real beans, they would not be so soft and cuddly.

4. If a baseball pitcher _____ a batter, he hits him in the head.

5. If you think someone is pulling your leg or talking nonsense, you might say, "You're _____.

B. *Corn* has been used throughout the world to name whatever crop was the most plentiful. In England this was wheat, but in Scotland and Ireland it was oats. In the United States, *corn* is used to make *corn syrup, corn meal, cornstarch, corn flakes, corn bread,* and tortillas.

| corn | Corn Belt | cornrow | corny |

1. The great farming states of the Midwest are known as the _____.

2. Vaudeville performers called the jokes appreciated by farm people *corn-fed* or _____.

3. In a _____ hairstyle, people braid their hair so finely that it resembles corn on the cob.

4. The *Hee Haw* comedy shows opened with performers standing in a field of _____.

C. Potatoes are such a basic food that they played a role in the history of the United States. In the late 1800s when the *potato blight* (a variety of different fungus diseases) caused a famine in Ireland, many Irish immigrated to the United States so that today one out of six Americans is estimated to have Irish ancestors. The Irish brought their love for potatoes with them. U.S. speakers refer to basic food and basic people as *meat and potatoes*. Every year, we eat literally tons of *mashed potatoes, potato salad, French fries, potato chips,* and even *potato pancakes. Sweet potatoes* are native to South America and are a favorite U.S. dish at Thanksgiving dinner.

| couch potato | hot potato | Potato Famine |

1. The Great _____ in Ireland was caused by the *potato blight*.

2. A _____ is someone who sits on a couch and vegetates by watching television and snacking.

3. In games of _____, something is quickly passed from one player to another. This can be either a real item or something like speech as in *hot potato humor,* when different people quickly contribute to the same joke.

D. Apples are the prototypical fruit as shows by the phrases *as American as apple pie* and *in apple pie order*. In Norse mythology, the gods had to eat one of Idun's apples every day to keep from aging. This is perhaps the source of our maxim, "An apple a day keeps the doctor away."

| Adam's apple | apple cart | apples of the earth | pineapples |

1. French and Persian speakers call potatoes _____.

2. People think that men's _____ were named from the Bible story of Eve tempting Adam with the apple, but the name really came about through a mistake in translation.

3. _____ are a kind of fruit that has stickers and are shaped like giant-sized pine cones.

4. If you upset the _____, you mess up someone's plans.

E. *Cherries* are a special treat because they are so seasonal and so fragile. This is the basis for the cliché about life being a *bowl of cherries*. Erma Bombeck made fun of this with the title of her book, *If Life Is a Bowl of Cherries, Why Am I in the Pits? Cherry* pie is popular in February when people remember the story about George Washington cutting down his father's cherry tree. In basketball, a *cherry picker* is a player left alone under his team's basket in hopes that someone will unexpectedly throw him the ball so he can score as easily as *picking a cherry*.

cherry on top of the sundae	**cherry pickers**	**cherry stem**

1. When a city reaches out and annexes a narrow strip of land and then a bigger piece that is a desirable suburb or a shopping center, critics call the practice _____ annexation.

2. The _____ is a metaphor for something special, but it is often used sarcastically.

3. City maintenance departments own _____, which are heavy-duty baskets that can be elevated to lift workers up to trim trees, repair traffic lights, and change the bulbs in street lights.

F. *Bananas* used to be considered much more of a luxury than they are today because they grow only in tropical climates so they have to be shipped to the United States from other countries. The popular song from the 1940s, "Yes, We Have No Bananas!" came out of this period when people were not at all sure that they would find bananas in a store. The phrase *Banana Republic* became an almost playful way to refer to small South American countries whose main export was bananas. The playful name was recently borrowed by a company that sells sporty clothes to young people.

banana seats	**banana splits**	**go bananas**	**top banana**

1. The _____ is a complimentary phrase from vaudeville where it was used to describe the "top" person, the one that didn't get bruised and banged up by being crushed under the bunch.

2. Bicycles with _____ are made for leisurely riding.

3. Since the 1920s, _____ have been a favorite treat at ice cream stores.

4. To _____ is to go crazy or nuts over something. The ideas is probably taken from the way monkeys act when they are given bananas to eat.

Baked and Cooked Food

Name: _____   **Period:** _____   **Date:** _____

Read these descriptions of some of food that has been prepared by a cook. Then choose the most appropriate words to write in the blank spaces of the more metaphorical sentences that follow. Talk about the food items and what they have in common with the way they are used in the metaphorical sentences.

A. *Bread* is such a basic food that its name is used to stand for more than what people eat. The scripture in the Bible, "Man does not live by bread alone," was not saying that besides eating bread, people should also eat meat, fruits, and vegetables. Instead, it was saying that in addition to food, people need spiritual and intellectual *feeding*. The Latin word for bread is *panis*. A *companion* is a person with whom you share bread.

> **breadbasket**   **breadline**   **breadwinner**   **pantry**

1. The Midwest is called the United States' _____ because it produces so much grain. The same term might be used for someone's stomach.

2. The _____ is where people keep their bread.

3. The _____ in a family is the one who brings home the bread, or at least the money (also called *dough* or *bread*) to buy the bread.

4. If homeless people get in a _____, they will be given more than bread.

B. *Toast* is bread that has been given an extra measure of baking, probably just before it is eaten. The idea of *toasting*, or drinking to someone's health, comes from an old custom of putting bits of toast in drinks to give them a special flavor or to absorb the bitterness from wine. Calling the person who is in charge of a program the *toastmaster* or *toastmistress* comes from the custom of *toasting* people, meaning that they are publicly given good wishes. In the 1950s, a popular comic strip about *Casper Milquetoast* furthered the idea that someone who ate pieces of toast swimming in hot milk (an old-fashioned dish for sick children) was a weakling.

> **Melba toast**   **milk toast**   **toasty**   **tostado**

1. In a Mexican restaurant, a _____ is a hard-cooked tortilla spread with beans or meat.

2. Australia's famous opera singer Dame Nellie Melba dieted by eating thin hard bread called

_____.

3. It is pleasant on a cold winter evening to curl up _____ and warm in front of a fireplace.

4. You probably don't want people to call you a _____ because you would rather be viewed as strong and assertive.

C. Cake is sweeter than bread and so is considered a luxury item. *Cakewalks* were made famous in minstrel shows where performers would prance and strut in a circle. People still play the game at parties and whoever is standing on a designated spot when the music stops wins or *takes the cake*.

caked on	cupcakes	a piece of cake	take the cake

1. If something is _____, it looks as if cake dough has dried or been baked on.

2. When someone describes something as _____, the person is saying it was easy or pleasant.

3. To _____ describes someone acting in an outlandish fashion.

4. People who are "soft and sweet" are sometimes called _____.

D. Cookies are considered to be treats, so when people ask what little reward they are going to get, they sometimes say, "What are the cookies?" On computers when companies make special offers to people based on what they bought last time, these are described as *cookies*. The *Cookie Monster* on "Sesame Street" inspired a name for people who on shared computers use more than their share of time.

cookie-cutter	cookie jar	tough cookie

1. A _____ is someone who is assertive or hard-nosed.

2. If a new employee is caught with his or her hand in the _____, that person is caught taking things he or she should not have.

3. Something described as _____ style is being criticized for being mass-produced or unoriginal.

E. Crumbs come from breads and pastries, but through comparison, speakers describe many things that are falling apart as *crumbling*. They also use *crumb* to mean something small, as when a mother complains that she has not heard *one crumb of news* from her child at summer camp. Because *crumbs* are small pieces that accidentally fall off and are brushed aside, they are considered worthless as when someone complains about having a *crummy* job or jokes about a friend being a *crumb bum*.

crumb	crumbled	crumbling

1. In Europe, you can see evidence of empires that have _____, both literally and figuratively.

2. After twenty years, their marriage seems to be _____.

3. They had to release the man because there was not one _____ of evidence.

F. Soup is cooked on top of the stove and is usually made with some kind of meat and vegetables. Because soup is usually served first, people use the term *from soup to nuts* to describe something as varied as a seven-course dinner. Perhaps because of the way a hot bowl of soup can revive a hungry person, *to soup up* something (such as a car) is to give it added power. A person *in the soup* is in some kind of trouble. The allusion might be to pilots flying in fog *as thick as pea soup* or, even more gruesome, to the image of missionaries being boiled by cannibals.

| soup kitchen | souped-up | thick as pea soup |

1. _____ cars aren't seen as often as they used to be.

2. There is no flying today because the fog is _____.

3. A _____ provides people with more than soup.

G. Stew is thicker than soup and usually has bigger chunks of meat and vegetables in it. This means that it must cook longer and so the name is also used for a process of slow cooking. For example, people talk about *stewed prunes* or other fruits and vegetables.

| shepherd's stew | a stew | stewing |

1. _____ can have in it whatever meats and vegetables happen to be available.

2. Someone in _____ is simmering and worrying about a problem of some kind.

3. People _____ in their own juices are fretting over trouble of their own making.

Eggs, Meat, and Milk

Name: _____ **Period:** _____ **Date:** _____

Read these descriptions of some basic proteins. Then choose the most appropriate words to write in the blank spaces of the more metaphorical sentences that follow. Talk about the food items and what they have in common with the way they are used in the metaphorical sentences.

A. Eggs, at least before the world learned about cholesterol, were considered the perfect food because they are fairly easy to get, they are filled with nutrition, they come in an efficient package, and they can be eaten in a form as plain as a boiled egg or as fancy as a soufflé. A company that makes a processed egg product alleged to be healthier than whole eggs named its product *Egg Beaters®*. This name is clever in saying that their product is better than real eggs. It also alludes to the kitchen tool used to *beat eggs* before putting them in a cake or an omelet.

eggheads	good egg	nest egg	walking on eggs

1. Because people's heads are egg-shaped, speakers refer to someone they like as a _____.

2. People who are called *high brows* or _____ have the same shape of heads as everyone else, but the metaphor implies that they have bigger brains.

3. A young couple working to acquire a _____ is saving money for the future.

4. If you have a delicate subject to discuss with someone, you could be described as _____ because you are being so careful about what you say.

B. Milk is the first food that both human and animal babies (if they are mammals) live on, so of course it is an important contributor to the English vocabulary. Metaphors based on the appearance of milk include the *Milky Way* galaxy visible on clear nights, *Milk of Magnesia®* medicine, and *milk glass*, which has a white sheen running through it. *Milkweed* is a plant that exudes a kind of white, *milky* substance, similar in appearance to what is called coconut *milk*.

cry over spilt milk	milk and honey	milks a situation

1. People who tell you not to _____ are saying there's no use worrying over things that cannot be helped.

2. If someone _____ for all its worth, the allusion is to the process of milking a cow and being sure to get out the very last drop.

3. In the Bible, people were always looking for the land of _____.

C. *Beef* is meat from cattle. Probably because it is the favorite meat of Americans, it connotes strength. When people talk about airports and other public places *beefing up* security, they are talking about more money being spent for personnel as well as for equipment. People who complain and demand action of some kind might be described as *beefing about* something. A successful commercial for a chain of hamburger restaurants joked with this idea by having two elderly sisters peer disgustedly into a large hamburger bun that was practically empty. One of them asked in a sneering tone, "Where's the beef?"

beef up	Beefeaters	beefing up

1. Athletes work out to _____ their bodies.

2. A school that is _____ its offerings is starting to give more solid, academic classes such as foreign languages and advanced math classes.

3. Since 1671, British _____ in their distinctive red uniforms have been Royal British Guards.

D. *Ham* is smoked or cured pork. *Bacon* is the smoked narrow pieces of pork that come from the sides of pigs. *Ham,* as in *ham radio operator* and in unskilled actors *hamming it up,* is thought to have come from the similarity in pronunciation to *amateur*. *Spam®* is a registered trademark for *SPiced hAM*. *Bologna* or *baloney* is an inexpensive kind of processed meat made mostly from pork. Metaphorically, it usually refers to something people think is worthless.

bacon	baloney	spam

1. Unwanted e-mail is referred to as _____. The name came from a funny skit by the Monty Python group where a waitress kept trying to sell spam.

2. If you are the one in your family who brings home the _____, you are the one earning the money the family lives on.

3. What he said was a bunch of _____.

WORKSHOP 5.4

Literal versus Metaphorical

Name: _____   **Period:** _____   **Date:** _____

The following terms related to eating are used both literally and metaphorically. Try to fit them into the appropriate blank spaces in the following sentences. In Part I, the words are to be used in a more basic or literal sense, while in Part II they are to be used in a more metaphorical sense. Each word is used once in each group.

PART I More Basic Sentences

| bite | chew | digest | nibble | savor | swallowing | taste |

1. My mother taught me to _____ each bite of food for ten seconds.

2. It's ironic that older people have a hard time _____ pills when they are the ones who need them the most.

3. I can still _____ that pepper steak I had for lunch.

4. When I study late at night, I have to have something to _____ on or else I fall asleep.

5. Nuts are said to be fairly hard to _____.

6. Once you _____ into one of their desserts, you will eat the whole thing.

7. Candy manufacturers have made millions of people _____ the taste of chocolate.

PART II More Metaphorical Sentences

| bitten | chewed | digest | nibbles | savored | swallow | taste |

1. Once she's had a _____ of a real job, she won't be so enthused.

2. She _____ the memory of her week in Canada.

3. Did you get any _____ from the flyers you passed out?

4. I don't believe in speed reading because it takes me a while to _____ any good story.

5. I got _____ out for parking in the host's driveway instead of in the street.

6. "Once _____, twice shy" is an old proverb.

7. It's hard to _____ that story about her sister being a movie star.

Literal versus Metaphorical   **85**

What's Cooking?

Name: _____   **Period:** _____   **Date:** _____

"What's cooking?" is one of the ways people ask "What's up?" or "What's happening?" Cooking-related metaphors are popular because most speakers have done enough cooking to have experienced such action-related terms as *to boil, to chop,* and *to beat.* If they have been careless in lifting off a lid and were burned by escaping steam, then they understand what is meant by someone being *steamed* or *needing to let off steam.*

   The boldfaced, italicized words and phrases in the lines taken from a recipe for Raisin Nut Cookies are *cooking* words that can also be used with extended meanings. Study the words and then choose which ones to write in the blank spaces of the metaphorical sentences given below the recipe. You will need to add endings (*-er, -en,* or *ed*) to some of the words to make them fit grammatically. After you figure out the answers, talk about the connection between the cooking-related meanings in the recipe and the extended meanings in the sentences.

RAISIN NUT COOKIES

Chop nuts and *mix* with raisins.   *Stir* in flour, nuts, and raisins.
Cream butter and sugar.   *Grease* the cookie sheet.
Beat eggs and *blend in.*   *Bake* at 350° for 10 to 12 minutes.

1. The lost hiker was picked up by a Forest Service _____.

2. To _____ an official's palm means to give a bribe.

3. He was badly _____ in the boxing match.

4. People snowed in sometimes complain about going _____ crazy.

5. He is so handsome it is impossible for him to just _____.

6. There was a good _____ of conservatives and liberals to discuss the issue.

7. After a week of rain, it felt good to sit in the sun and _____.

8. Our car was absolutely _____ when we collided with the truck.

Make a Metaphor Sandwich

Name: _____ **Period:** _____ **Date:** _____

As a demonstration of how often speakers use metaphors based on food, fill in Figure 5.1 with words and little pictures to make a metaphor sandwich. You can choose from the ideas below or think up others of your own.

On the **bread** part of your sandwich, you might draw a picture of one or more of these bread-related metaphors:

- A woman with her hair in a *bun*.
- A person with a big *breadbasket* (a big stomach).
- Someone at the bank getting *bread* or *dough*.
- Homeless people standing in a *breadline* for supper.
- The earth's *crust*.

- A *crust* that formed overnight on slightly melted snow.
- Someone who is *upper crust*.
- A *crustacean* (e.g., a lobster or a shrimp).
- A *crusty* person.

For the **spread** part of your sandwich, you might draw:

- A friend who is all *butterfingers*.
- A flatterer trying to *butter someone up*.
- A *bread-and-butter* thank-you note.

- A *mustard plaster*.
- A canister of *mustard gas*.

For the **trimmings,** you could draw a *cute tomato,* someone *in a pickle*, or someone who is as *cool as a cucumber*. Glue on play dollar bills for the *lettuce*. If you want some *pepper*, you can draw:

- A man with a *salt-and-pepper* beard.
- Someone giving a *pep talk*.

- A *peppy* cheerleader.
- A slice of *pepperoni sausage*.

For other **meats,** you might draw:

- A friend *beefing* about how much homework she has.
- An airport manager *beefing up* security.
- A football player *beefing up* for the fall season.
- A *ham* radio operator.

- Two kids *hamming* it up.
- A copy of some *spam* e-mail.
- Someone *bringing home the bacon*.
- A bunch of *baloney*.

If you do not want a meat sandwich, you can draw:

- A *traffic jam*.
- A *log jam*.
- A *big cheese*.

- One of the *cheese head* fans of the Green Bay Packers.
- Something *cheesy*.

If you want a *toasted* sandwich, you can draw a picture of the guests at a wedding *toasting* the bride and groom, but if you would rather have a *grilled* sandwich, you can draw a picture of parents *grilling* a teenager who came home late.

Figure 5.1 A metaphor sandwich

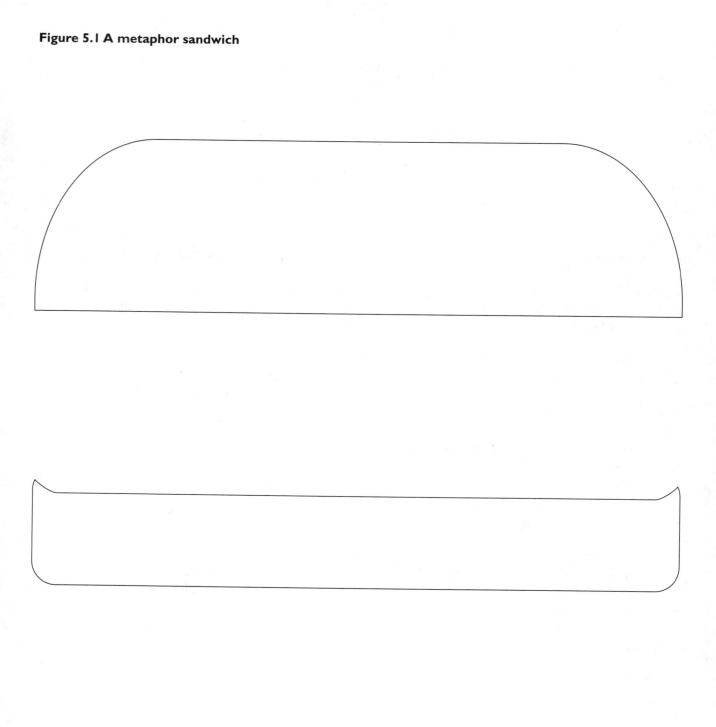

Food as Sources and Targets of Metaphors

Name: _____ **Period:** _____ **Date:** _____

This chapter has been about how the names of foods have been metaphorically applied to other ideas. However, the process also works the other way around so that foods are named because of their similarity to something that is better known. For example, *crackers* got their name because they *crack* and *crackle*, while *popcorn* and *Pop Tarts*® were named because they puff up. The sentences below illustrate how food can serve both of these roles. The italicized items have metaphorical names based on their shapes. However, four of the items are foods that have received their names from miscellaneous sources, while three are miscellaneous items that have received their metaphorical names from food. Show that you can figure out the difference by reading the sentences and then drawing little pictures of the items. In the box on the left, put the food items with names based on shapes. In the box on the right, put the miscellaneous items that happen to look like food.

1. The man was convicted because of a single footprint left by the *waffle print* on the sole of his sneakers.

2. *T-bone steaks* are my Dad's favorite.

3. The school dress policy disallows the wearing of tank tops by boys and tops with *spaghetti straps* by girls.

4. Nikki eats *bell peppers* like some people eat apples.

5. The name of the Subway® Sandwich shops is a pun on the *submarine sandwiches* they sell.

6. There are a lot of *pie charts* in this book.

7. I like *shoestring potatoes* better than potato chips.

Figure 5.2

Foods named after the shape of miscellaneous items

Miscellaneous items named after the shape of foods

Illustrate the Menus

Name: _____ **Period:** _____ **Date:** _____

When words are borrowed from other languages, many English speakers do not know the meanings of the words and so miss out on the underlying metaphors. Here are food names that you are likely to find on the menus of Mexican and Italian restaurants. Draw a little picture by each one to illustrate the underlying metaphors. If you have never eaten one of these items of food, maybe a classmate can describe it for you. After you draw these pictures, try to think of some other foods whose names are metaphors based on their shapes.

1. At Mexican restaurants, *burros* can be filled with almost any kind of spicy food.

2. *Burritos* are similar to *burros* except smaller.

3. At Italian restaurants, *tortellini* is a stuffed pasta that resembles tortoises or little turtles.

4. If you order a bowl of *vermicelli* at an Italian restaurant, you are literally ordering "little worms."

5. A *tostado* at a Mexican restaurant is sort of like a piece of toast except it does not have butter and jelly on it.

6. You can hardly eat at an Italian restaurant without having *pasta*, which is cognate with such English words as *paste* and *pastry*.

Common Features: 1. shape and size, **2.** shape, **3.** provide choices, **4.** small and efficient, **5.** all smashed together, **6.** green and crisp.

Workshop 5.1: A. 1. jelly beans, **2.** string bean, **3.** Beanie Babies®, **4.** beans, **5.** full of beans. **B. 1.** Corn Belt, **2.** corny, **3.** corn row, **4.** corn. **C. 1.** Potato Famine, **2.** couch potato, **3.** hot potato. **D. 1.** apples of the earth, **2.** Adam's apples, **3.** pineapples, **4.** apple cart. **E. 1.** cherry-stem, **2.** cherry on top of the sundae, **3.** cherry pickers. **F. 1.** top banana, **2.** banana seats, **3.** banana splits, **4.** go bananas.

Workshop 5.2: A. 1. breadbasket, **2.** pantry, **3.** breadwinner, **4.** breadline. **B. 1.** tostado, **2.** Melba toast, **3.** toasty, **4.** milk toast. **C. 1.** caked on, **2.** a piece of cake, **3.** take the cake, **4.** cupcakes. **D. 1.** tough cookie, **2.** cookie jar, **3.** cookie-cutter. **E. 1.** crumbled, **2.** crumbling, **3.** crumb. **F. 1.** souped-up, **2.** thick as pea soup, **3.** soup kitchen. **G. 1.** shepherd's stew, **2.** a stew, **3.** stewing.

Workshop 5.3: A. 1. good egg, **2.** eggheads, **3.** nest egg, **4.** walking on eggs. **B. 1.** cry over spilt milk, **2.** milks a situation, **3.**

milk and honey. **C. 1.** beef up, **2.** beefing up, **3.** Beefeaters. **D. 1.** spam, **2.** bacon, **3.** baloney.

Workshop 5.4: Part I: 1. chew, **2.** swallowing, **3.** taste, **4.** nibble, **5.** digest, **6.** bite, **7.** savor. **Part II: 1.** taste, **2.** savored, **3.** nibbles, **4.** digest, **5.** chewed, **6.** bitten, **7.** swallow.

Workshop 5.5: 1. chopper, **2.** grease, **3.** beaten, **4.** stir, **5.** blend in, **6.** mix, **7.** bake, **8.** creamed.

Workshop 5.7: *Foods named after the shape of miscellaneous items*: T-bone steak, bell peppers, submarine sandwich, shoestring potatoes. *Miscellaneous items named after the shape of foods*: waffle print sneakers, spaghetti straps, pie charts.

Workshop 5.8: Discussion ideas: Some other foods named because of their shapes are bear claws, sweet rolls, corn flakes, hot-dogs, round steaks, T-bone steaks, and chocolate pecan turtles.

End-of-Chapter Activities

Aesop was a Greek slave who lived more than 2,000 years ago. He became famous for telling little stories that taught lessons. He probably did not really tell all the stories that are attributed to him; nevertheless, his name is recognized around the world because the stories, supposedly about animals, were really about the characteristics of the powerful, and often greedy and obnoxious, people that he observed. Many of his stories, besides being about animals, were about food, because everyone relates to food. His most famous story, "The Fox and the Grapes," is so well known that speakers do not need to tell the whole story when they see a similar situation. All they say is *sour grapes* and listeners know what is meant. Speakers also use the phrase *sweet lemon* to describe an opposite situation. When something bad happens, the person insists it was a good thing—that is, the lemon was sweet instead of sour.

After we read "The Fox and the Grapes," there are three other food-related parables for you to read, plus some proverbs related to food. Read the parables and the proverbs and choose one to illustrate. It would be fun if

you could use your picture as a visual aid to help you tell your story to a small group of students from another class or to someone at home.

THE FOX AND THE GRAPES

A hungry fox was walking down a country road. He was passing a grape arbor when he noticed that a branch of a grapevine had worked itself into a tree by the side of the road. As a result, a beautiful bunch of grapes was hanging right there over the fox's head. "This is my lucky day," thought the fox as he reached up to get the grapes. However, they were higher than he thought. He stood on his tiptoes, but still could not reach them. He went back down the road a little ways and took a running leap at the grapes. Still he missed them. He tried again and again, until finally exhausted and sweaty, he looked at the grapes and decided they were sour anyway.

Moral: It is easy to say that what you cannot get is not worth having.

Three Fables

Here are three other Aesop's Fables and the morals. This time, you will need to figure out which moral goes with which story. Write it in the space after the story.

☐ Do not count your chickens before they are hatched.
☐ Greediness is its own reward.
☐ One good trick deserves another.

THE BOY AND THE ALMONDS

A hungry farm boy loved the almonds that his family grew and took to market every week. One day just before his father was leaving for the weekly trip, his mother told him that he could reach into the jug and take as big a handful as he could hold. The boy was delighted. He reached in and stretched out his fingers to close his fist over what he thought must be one-fourth of all those in the jug. However, he soon discovered a problem. He could not take his hand out of the jug. His mother advised him to let go of a few of the nuts, but he refused. So there he stood all afternoon hungry and miserable, but holding onto more almonds than he ever dreamed he could have.

Moral: _____

_____

THE AMBITIOUS MILK MAIDEN

A girl was carrying a bucket of good, fresh milk to sell at the market. She held it on her head with one hand, and on the long and boring walk began dreaming of what she would buy with the money. She decided on eggs that she could put behind the stove in her kitchen to keep them warm until they hatched. Then when they hatched, she would let them grow until they laid eggs themselves. Each week she would be able to take a basket of eggs to market to sell. Oh, what fine clothes she could have with the money and what an elegant lady she would become! With this

thought, she took her hand from the milk bucket so that she could practice a little curtsy, and of course the bucket tipped off and spilled every bit of the milk.

Moral: _____

_____

THE FOX AND THE STORK

A sly old fox invited his friend, the stork, for dinner. The fox cooked a wonderful broth soup, rich with little pieces of meat and savory vegetables. It smelled so good the whole neighborhood wished they had been invited. However, when the stork arrived at the dinner table, he found the dinner served on a wide, shallow plate. The fox lapped it up hungrily, but all the stork could do was to wet the end of his beak. He was a gracious guest and said nothing about his problem. However, the next week, when he invited the fox to dinner, he cooked an equally wonderful fish chowder, which he served in a tall bottle with a narrow neck. When the two sat down to eat, the stork put in his bill and enjoyed the feast to its fullest. But all the fox could do was to lick the outside of the bottle.

Moral: _____

_____

Here are some other proverbs. Pick one that you like and write a food-related story that will illustrate it.

☐ The cream rises to the top.
☐ Don't bite off more than you can chew.
☐ Feast today; famine tomorrow!
☐ Don't jump out of the frying pan into the fire.
☐ Don't put all your eggs in one basket.
☐ You have to crack some eggs to make an omelet.

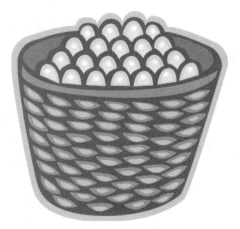

CHAPTER SIX

Containers and Shelters

Background Reading for the Teacher

How people refer to containers is a good illustration of how language changes more slowly than does technology. While speakers are using the same names for containers as did people two or three centuries ago, the actual items are likely to be very different. For example, we still talk about *boxing rings* from the days when whoever set up a match would simply draw a ring in the sand. Today, boxing *rings* are squares; with their sides made from posts and ropes they look more like *boxing boxes*. However, there is little likelihood that a change will occur because the term is so firmly established. For the most part, U.S. speakers shy away from terms that sound as though they are repetitious, even though the two meanings of *box* are different.

The most dramatic example of how speakers use old names for new items relates to computers where people talk about *folders, files, clipboards,* and *bulletin boards*. Computers have functions that play the roles of these pieces of office equipment, but they do not have the kinds of concrete items that in a real office people pick up and touch.

The pronunciation of *clipboard* illustrates another principle of language change. Because *clipboard* has been in the language only since the late 1800s, speakers pronounce it distinctly so that the images of a *clip* and a *board* come through. The word *cupboard*, a board on which people set cups or from which they hung cups, has been in the language from the 1500s.

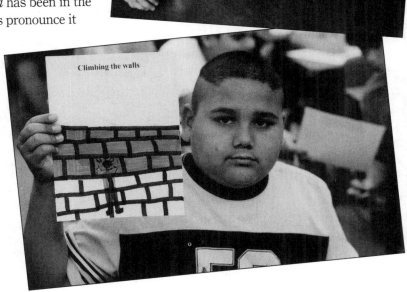

Climbing the walls

Six-year-old Angie (top) explains *bucket* metaphors at the *Hands-On* table, while seventh-grader Jacob (bottom) shows what it means to be "climbing the walls." An advantage of providing students with choices to illustrate is that since they are not drawing the same things, they are not competing with each other and are genuinely interested to see what their friends are doing.

That word has evolved both in meaning and pronunciation so that many speakers are surprised to recognize its origin as *a board for cups*.

We are including *shelters* in this chapter, because they too are containers, only bigger than what most people think of as containers. Another difference is that both people and animals choose to go into shelters, while with containers an outside force puts things into containers.

Notes to Help Teachers Elicit Ideas from Students

It must be human instinct for people to want to extend their power by carrying things around. Depending on your class and the atmosphere you want to establish, you might have a contest to see who has the most pockets or who is carrying around the most unusual items in pocket, purse, billfold, or backpack. Having students take everything out to pile on their desks could cause embarrassment, so you probably won't want to do that. You could, however, ask for volunteers to tell about their most unexpected items or about what they carry around just for pleasure or emotional "comfort." If your students do journal writing, a topic could be what they would miss most if they lost their backpack or purse, or they could contrast the most "essential" thing they carry with the most "useless" thing.

To move more directly into the topic of this chapter, here are some questions to ask about especially interesting container words. We have also included possible comments that either you or your students could make.

Question	Desired Comments from You and from Students
Do you know how to *purse* your lips? It is almost like getting ready to kiss, except that it is accompanied by a frown and means that the person is concentrating. How do you think the name developed?	When a person's mouth is pursed, it looks like the top of a drawstring bag or purse. (If you have a drawstring bag, bring it in as an illustration.)
Does anyone here live on a *cul de sac*? Can you draw a picture of your street? What does its shape look like?	A *cul de sac* is French for *dead end* street. It literally means "bottom of the bag," but it sounds more appealing than *dead end*. A *sack* in football is when the quarterback is knocked down behind the line of scrimmage. He is *in the sack*.
When people lose their jobs, as when the Enron Corporation closed, they were shown on TV walking away with their belongings in cardboard boxes. But before boxes were plentiful, people used sacks. Can you think of a related metaphor about someone losing a job?	Getting *sacked* is a common way of describing getting *fired*. It is a kinder description than *getting fired*, which is based on an old custom of burning people's houses or belongings when they were no longer wanted. During wars when soldiers *sack* a city, they carry off the valuables in sacks. Today's robbers sometimes steal a pillowcase to use as a *sack*. Another way to say you have been *sacked* is to say you have been *canned*, which means you have been "shelved" or "put away."

Another good conversation starter is to look at the fairly basic container words on the left and the more metaphorical words on the right and ask students to decide whether the similarity is one of SHAPE or ACTION. In the interest of saving paper, this could be done orally or with help from an overhead or a chalkboard.

TO HOLD THE FLOOR

More Basic		**More Metaphorical**
1. A lipstick tube	_____	A tube top
2. A saucer	_____	A flying saucer
3. A bottleneck	_____	A bottleneck in traffic
4. A frying pan	_____	The Oklahoma panhandle
5. A kettle	_____	A kettle drum
6. A cardboard box	_____	A railroad boxcar
7. An ice cream scoop	_____	A scoop in journalism
8. A kitchen sink	_____	A sinkhole in Florida
9. A water bucket	_____	Bucket seats in a car
10. A bull pen on a farm	_____	A bullpen in baseball

Continue the conversation by talking about the relationships between the names of containers and actions that are associated with them. Listed here are some common containers. Work with students to create sentences in which the container words are changed into verbs. A sample sentence is given for each sentence, but to give students more time to understand the concept, encourage the class to create three or four different sentences for each of the container words.

TO GO THROUGH THE ROOF

1. A *pack*age of cookies (Suzie *packaged* the cookies.)

2. A *cart*on of eggs (We *carted* off the eggs.)

3. A *stow*away (Please *stow* your luggage in the overhead compartments.)

4. A *sack* of popcorn (Can you *sack* the popcorn for the trick-or-treaters?)

5. A pile of *lug*gage (Do we have to *lug* our own stuff?)

6. A *clip*board (The coach *clipped* her notes on that board.)

7. A *bottle* of cherries (We *bottle* cherries every summer.)

8. A *packet* of trail mix (It's a good thing we *packed* some trail mix.)

9. A *pocket* full of change (He always *pockets* the change.)

10. A *bag* of sand (Volunteers are needed to *bag* sand to help prevent flooding.)

Other seventh graders enjoyed making posters that literally interpreted such expressions as *holding the floor* and *going through the roof.*

Holding the Bag— from Literal to Metaphorical

Name: _____ **Period:** _____ **Date:** _____

Some of the first toys that toddlers enjoy are boxes, purses, baskets, and miniature trucks and wagons that can be filled with things. The manufacturers of children's clothing have discovered that kids love pockets, so they sew them into overalls, pants, skirts, and shirts. *Pocket* is the diminutive form of *poke*, which is an old word for *sack*, as seen in the cliché about not buying *a pig in a poke*. Pockets were originally separate little sacks as shown by the nursery rhyme,

> Lucy Locket lost her pocket.
> Kitty Fisher found it.
> Nothing in it; nothing in it,
> Just a ribbon round it.

After this nursery rhyme was created, someone had the good idea of sewing pockets into clothing both for convenience and for security. *Pocket* is related to *pouch*, *packet*, and *package*, all of which have similar meanings. Read these basic descriptions of some common containers and then choose the most appropriate terms to write in the blank spaces of the sentences that follow. Talk about the relationships between the basic and the more metaphorical meanings.

A. Bags are larger and stronger than sacks. Although you check your *bags* at the *baggage area* in an airport, the majority of *bags* are not as big or as sturdy as suitcases. They are like *sandbags* or *grocery bags*. Small plastic *bags* are called *baggies*, while *handbags* are also called *purses*. *Bag women* or *bag ladies* are homeless women who carry their belongings in shopping bags. Metaphorically, people who are described as carrying *too much baggage* have a troubled past.

baggy clothes	bags	holding the bag	out of the bag

1. If you let the cat _____, you gave away a secret.

2. Parents wonder why their children like to wear _____.

3. If you are left _____, you have been abandoned in some enterprise.

4. People without enough sleep have _____ under their eyes.

B. *Case* is related to *chest*. Both words come from Latin *capsa*, which is related to carrying or heaving things. The things being carried can be literal, as when people buy their groceries *by the case*, or they can be metaphorical, as when people make a *case* for something. The *briefcases* that people carry around were first designed for lawyers to take their *briefs* (their notes on their *cases*) to court. *Casings* are also protective coverings as those around doors and windows.

casings	encased	your case

1. In Arizona, tourists can buy scorpions _____ in plastic.

2. If you want to borrow money from someone, you lay out _____ explaining why you need the money and how you will pay it back.

3. _____ from ammunition are sometimes used as evidence in court.

C. *Baskets* are usually woven from straw, but today they might also be made from plastic, or, in the case of *wastebaskets,* from metal or wood. They vary in purpose from the playful uses of *Easter baskets* to the practical uses of *laundry baskets*. The first games of *basketball* were played with *bushel fruit baskets* attached to posts.

basket cases	basket weaving	wastebasket

1. When people want to insult a college class as being too easy, they call it _____.

2. Physically, _____ are people so damaged that they must be carried around by others. Metaphorically, *basket cases* are emotionally troubled people who at the moment need help and care from others.

3. To put something in the round file is to put it in the_____.

D. *Packs* and *packages* can be almost any size. What distinguishes them from other containers is that, except for *backpacks*, they are not usually premade. They are like the "brown paper packages tied up in string" that Julie Andrews sang about as "one of her favorite things" in *The Sound of Music*. Although the U. S. Postal Service no longer lets people use string because it gets tangled in the machines, many people still love to get *packages* in the mail, especially around birthdays and Christmas.

pack their children	packets	packing

1. Parents who _____ off to summer camp know that a lot of *packing* is involved.

2. _____ are small *packages*.

3. Styrofoam _____ is so lightweight that it flies all over when you open a *package*.

E. *Bottles* have an advantage over cans in that people can see what they are buying. This was especially important in the 1800s when people were suspicious of buying anything they could not see. *Bottles* for babies, as well as *water bottles* for adults, are now made out of plastic because it weighs less and will not break and cut people. The *bottlebrush tree* has a unique blossom that looks like the kinds of brushes used to clean out narrow-mouthed bottles.

> **bottlenecks**　　　　　　**bottle-nosed**　　　　　　**bottle up**

1. _____ occur in traffic when four lanes turn into only one or two.

2. Some families tend to _____ their emotions.

3. The _____ dolphin has a prominent beak.

F. *Cans* have an advantage over bottles: If they are dropped, they probably will not break. In England, *canned food* is called *tinned food*. Both toilets and jails are sometimes referred to as *cans*, while if you get *fired* from a job, you might say you have been *canned*.

> **can it**　　　　　　**canned**　　　　　　**canned jokes**

1. If someone tells you to _____ or put a lid on it, you are being told to be quiet.

2. On television and radio _____ applause (from old recordings) is often added to the studio audience's reaction.

3. Because _____ do not fit into the immediate situation, they are not as surprising and funny as are spontaneous jokes.

From Literal to Metaphorical

Name: _____ **Period:** _____ **Date:** _____

The following container terms are used both literally and metaphorically. Try to fit them into the appropriate blank spaces in the sentences. In Part I, the words are to be used in a more basic or literal sense, while in Part II, they are to be used in a more metaphorical sense. Talk about the relationships between the two different uses.

bag	bottled	canned	case	pack	pockets	purses	sacks

PART I Basic Sentences

1. Civil War soldiers considered _____ meat a luxury.

2. The gang steals _____ from elderly women.

3. Today even little kids have to carry a back _____.

4. When my brother carried a book _____, he would set it down and forget it.

5. We are to bring our lunches in paper _____ with our names written on the outside.

6. High-fashion overalls for babies have four or five _____.

7. We need a _____ of pop for the party.

8. My grandmother _____ 40 quarts of peaches this year.

PART II Metaphorical Sentences

1. Three passengers were injured when the plane hit a couple of air _____.

2. His attorney says the defense has no _____.

3. When his partner quit, he was left holding the _____.

4. When our teacher _____ her lips, we know she is thinking about giving us more homework.

5. I don't like _____ humor.

6. It's not healthy to keep your emotions _____ up.

7. That is such a _____ of lies.

8. When an army _____ a city, the soldiers carry off valuables.

Containers in the Home

Name: _____ **Period:** _____ **Date:** _____

Read the following paragraphs carefully and pick the appropriate words from those listed and write them in the blank spaces. Talk about the meanings and try making up some new sentences using the words with their extended meanings.

PART I Pots and Pans

balancing pans	flash	frying pan	pan out	pan for gold
potbellied	pot shots	Texas Panhandle	to pan	

Pots and *pans* provide English with dozens of lexical extensions. A *pan* is a broad, shallow container used in kitchens for many purposes. Well-stocked kitchens have *baking pans, cookie pans, warming pans, frying pans,* and *dishpans*. People are probably thinking of the shape of a **(1.)** _____ when they talk about the Oklahoma and the Florida *Panhandles*. They are probably thinking of a *sauce pan* with a shorter handle when they talk about the **(2.)** _____. Scales have **(3.)** _____, while some old-fashioned guns and old-fashioned flash cameras have *pans* to hold the powder that is to be lit. This is where the phrase a **(4.)** _____ in the pan comes from to refer to something dramatic but short-lived.

The history of the western United States was changed dramatically in the mid-1800s when thousands of adventurers flocked to California, Colorado, and Nevada to **(5.)** _____. All that was needed was a large pan with gently sloping sides. Hopeful miners would scoop up a pan of water, sand, and gravel and swirl the contents around. The heaviest material would sink to the bottom, to be examined for gold nuggets or flakes. This method of looking carefully to separate the gold from the refuse is the grounding for the verb **(6.)** _____, as when a critic *pans* a movie or a play or when speakers say something did not **(7.)** _____.

Pots are larger containers. The ones made from clay are called *pot*tery as with *crock pots*. Both **(8.)** _____ people and *potbellied* stoves are fully rounded out. A *pot licker* is stingy, while someone who takes *potshots* is killing a domesticated animal for food. In a similar way, snipers on tops of buildings are described as taking **(9.)** _____, because they are shooting people without giving them a chance to escape.

PART II Cupboards and Cabinets

> Cabinet Room   cupped   drawers   dresser
> kitchen cabinets   metaphorical   shelf life   shelving

The first *cupboards* were literally a board attached to a wall. Dishes could be set on them and cups hung from them. The fact that *cupboards* were named for *cups* shows the importance of cups for drinking. While food can be picked up and eaten, it is relatively hard to *cup* your hands for drinking. Babies and young children would be especially challenged. Also, no one wants to have hot drinks from **(1.)** _____ hands. Even in prehistoric times, people made cups out of the tusks of animals and out of hollow bones whose ends would be plugged. The Biblical phrase, "My cup runneth over," to mean that someone has been greatly blessed, hints at how long container words have been given **(2.)** _____ meanings.

Cabinets are small *cabins* where people store things. **(3.)** _____ _____ are used for food, dishes, and cooking utensils. People put papers in *filing cabinets* and other items in *gun cabinets, medicine cabinets, china cabinets,* and *knick-knack cabinets*. The White House undoubtedly contains many *cabinets* of these kinds, but the one that most people think about when they hear someone refer to *The President's Cabinet* is not a container, but a group of Presidential advisors. This metaphorical name may be based on the fact that these people meet in closed sessions in the **(4.)** _____ or that the President goes to them for important advice, similar to the way that he would go to an actual cabinet to retrieve crucial documents.

A specialized kind of cabinet is the one we get dressed in front of, so we call it a **(5.)** _____. The *drawers* in dressers or desks are the parts that get pulled out, as when, in a western movie, the sheriff *draws* his gun or a cowboy pulls on his long underwear, also called **(6.)** _____.

Shelves are flat boards attached to a wall or to the inside of a *cabinet* or *closet*. When speakers talk about **(7.)** _____ a project that no longer interests them, most likely they do not actually put anything on a shelf. Instead, they just stop working on whatever the project was. When speakers talk about something as being *off the shelf*, they are saying that it is ordinary rather than being custom made. The **(8.)** _____ of something alludes to how long it can sit on the shelf in a pantry or in a grocery store and still be good. More metaphorically, speakers might talk about the *shelf life* of a topic that is current news. The metaphor hints that the public sooner or later gets tired of particular news topics.

The Relative Sizes of Food

Name: _____ **Period:** _____ **Date:** _____

Shape is the most common basis for container metaphors. The shapes of items with similar names are fairly consistent, but the sizes depend on what the items are being compared to. For example, *cupolas* are those little caps that look like upside down *cups* on the tops of ornate buildings. They are nearly always described as small, but that is in relation to the dome or the roof that they decorate, not in relation to a cup, from which they are named.

One of the suffixes that English uses to indicate smallness is *-et*, as when a *pocket* is a small *poke* or *sack* and a *tablet* is round and flat, but much smaller than a tabletop. *Closets* are small *enclosures*, but no one thinks it odd to have a *walk-in closet*. A *bassinet* is a small *basin* to hold babies. Actually, *bassinets* are bigger than the *basins* that people have in their bathrooms, and so the idea of smallness is probably more closely connected to the baby than to the container.

Packets are small packages, as with pills that come in *packets* or the *packets* of dehydrated foods that campers take with them. Even though *packets* of food are usually bigger than *packs of cards* or *packs of cigarettes,* people use a word meaning "little package" for food because it is expected to come in bigger packages than cards or cigarettes.

The biggest mismatch in size comes when talking about *The Big Dipper* and *The Little Dipper*. These constellations include the seven principal stars in Ursa Major and the seven principal stars in Ursa Minor. Since these are bigger than our whole universe, neither one should be called *little,* except in relation to each other.

To give you practice in thinking about the relative size of containers, listed below are some basic containers followed by lexical extensions given in alphabetical order. Draw a little picture of what you envision for each of the main words. Then look at the alphabetical listing of extended uses, and on the space to the right put the words in a new list arranged by the typical sizes of these items.

If you do not know the meanings of the words, talk to people about the words or look them up in a dictionary. In the first set, for example, you probably know most of the words, but you might not know that *bowling balls* are heavier on one side than the other as if they are made from a bowl (the heavier side) and a matching lid (the lighter side with the holes for fingers). Because bowling balls look like spheres rather than bowls, most speakers do not make the connection.

While metaphors based on shape are fairly easy to see, metaphors based on actions are usually more abstract and therefore harder to picture. For example, the dipping action associated with *scooping* something up is the basis for a *scoop* in journalism. But such a *scoop* cannot be measured by size or weight, so it is not in the list. Nevertheless, it is a good word to use in a metaphorical sentence. Underneath each set of words, write a sentence using a form of the word as a metaphor. To help you think about metaphors we have listed several more abstract metaphors, but you are also welcome to use one of the metaphors in the lists.

Basic item and extensions	Rearranged by size (starting with the smallest)

1. Bowl

A bowler hat

A bowling ball

A punch bowl

a. _____

b. _____

c. _____

Metaphors: *(to bowl someone over, the Oklahoma dust bowl, a bowl game)*

2. Box

A box camera

A cereal box

A pillbox

A railroad boxcar

a. _____

b. _____

c. _____

d. _____

Metaphors: *(to feel boxed in, to think outside the box, a boxing match)*

3. Dish

A casserole dish

A satellite dish

Toy dishs

a. _____

b. _____

c. _____

Metaphors: *(to dish it out, a covered dish supper, calling a beautiful woman a dish)*

4. Kettle

A kettle drum

A kettle hole (made by a glacier)

A tea kettle

a. _____

b. _____

c. _____

Metaphors: *(a fine kettle of fish, the pot calling the kettle black, kettle corn)*

5. Scoop

An ice cream scoop

A scoop neckline

A scoop shovel

a. _____

b. _____

c. _____

Metaphors: *(a scoop in journalism, to scoop someone up in your arms)*

Shelters

Name: _____ **Period:** _____ **Date:** _____

The difference between containers and shelters is that both people and animals make shelters for themselves. A container has been made, or adapted from nature, by a person who uses the container to hold or to carry things. Shelters are also made or adapted from nature, but people and animals go into them willingly because shelters protect them from bad weather and make their lives more comfortable.

The following paragraphs tell about basic kinds of shelters and their parts. Because the names for these ideas are so basic, they have been given many extended meanings. Talk about the basic meanings of the italicized boldface words at the beginning of each paragraph. Then read the more metaphorical terms and the sentences that follow the paragraphs. Write the most appropriate terms in the blank spaces. Talk about the relationships between the literal and the metaphorical meanings and what clues help you figure out the connections.

A. *Caves, shacks, cabins, cottages,* and *houses* have all served as homes, or at least as basic shelters, for people. The most unusual extension from these words is *caboose,* the name for the last car on trains that was traditionally used as living quarters by the staff. It is a combination word from *cabin* and *house.* Modern trains no longer have *cabooses,* but metaphorically speakers call a baby a *caboose* if it is born to a family after the other children are teenagers. The idea is that this is the last one in the line and that it is smaller than the other children, just as *cabooses* are smaller than the regular cars on a train.

> **cabin fever**   **cavernous**   **cottage**   **home page**   **house**   **Shack**   **sheltered**

1. I'm not sure that she should go on trip by herself because she has lived such a _____ life.

2. The _____ on a website is the one that serves as the place where viewers start from.

3. There is a _____ feeling to a sports arena if few spectators turn out.

4. _____ industries are small businesses or services. The idea comes from people being hired to knit gloves, make candles, or do other crafts at home and then bring the items into a boss.

5. A national electronics store named itself *Radio* _____ ® probably to give buyers a sense that it was small and friendly instead of a national chain.

6. The _____ of Representatives is the biggest U.S. legislative body at the national level.

7. People who cannot go out can get _____ even if they live in a mansion.

B. *Roofs, ceilings, floors,* and *walls* make up the basic parts of a house. The roofs on most houses extend beyond the walls for a foot or more. This overhanging part, called the *eaves,* is built to protect the house from weather. A person who is *eavesdropping* is listening in on other people's conversations. The name comes from the image of people standing under the eaves of a house pretending to be staying out of the rain, but really listening to what people inside the house are saying.

cloud ceiling   floor   floored   glass ceiling   ocean floor   roof   through the roof   walled in

1. Because I grew up on a prairie, living in a forest makes me feel _____.

2. When she told her father about the fender-bender, he went _____.

3. I was _____ when I heard they were sisters because they are so different.

4. The _____ was so low that pilots of small planes were advised not to take off.

5. Whoever is holding the _____ in a meeting is the person who is talking.

6. Women complain that a _____ keeps them from getting the highest jobs.

7. I hate the way peanut butter sticks to the _____ of my mouth.

8. The _____ is just as varied as is dry land.

C. *Rooms, closets, kitchens,* and *porches* are the *parts* of houses that are *partitioned off* for special purposes. *Rooms* are usually named for their purposes, as with *bedrooms, living rooms, bathrooms,* and *dining rooms.* An old-fashioned name for the *living room* was the *parlor,* which comes from the French word *parler* meaning "to speak." *Closets* are *enclosures* for clothing. Their alternate name is *wardrobe,* meaning a place that *guards* (wards off dangers) your clothes. *Kitchens* get their name from the Latin word *cokere,* meaning "to cook." A *kitchen garden* is a small garden where spices and vegetables are grown for use by only one family. *Kitchenware* and *kitchen cabinets* make it easier for people to do their work. When anthropologists study sites of primitive humans they look for the *kitchen midden,* which is the mound containing such things as pottery shards, bones from meat, and remnants of kitchen utensils. *Porches* are named from *port,* meaning *door.* They used to be called *porticos* or, in some parts of the country, *verandas.*

in the closet	kitchen cabinets	kitchen sink	porch light
room	room in	room for one more	roomy

1. An old Irish saying is that there is always _____.

2. Most families have some kind of skeletons _____.

3. Presidents have always had _____ made up of their friends, people they are so comfortable with that they will invite them into the kitchen.

4. If you go on a trip and are accused of taking everything but the _____, you have overpacked.

5. Clothes that are _____ are usually more comfortable than those that fit skintight.

6. Leaving the _____ on is a welcoming gesture.

7. If someone tells you there is always _____ for improvement, the person is probably getting ready to make a suggestion.

8. It is the new fashion at hospitals for the babies to _____ with the mothers instead of being placed in a separate nursery.

D. *Doors, windows, curtains,* and *drapes* all make it easier to live in houses. *Doors* are often viewed metaphorically as when something like college is viewed as *the door to success*. The little rise at the bottom of doors is called the *threshold*, because when people had straw on their floors (straw is left over from *threshing*), this little rise kept the threshing material inside the house. Someone standing on the *threshold* of a new career is about to step through a *door of opportunity*. The most significant feature of *windows* is that people can see through them. The word originally came from the idea of an *eye for the wind*, so both sight and ventilation were important. *Curtains* are soft window coverings or decorations. When people use the term *It's curtains!* to mean the end, or the death, of something, the allusion is to way *stage curtains* fall at the end of a play. All during the Cold War (the 1950s to the 1990s), people talked about the *Iron Curtain* that seemed to close off communication between the United States and the Soviet Union. *Stage curtains* are big and heavy and thus really like *drapes.* The earlier meaning of *drape* was the folds of cloth or the way it hung. In hospitals patients are *draped* with sterile coverings before having surgery.

> **back door   bay windows   curtains   door   draping   knocks   threshold   window**

1. Basketball players sometimes surprise the defense by going through the _____.

2. Blame for the financial troubles was laid at the _____ of the governor.

3. Someone who is described as having a clear _____ on the future is respected for considering the facts and having sound judgment.

4. If opportunity _____ at your door, you'd better answer.

5. Grooms are shown carrying their brides across the _____ as a symbol of their entering a new life.

6. Flirtatious women are sometimes described as _____ themselves all over men.

7. The scandal was _____ on his political ambitions.

8. Men with big bellies are said to have _____ because of the way their bodies extend outward as do windows designed to let people see in three directions.

E. *Tables, chairs, beds, couches, carpets,* and *rugs* are such basic pieces of furniture that they too have inspired metaphorical uses. When people have something unpleasant to say or when they want to be extra careful as in asking their boss for a raise, they will *couch* their message very carefully. They are trying to *soften* or *cushion* what they say. Do you see how all three of these terms (*couch, soften,* and *cushion*) are related both in their basic and their metaphorical senses?

bedrock	carpet	chairs	couch potato	cushion
flower beds	rug	table of contents	to bed	water table

 1. In cold climates, people cover their _____ with mulch and straw to get ready for winter.

 2. A team that has a _____ has a comfortable lead.

 3. If you are called on the _____, the idea is that you are called in and scolded by someone important enough to have a carpeted office.

 4. The _____ is the depth at which well drillers will find water.

 5. If someone pulls the _____ out from under you, that person suddenly dashes your hopes.

 6. The person who _____ a meeting is in charge based on the old idea that only important people get to sit down.

 7. When a bridge is being built over a river, engineers like the foundations to be built on _____.

 8. A _____ sits all day watching TV and eating snacks.

 9. In newspaper offices the paper is _____ when it is sent to the printing press.

 10. A _____ tells you what is in a book.

Human versus Animal Shelters

Name: _____ **Period:** _____ **Date:** _____

Because people consider themselves to be higher-level creatures than animals, it is a little surprising that people borrow the names of animal homes and use them in relation to themselves. See if you can figure out which of the following terms should go in the blank spaces of these sentences. Then talk about the animal or animals that each name relates to. Can you think of what the human action has in common with the animal whose home is alluded to?

> **beehive   burrowing   cages   cooped up   corral   den   doghouse   nest   pigpen   rat hole**

1. When my mother's quilting group arrives, our house is as busy as a _____.

2. On weekends my father hibernates in the _____ and watches sports on TV.

3. Young mothers with little children often feel _____.

4. You've got to_____ your emotions or you will get in trouble.

5. Loaning money to Erik is the same as putting your money down a _____.

6. On the first snowstorm of the winter, I feel like _____ down in bed and reading a good book.

7. The newlyweds are working hard to feather their _____.

8. My cousin is always in the _____ because he makes promises and then forgets about them.

9. I should think the people who work in teller's_____ in banks would feel like magnets for robbers.

10. His room is always a _____.

A Container Crossword Puzzle

Name: _____   **Period:** _____   **Date:** _____

Use these clues to work the crossword puzzle on the next page.

ACROSS

4. Today's _____ hold lots more than cups.

7. Most houses today have built-in _____ (small *enclosures*).

8. The Little _____ is not so little.

9. Purses are also called _____ because women carry them in their hands.

12. People who _____ their lips are probably thinking.

13. Even if you get _____ at work, you will probably carry your belongings home in a box.

DOWN

1. Small cabins are _____.

2. People like to buy food in a _____ so they can see it.

3. In the 1850s, a gold miner went to work with a shovel and a _____.

5. A cul de sac is really a _____ street.

6. In old movies, train-riding hoboes often jump into empty _____.

10. Doctors are cautioning kids not to overload a _____.

11. A _____ can be an area hundreds of miles wide that slopes down to something like the Great Salt Lake in Utah.

Shape or Action: 1. shape, **2.** shape, **3.** shape, **4.** shape, **5.** shape, **6.** shape, **7.** action, **8.** shape, **9.** shape, **10.** action.

Workshop 6.1: A. 1. out of the bag, **2.** baggy clothes, **3.** holding the bag. **4.** bags. **B. 1.** encased, **2.** your case, **3.** casings. **C. 1.** basket weaving, **2.** basket cases, **3.** wastebasket. **D. 1.** pack their children, **2.** packets, **3.** packing. **E. 1.** bottlenecks, **2.** bottle up, **3.** bottle-nosed. **F. 1.** can it, **2.** canned. **3.** canned jokes.

Workshop 6.2: Part I: 1. canned, **2.** purses, **3.** pack, **4.** bag, **5.** sacks, **6.** pockets, **7.** case, **8.** bottled. **Part II: 1.** pockets, **2.** case, **3.** bag, **4.** purses, **5.** canned, **6.** bottled, **7.** pack, **8.** sacks.

Workshop 6.3: Part I: 1. frying pan, **2.** Texas Panhandle, **3.** balancing pans, **4.** flash, **5.** pan for gold, **6.** to pan, **7.** pan out, **8.** potbellied. **Part II: 1.** cupped, **2.** metaphorical, **3.** kitchen cabinets, **4.** Cabinet Room, **5.** dresser, **6.** drawers, **7.** shelving, **8.** shelf life.

Workshop 6.4: 1. Bowl: a. a bowler hat, **b.** a bowling ball, **c.** a punch bowl. She was *bowled over* by his British accent. **2. Box: a.** a pillbox, **b.** a box camera, **c.** a cereal box, **d.** a railroad boxcar. She has felt *boxed in* ever since her father moved in with them. **3. Dish: a.** toy dishes, dishes, **b.** a casserole dish, **c.** a satellite dish. The coach really knows how to *dish it out* when we make a stupid mistake. **4. Kettle: a.** a tea kettle, **b.** a soup kettle, **c.** a kettle drum, **d.** a kettle hole. My mother always said, "The pot shouldn't call the *kettle* black." **5. Scoop: a.** an ice cream scoop, **b.** a scoop neckline, **c.** a scoop shovel. Little Cindy loves to be *scooped up* and spun around.

Workshop 6.5: A. 1. sheltered, **2.** home page, **3.** cavernous, **4.** cottage, **5.** shack, **6.** house, **7.** cabin fever. **B. 1.** walled in, **2.** through the roof, **3.** floored, **4.** cloud ceiling, **5.** the floor, **6.** glass ceiling, **7.** roof, **8.** ocean floor. **C. 1.** room for one more, **2.** in the closet, **3.** kitchen cabinets, **4.** kitchen sink, **5.** roomy, **6.** porch light, **7.** room, **8.** room in. **D. 1.** back door, **2.** door, **3.** windows, **4.** knocks, **5.** threshold, **6.** draping, **7.** curtains, **8.** bay windows. **E. 1.** flower beds, **2.** cushion, **3.** carpet, **4.** water table, **5.** rug, **6.** chairs, **7.** bedrock, **8.** couch potato, **9.** to bed, **10.** table of contents.

Workshop 6.6: 1. beehive, **2.** den, **3.** cooped up, **4.** corral, **5.** rathole, **6.** burrowing (rabbits, prairie dogs, moles, etc.), **7.** nest, **8.** doghouse, **9.** cages, **10.** pigpen.

Workshop 6.7: Across: 4. cupboards, **7.** closets, **8.** dipper, **9.** handbags, **12.** purse, **13.** sacked. **Down: 1.** cabinets, **2.** bottle, **3.** pan, **5.** deadend, **6.** boxcars, **10.** backpack, **11.** basin.

End-of-Chapter Activities

1. Read Louis Sachar's *Holes* (Farrar, Straus and Giroux, 1998). After you have read and enjoyed the book, think back and find three or four examples of containers that played important roles in the plot. You can start with the holes themselves. What did they contain? What were they supposed to contain? What does Sachar mean when he names the last part of the book "Filling in the Holes"? What about the gold tube with *K B* engraved on it? What kept the *sploosh* more or less "good" all those years? And how did Sachar describe the shape of *Camp Greenlake*? And what container is at the center of the whole story?

2. Here are some old proverbs that relate to containers or shelters. Choose one to illustrate with a drawing, a cartoon, or a short, short story. Perhaps you can think of a contrasting proverb to put with the one you choose. Be ready to tell the class whether your illustration is a literal or a figurative one.

☐ Don't jump out of the frying pan and into the fire.

☐ The pot shouldn't call the kettle black.

☐ They've got him over a barrel.

☐ There's no use shutting the barn door after the horse is out.

☐ We can see the light at the end of the tunnel.

☐ Be wary of a flash in the pan.

☐ Don't buy a pig in a poke (it might turn out to be a cat).

☐ People who live in glass houses should not throw stones.

☐ Don't go through the roof.

CHAPTER SEVEN

Clothing

Background Reading for the Teacher

Good stories to start students thinking about clothing include Hans Christian Andersen's *The Emperor's New Clothes* (there are many editions), Dr. Seuss's *The 500 Hats of Barthlomew Cubbins* (Vanguard Press, 1938 and 1965), and Harve and Margot Zemach's *Duffy and the Devil* (Farrar, Straus and Giroux, 1973). This latter book is a Cornish version of the old story of Rumplestilskin and the princess who had to spin straw into gold. A longer book that students might enjoy hearing and talking about is Eleanor Estes's classic *The Hundred Dresses* (Harcourt Brace, 1944).

While today most people buy their clothes ready-made, they still have enough experience with mending and sewing to understand and appreciate the many sewing-based metaphors that are part of everyday English. Someone who puts off fixing a hem that has started to come undone and, as a consequence, must redo practically the whole hem is in a good position to appreciate the proverb, "A stitch in time saves nine." Similarly, someone who goes to the trouble of sewing something out of cheap cloth and is then disappointed can understand the old saying, "You can't make a silk purse out of a sow's ear."

This is a wonderful chapter for hands-on experiences. Have students turn their jackets inside out to examine *frayed seams* and figure out why something *on the seamy side* is to be kept hidden. Bring your sewing basket to class and provide embroidery floss (it shows up better than just plain thread) and needles (large eyes are easier to thread), pins, buttons, and zippers to encourage students to experiment with actual sewing when they illustrate some of the metaphors. We know a Cub Scout leader who, on the day she taught a lesson on sewing, cut the buttons off each boy's shirt and then taught the boys how to sew them back on. You probably won't want to go that far, but accomplishing something with a needle and thread can be a memorable experience.

Of all the lessons we taught, this was the one that parents got the most involved with. We provided printed word strips and card stock for children to take home for posters. Their mothers contributed zippers, needles, embroidery thread, and all kinds of other supporting materials for posters. At least one father also made a contribution— perhaps unknowingly—of his *Troop Committee Chairman* badge, which came back on *A Crosspatch* poster.

TO EMBROIDER THE TRUTH

The Truth

A CROSSPATCH

THE THREAD OF THE STORY

Once upon a time there was a beautiful princess

The poster at the top was written in ink, but with a real needle taped on. On the bottom, 7-year-old Madeleine demonstrates her *Zip Your Lips* poster.

Notes to Help Teachers Elicit Ideas from Students

A good point to make with students is that the kinds of clothing that have been around the longest (robes, gowns, coats, shoes, hats, etc.) are the items that have been given extended meanings and have served as the sources for metaphors. Articles of clothing more recently designed are likely to have been the receivers, rather than the sources, of metaphors. One way that speakers choose names for new items of clothing is to describe what the clothes enable people to do. Give the following descriptions and see if students can figure out the item of clothing. Thoughts to solicit from students or to share with them are in parentheses. One way to slow down the action so that children will spend more time thinking about the connections is to ask children to draw the item (either on paper or on their white boards) and then hold up their pictures.

1. These are good shoes to wear if you want to *sneak up* on someone. (Because they are made from cloth and rubber, *sneakers* are "quiet" shoes. Detectives used to be called *gumshoes* [*gum* was an early word for *rubber*] because they wore rubber-soled shoes as they crept about spying on people.)

2. If you want to *jump* out of an airplane or even from the top of the monkey bars, it is a good idea to wear something firmly attached over your shoulders so that you won't jump out of your clothes. (The straps on girls' *jumpers* are an integral part of the garment. *Jumpsuits* are one-piece garments, making it even less likely that people will lose their clothes while jumping.)

3. What do you wear if you are chilly and would prefer to *sweat a little*? (*Sweaters, sweat suits,* or *sweatshirts*) The word *sweater* has been in the language since the 1500s, but *sweat suit* can be traced only to about the 1950s.)

4. What do women wear that allows them to *slip into* their clothes more easily? And what is a similarly named item designed so that people can *slip* their feet into them when they first get out of bed? (Women wear *slips* that are made from lightweight, *slippery* cloth. Most bedroom *slippers* are soft and loose enough, perhaps with no backs, so that people can *slip into them* without bending over or fastening anything.)

5. What do some men use to *suspend* or hold up their trousers? (*Suspenders* have been used for this purpose since the 1500s. You might compare *suspenders* to the supports on *suspension bridges* and to the hanging *pendants* that women wear as jewelry. More metaphorically, you could talk about a *suspenseful situation*, in which people are left *hanging.* The connection to *hanging* is further emphasized in the old-fashioned name for *suspenders*, which is *galluses*, a cognate of *gallows*.)

Clothing as Metaphorical Targets

Name: _____   Period: _____   Date: _____

As you will see in this chapter, speakers have given many extended meanings to the names of such basic items as *capes, robes, coats, jackets, hats, caps, hoods, dresses,* and *skirts*. However, in this first workshop, the focus will be on how speakers find names for more recently developed items of clothing. This workshop presents examples of five different sources from which speakers have created the names of articles of clothing. After you read about these, write at least three examples in each section of the pie chart on page 114, identified as A. a geographical allusion, B. the name of a person, C. a descriptive feature of the item, D. the body part that the item is associated with, or E. an allusion to a profession where the item is worn.

Some articles of clothing are named by fashion designers and marketing experts, but others are given names through a kind of folk creativity that describes a characteristic of the item. For example, *bowler hats* are shaped like bowls, while *pillbox* hats are shaped like pillboxes. *A-line* dresses are shaped like a capital *A*, while *T-shirts* are shaped like a capital *T*. If you want to keep warm on a ski trip, you will probably wear long underwear, commonly referred to as *long johns* or *drawers*. The connection to *draw* is that people have to pull them on, much like you *draw* the drapes or pull out a dresser *drawer*.

Some names are based on a connection with the geographical location where they first appeared, as with *Bermuda shorts* and *Bikini swimsuits*. *Oxford* shoes are named for Oxford, England, while *cordovan* shoes are named for Cordoba, Spain, where shoemakers use leather tanned from the inside layer of horsehide and stained a dark red. *Mackinaw blankets* were used by Native Americans in the 1800s when they were distributed by the U. S. government at the trading post on Mackinaw Island in upper Michigan. These heavy wool blankets, often with a red plaid design, were used first as blankets and then later sewn into *mackinaw coats*, which are still worn by hunters and outdoorsmen in cold weather. Perhaps one of the reasons the name caught on is that it is similar to *mackintosh*, a name that was also coming into fashion to name the raincoats that sailors wear. These are named for the Scottish chemist and inventor Charles Macintosh, who in 1836 figured out how to get rubber to stick to heavy cotton cloth. *Bloomers* are named for feminist Amelia Jenks Bloomer, who in the mid-1800s advocated that women be allowed to wear long, blousy pants instead of the cumbersome hooped skirts that were fashionable.

In the mid 1900s, the *Nehru jacket*, with its short stand-up collar, was named for the first prime minister of India, while the *Eisenhower jacket* was named for the military uniform preferred by General Dwight D. Eisenhower during the Second World War.

If an item of clothing has a feature that is considered unusual, then a description of this feature might serve as the name. Women's *tights* were obviously named because of the way they fit, which is opposite to the *slack* or loose fit of men's *slacks*. Once such descriptive names are given, they stick long after the feature has changed from unusual to expected. For example, most men used to wear long underwear, so *briefs* or *shorts* was the descriptive name attached to the newly designed underwear that became fashionable in the early 1900s. In a similar way, even through the "roaring twenties," women were expected to keep their legs covered with long stockings, but in the 1940s, as the United States concentrated on the war effort, short stockings became acceptable. They were called *bobby sox*, taken from the verb to *bob*, meaning "to cut." Teenaged girls were called *bobby soxers* because they wore stockings that had been *bobbed*; they also used *bobby pins* on their *bobbed hair*.

An alternate name for *bobby sox* is *anklets*, named for the part of the body with which they are most associated. Other items named in relation to the part of the body they cover are *necklaces, neckties, backpacks, earrings, shoulder straps, knee pads,* and *overalls* or *coveralls*.

Another system is to name items of clothing after a profession or an activity where they have been worn as with *ballet slippers, tennis shoes, baseball caps,* and *boxer shorts,* which are the outside pants worn by boxers. *Jockeys,* the men who ride race-horses, were the first ones to wear *jock straps* and underpants with built-in support. It is from these men that we get the name for *jockey shorts* and the custom of referring to all male athletes as *jocks*.

Write at least three examples in each section of this pie chart.

Figure 7.1 Origins of clothing names

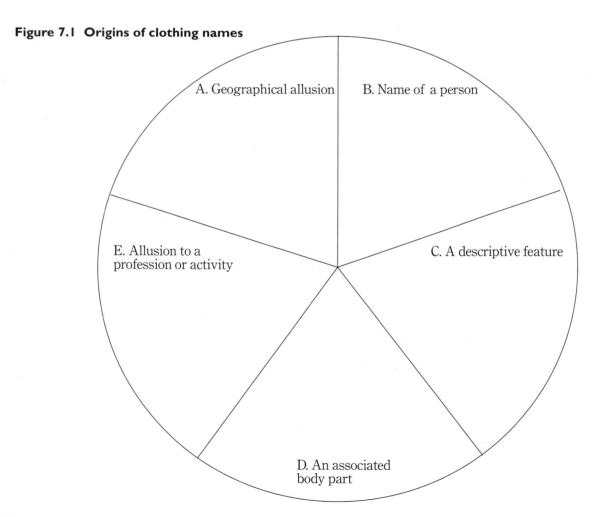

Hats Off

Name: _____ **Period:** _____ **Date:** _____

It is ironic that sometimes people are expected to show respect by removing their hats as when they come to dinner or to class or when they salute the flag. In other circumstances, as when entering particular religious buildings, covering one's head is a mark of respect. Some religions teach that a person's head should always be covered.

Hat has been in English for more than 800 years, and from the earliest history, the kind of hat someone wore told what kind of job the person did. Morris Udall, an Arizona politician who once ran for President, told about going to such a small high school that in the middle of a football game, he had to quickly take off his helmet and put on his band hat so that he could play for the half-time show. This is a literal example of someone *wearing two hats*, but the term is more often used figuratively. It is like the metaphor of *pulling a rabbit out of a hat*, which might describe a magician's trick, but might also describe someone unexpectedly coming up with a solution to a problem.

A *hat* word that most of us do not recognize is the word *tulip*, which comes from the Turkish word for *turban*. Although most of us think that tulips come from the Netherlands, they were actually a Turkish flower exported to Holland. The name comes from the way a field of tulips nodding in the wind looks like a large group of men wearing colorful turbans. But since neither Dutch nor English speakers were familiar with turbans or the word *tülbent,* the pronunciation was changed to the more familiar sounding *tulip (two lips)*, and the metaphor was lost.

The word *bonnet* is related to the word *bound* and has been in English since the thirteenth century. *Bonnets* are *bound* or tied under the wearer's chin. The *sun bonnets* that pioneer women wore were sewn from cloth. They had a large, stiff brim in the front to protect the wearer's face and a hanging ruffle in the back to protect her neck. More fashionable *bonnets* were woven from straw and decorated with flowers and tied under the chin with ribbons.

Caps probably got their name because of an association with the Latin word for *head*, which is *caput. Baseball caps, nurses' caps,* and the *caps* worn at graduation serve very different purposes, but even more different are *bottle caps* or the *caps* for toy guns, which are little bits of dynamite, *capped* with paper. The tops of columns are called the *capitals*, while the highest part of a building is its *capstone*. If a person *caps* an accomplishment, they have done something even better.

Hoods are bigger than caps. We know they were commonly worn because of stories about *Robin Hood* and the old folktale about *Little Red Riding Hood*. Birds are said to be *hooded* if their neck and head feathers are colored differently from their bodies. Falconers put real *hoods* on their birds to keep them from being visually stimulated. At universities people are *hooded* in honor of having earned advanced degrees. This custom goes way back in time as shown by words that include *hood* marking such designations as *childhood, adulthood, neighborhood, priesthood,* and *widowhood*. In a less positive sense, people wear *hoods* when they do not want to be recognized as with members of the Ku Klux Klan and with executioners, who did not want to be recognized by the families of those they were killing.

Veils took their name from Latin *vela*, which referred to sails, curtains, and awnings, all pieces of cloth that hang from something. In religions, people talk about the *veil* that separates earth from heaven. An old-fashioned way to say that a Catholic woman has entered a convent is to say *she took the veil*. Muslim women are sometimes referred to as *women of the veil* because of the way they keep their heads—and, in some countries, their faces—covered when they are out in public. The idea of brides wearing *veils* at their weddings can be traced back to ancient beliefs about a woman's face being special for her husband.

Read these more metaphorical allusions to head coverings. Choose the most appropriate of the terms to write in the sentences; talk about what the metaphors have in common with the head coverings.

PART I Veils, Hoods, and Bonnets

> **bonnet**   **Bridal Veil**   **hoods**   **hoodwink**   **neighborhood**   **veiled**

1. There must be nearly a dozen _____ waterfalls in the United States.

2. You naturally have things in common with people from your own _____.

3. To _____ people is to keep them from knowing that you are pulling a trick.

4. She interpreted what he said to be a _____ threat.

5. What American speakers call a hood on a car, British speakers call a_____.

6. Cooking counters in restaurants are required by safety laws to have ventilation _____.

PART II Caps and Hats

> **cap**   **capped**   **capstone**   **hat trick**   **hats into the ring**   **old hat**   **pass the hat**   **which hat**

1. To _____ is to ask for donations.

2. A _____ experience in college is something like defending a thesis or putting on an exhibition.

3. Snow- _____ mountains are gorgeous especially in the summertime.

4. When politicians throw their _____, they are announcing their candidacy.

5. Teachers/coaches are treated differently depending on _____ they are wearing.

6. A girl who has her _____ set for a boy wants him to be her boyfriend.

7. Something that is _____ is common or out-of-date.

8. In ice hockey, it is called a _____ when specators throw their hats onto the rink to celebrate a player's scoring three goals.

From Rags to Riches

Name: _____ **Period:** _____ **Date:** _____

As far as clothing goes, speakers think of *rags* as being the worn-out clothes that a homeless person or someone who has been abandoned at sea or lost in a war zone might wear. Even though a *rag picker* is someone who goes through other people's garbage and a *ragamuffin* is a dirty and unkempt child, people jokingly refer to their own clothes as *rags* or *glad rags*. They also refer to the manufacturers of clothing as the *rags industry*.

Rag and *ragged* come from a word meaning shaggy, uneven, or rough, an idea transferred to *ragtime music*, which has strong syncopation in the melody with a different beat in the accompaniment. This shows how not all words made from *rag* have negative connotations. *Raggedy Ann* and *Raggedy Andy* are well-loved stuffed dolls made from scraps of cloth. Another example is the high-quality paper that contains small amounts of cotton and linen and is identified by its *rag content*.

On a prestige scale, *robes* are far removed from *rags*, especially the kind of royal robes shown in old pictures of kings and queens. But this word too has its surprises. It is related to a thirteenth century Germanic word for *robbing*. People who came through towns wearing big, loose garments were suspected of hiding stolen goods in their loose clothing. It is ironic that today the people we would least suspect of being robbers—judges and ministers—are people who wear robes in public. Other people wear *bathrobes* and go outside in them only if there is some kind of an emergency. However, the historical importance of robes is shown through the word *wardrobe* as a way to refer to all of people's clothes. *Ward* is cognate with *guard*, and so *wardrobes* are closets that guard people's *robes* or their clothing.

Gowns are loose-fitting like a robe, but lighter in weight. *Gowns* used to be worn by both men and women, but today they are mostly thought of as women's wear as in *evening gowns* for formal occasions and *nightgowns* for sleeping. This is why some judges and ministers talk about their *robes* instead of their *gowns*, but actually what they wear are more like *gowns*.

Even though only women wear *dresses,* men also get *dressed* and keep their clothes in *dressers*. And both men and women who want particular hairstyles use mousse as *hair dressing*. This idea of fixing something to be its best is the underlying idea behind the *turkey dressing* that you eat at Thanksgiving.

In the history of clothing, most *capes* were not as elegantly tailored as those worn in movies by Count Dracula, Sherlock Holmes, Superman, and Batman. *Cape* is related to the Latin word for *head*, and such land masses as The *Cape of Good Hope* and *Cape Cod* resemble heads sticking out into oceans. The word *escape* is also related. It comes from the idea that if someone grabs your *cape*, you can just slip out of it (*ex*=from). The spelling was changed to *escape* for ease in pronunciation.

Coats require more tailoring than capes because they have sleeves, buttons, and pockets. *Overcoats* have to be big enough to fit over suits and jackets. During the U.S. Civil War, soldiers who found themselves in enemy territory would turn their coats inside out in hopes of keeping their "true colors" from being recognized. This is how *turncoat* came to be used to identify a traitor.

Jackets are short, lightweight coats. They are such common pieces of clothing that their name comes from the French *Jacque* and English *Jack*, a generic name for the common man. Metaphorically, *book jackets* and *record jackets* provide lightweight protection to books and records similar to what the cloth jackets provide for people.

Read these sentences and the listed terms and see if you can figure out the most appropriate terms to write in the blank spaces. Talk about the relationships between the clothing-related meanings and the more metaphorical meanings illustrated here.

PART I Rags, Robes, Gowns, and Dresses

dressing	ragging	rags	ragtag	town-gown	wardrobe

1. _____ people and attitudes are on the fringes of respectability.

2. People have to buy a new _____ if they move from Florida to Canada.

3. If someone is said to be hired as window _____, the idea is that the person is hired to look good rather than to do real work.

4. _____ someone is giving that person a hard time.

5. In college towns, people talk about _____ relationships in reference to how professors and students get along with the townspeople.

6. Newspapers, especially tabloids, are sometimes referred to as _____.

PART II Coats, Jackets, and Capes

book jacket	coats	coats of arms	coats of paint
escape	jacketed	to coat	turncoat

1. It is hard to remember _____ little kids with sunscreen.

2. When we write reports on our reading, our teacher will not let us quote from the _____.

3. Superman uses his cape to _____, but not in the way the word implies.

4. In restaurants, _____ potatoes have the skins left on.

5. People have to use more than one _____ to change a dark wall into white.

6. Several Internet companies sell _____ to families.

7. Folk wisdom says that in the fall the thickness of animals' _____ predict how hard the winter will be.

8. A _____ is a traitor.

To Sew a Fine Seam

Name: _____ **Period:** _____ **Date:** _____

When people interact with things, they are more likely to internalize and remember the words. As these workshops keep demonstrating, it is usually the oldest, most basic items of clothing that serve as the source for extended meanings. But if something is dramatic enough, it will find its way into the language. For example, the word *zip* to describe something moving fast has been in the language for only a hundred and fifty years. Zippers were invented in 1893, but they were called such names as the *Universal,* the *Hookless,* and the *C-Curity* fastener. In 1921 the B. F. Goodrich rubber company in Akron, Ohio, started manufacturing overshoes with slide fasteners. After a couple of years, one of their engineers coined the name *zipper.* It was such a good name that it was immediately adopted all over the country. By the time Goodrich tried to claim it as its own trademark, the courts said it was already the generic name for the item.

Because everyone has experience with *zippers,* it quickly found a place in the language. Even little kids understand what is meant if they are told to *zip* their lips (shut their mouths) or asked if they just *zipped through* their homework (did it quickly and without effort). In the 1960s, the clever name of *ZIP Code* for the U. S. Postal Service's *Zone Improvement Plan* helped the U. S. Postal Service convince customers that if they would go to the trouble of adding new numbers to old addresses, their mail would be delivered in a *zippy* fashion.

There are other words related to clothing that, although they are not as dramatic as the *zipper,* have been around a lot longer and so have had more time to acquire extended meanings. Read the basic definitions and then figure out which of the terms is the most appropriate to write in the blank spaces. Talk about the relationships between the basic meanings and the more metaphorical ones.

A. *Pins* are made from pieces of fine wire sharpened on one end so they can be poked through cloth or into other soft materials. Some historians have said that the invention of the *safety pin,* in which the sharp point is covered, should be considered among the top twenty inventions of the world. The expression *neat as a pin* tells something about the history of pins. Today we view people who *pin* their clothes as sloppy, but a few hundred years ago most people wore loose-fitting robes tied with sashes or belts. When fitted clothing became fashionable, the person with pins was the tidy person. Pins were so expensive that families had to save up their money. This means that *pin money* was not the small change it is considered to be today.

| center pin | pin-striped | to pin |

1. A wrestler gets points every time he manages ⸻ an opponent.

2. ⸻ suits are usually navy blue with tiny white stripes.

3. In various pieces of machinery, different parts hook onto the ⸻.

B. *Needles* were even more expensive than pins because the metal had to be strong enough to withstand continuous pushing and bending while still being fine enough to go through cloth, leather, or fur. As comparisons to *sewing needles*, speakers talk about *pine needles, phonograph needles, injection needles, needles* on a compass, and the *needles* on pumps used to blow up footballs and bicycle tires. The challenge in making sewing or injection needles is making either vertical or horizontal holes through the metal. Especially before the industrial revolution, needles were a rare and expensive commodity. Today we use the phrase *hunting for a needle in a haystack* only metaphorically, but when needles were so much more valuable than they are today, people would hunt for a dropped needle no matter where they lost it.

| needlenose | Needles | needling | sitting on pins and needles |

1. "Quit ⸻ me!" is a way to tell people to leave you alone.

2. ⸻ pliers have long narrow prongs to grasp things in tight places.

3. ⸻, California, is named for a geological formation of tall, pointed rocks.

4. People waiting for the results of medical tests are ⸻.

C. *Stitches* are made by using a needle to pull thread in and out of cloth. The sewing machine made the process easier because thread from one side of the cloth catches the thread from the other side and holds it.

| a stitch | in stitches | stitches |

1. Having a ⸻ in your side means your muscles have contracted.

2. Something similar happens when a comedian leaves you ⸻.

3. People talk about how many ⸻ they have even if the doctor used metal clamps or some other kind of fastener to close a cut.

D. *Thread* is finer than string and is used either in sewing cloth together or in weaving cloth on a loom. *Thread* comes from a word meaning "to twist or turn," which probably relates to how thread is made, but it also describes what people do with *thread*. When *threading their way* through heavy traffic or through an underground set of caverns or caves, people use similar instincts as in *threading* a needle. When people jokingly refer to their clothes as their *threads*, they are saying their clothes aren't even worthy to be called *rags*.

thread of a story	threadbare	threading

1. The _____ on screws and bolts is fine like a thread and also twists and turns.

2. If you are following the _____ or figuring out a common thread in two stories, you are following the twists and turns of an author's mind.

3. A _____ existence is based on the idea of people being so poor that their clothes are worn down to the individual threads.

E. *Embroidery floss* is heavier than the thread used for regular sewing. It is brightly colored and shiny because the purpose of *embroidery* is to add ornamental designs to cloth. *Floss* is made from separate threads twisted together so that if a woman wants to sew a finer design, she can divide the strand and work with only one or two threads. The dental *floss* used to clean teeth is similar in size and strength, but it is coated with wax to keep it from cutting into people's gums. When something is described as *flossy*, it is probably being criticized as overdone, based on the fact that *floss* is so much "fancier" than thread.

embroider	embroidery	embroidery floss

1. When people embellish or _____ the facts, they add additional details.

2. Critics who describe public art as _____ mean that it is an unnecessary luxury.

3. You should not use _____ on your teeth because it will cut your gums.

F. *Knots* are both a plague and a benefit to people who sew by hand. Sewers need to tie knots at the end of a thread to keep it from pulling through the cloth. But once the sewing has started and the thread accidentally becomes *knotted*, then whoever is sewing has to cut the thread off and start over again. *Knitting* is cognate with *knotting*, which is an appropriate description of the process because knitters use their needles to twist or tie strands of yarn together. Metaphorically, speakers talk about *close-knit* families and about people *knitting their brows* in concentration.

in knots	knit	knotty	petrified wood

1. A _____ problem is one that is as hard to solve as it is to untie a knot in thread.

2. The knots in many ancient trees have been preserved in _____.

3. Someone whose stomach is constantly _____ may be getting ulcers.

4. Doctors set broken bones in hopes that they will _____.

G. *Seams* are the lines of sewing that join two or more pieces of cloth. Some cloth is woven in a continuous tube so that stretchy shirts and dresses can be made without side *seams*. This *seamless* technique results in a smooth appearance and in the metaphor of calling smooth transitions *seamless*. For example, European countries are hoping that the Eurodollar will help tourists move *seamlessly* from one country to another. The *seamy side* of a piece of sewing shows the cut edges and the loose threads. This is why people describe things that are meant to be kept out of sight as being on the *seamy side*.

in the seam	seams	seams of ore	seamy

1. Prospectors hope to find _____ running through mountains.

2. When pipes have been welded together, the _____ show.

3. Football quarterbacks try to throw the ball to a receiver _____, meaning someone in the space between coverage.

4. Tabloid newspapers often focus on the _____ side of life.

H. *Frayed edges* are those with loose threads that have not been hemmed. These *frayed edges* give negative connotations to things that are *on the seamy side*. *Friction* and *frazzle* are related words. A distraught person can be described as having either *frazzled* or *frayed* nerves. A young mother who says that her nerves are *frayed* is saying that her children *rub her the wrong way;* they are *wearing her down*.

fray	frazzled	into the fray

1. If someone enters _____, that person is jumping into a brawl or a quarrel.

2. Too much competition can _____ children's friendships.

3. Homeless people tend to have clothes that are _____ and worn.

I. *Patches* are small bits of cloth sewn on a garment to cover a hole or snag. The smallness of *patches* is emphasized in such metaphors as *eye patches, beauty patches,* and *Boy or Girl Scout patches*. When people talk about a *pumpkin patch* or a *cabbage patch*, they are referring to a small garden. With cloth, a *crosspatch* does not blend in, as when the stripes go one direction and the patch is made from cloth going a different direction. Metaphorically, a person who is a *crosspatch* is someone who does not fit in with the culture of a group.

patch through	patch up	patchwork

1. *Patched together* can describe more things than _____ quilts.

2. People can literally *patch* a tire, while more metaphorically they _____ relationships.

3. Sometimes people have to _____unusual connections on telephone or computer lines.

J. *To mend* something is to repair it. Although this usually refers to repairing a hole or a tear in cloth, it might also be used in broader contexts. A World War II slogan, "Make do and mend," encouraged people to mend more than their clothing as does the slogan, "It's never too late to mend."

amendment	mend	on the mend

1. People who have been sick are happy to report that they are _____.

2. Adding an _____ to a motion is to *mend* or fix it.

3. When politicians _____ political fences, they apologize to people they might have offended.

K. *To unravel* something is to pull it apart. The word *ravel* comes from a Danish word for "loose thread," so actually the word *ravel* means the same thing as *unravel*, but most English speakers prefer to say *unravel*. With woven cloth this is not so easy, but with knitted material and with the kind of chain stitching sometimes used for hems, pulling on a single thread can sometimes *unravel* a whole hem or any part of a sweater that has been knitted from one piece of yarn.

unravel	unravels	unraveling

1. In court trials, cases are often lost when a defendant's story _____ or falls apart.

2. She was so nervous while taking the test that she didn't realize she was _____ the sleeve to her sweater.

3. A person's career will probably begin to _____ if suspicions are aroused that the person has been sharing trade secrets.

A Sewing-Related Crossword Puzzle

Name: _____   Period: _____   Date: _____

Use these clues to fill in the crossword puzzle.

Across

4. The job of probation officers is to help people _____ their ways.

5. It helps broken bones to _____ if they are kept in a stationary position.

7. _____ were named from an onomatopoeic word describing something moving fast.

8. Knowing how to_____ has been an important skill for as long as people can remember.

9. Someone who has _____ nerves is worn out.

10. Looking for Britton and Taryn at Six Flags was like hunting for two_____ in a haystack.

12. The newest way for people to take certain medicines is through skin _____.

Down

1. When a college boy _____ a girl, he gives her his fraternity pin as a pre-engagement gesture.

2. Parents tend to _____ stories about their children's accomplishments.

3. For our test, we had to _____ the plot of the latest book we read.

6. When people have a _____ discussion on a computer, they communicate one after the other rather than all at the same time.

11. Prospectors are eager to discover _____ of ore because they can run for miles.

Workshop 7.1: A. (Geographical allusion): bermuda shorts, bikini swimsuits, oxford shoes, cordovan shoes, mackinaw blankets. **B. (Name of a person):** mackintosh raincoats, Nehru jackets, Eisenhower jackets, bloomers. **C. (Descriptive feature):** bowler hats, pillbox hats, A-line dresses, T-shirts, long johns or drawers, tights, slacks, briefs, shorts, bobby sox. **D. (An associated body part):** anklets, necklaces, neckties, backpacks, earrings, shoulder straps, knee pads, overalls, and coveralls. **E. (Profession or activity):** ballet slippers, tennis shoes, baseball caps, boxer shorts, and jockey shorts.

Workshop 7.2: Part I: 1. Bridal Veil, **2.** neighborhood, **3.** hoodwink, **4.** veiled, **5.** bonnet, **6.** hoods. **Part II: 1.** pass the hat, **2.** capstone, **3.** capped, **4.** hats into the ring, **5.** which hat, **6.** cap, **7.** old hat, **8.** hat trick.

Workshop 7.3: Part I: 1. ragtag, **2.** wardrobe, **3.** dressing, **4.** ragging, **5.** town-gown, **6.** rags. **Part II. 1.** to coat, **2.** book jacket, **3.** escape, **4.** jacketed, **5.** coats of paint, **6.** coats of arms, **7.** coats, **8.** turncoat.

Workshop 7.4: A. 1. to pin, **2.** pin-striped suits, **3.** center pin. **B. 1.** needling, **2.** needlenose, **3.** Needles, **4.** sitting on pins and needles. **C. 1.** a stitch, **2.** in stitches, **3.** stitches. **D. 1.** threading, **2.** thread of a story, **3.** threadbare. **E. 1.** embroider, **2.** embroidery, **3.** embroidery floss. **F. 1.** knotty, **2.** petrified wood, **3.** in knots, **4.** knit. **G. 1.** seams of ore, **2.** seams, **3.** in the seam, **4.** seamy. **H. 1.** into the fray, **2.** fray, **3.** frazzled. **I. 1.** patchwork, **2.** patch up, **3.** patch through. **J. 1.** on the mend, **2.** amendment, **3.** mend. **K. 1.** unravels, **2.** unraveling, **3.** unravel.

Workshop 7.5: Across: 4. mend, **5.** knit, **7.** zippers, **8.** sew, **9.** frayed, **10.** needles, **12.** patches. **Down: 1.** pins, **2.** embroider, **3.** unravel, **6.** threaded, **11.** seams.

End-of-Chapter Activities

Choose one of these sewing-related proverbs or phrases to illustrate with a poster. You may find that one of the best ways to illustrate your idea is to use real needles, thread, buttons, zippers, pins, and pieces of cloth. You can draw a picture or use cutouts. When you explain your poster to the class, be ready to tell them whether you have (1) made a literal interpretation of the idea, (2) made a metaphorical interpretation, (3) created a pun, or (4) taken a different approach that you will explain.

- ☐ A stitch in time saves nine.
- ☐ A threadbare existence.
- ☐ To button your lips.
- ☐ To zip your lips.
- ☐ To be at loose ends.
- ☐ All patched together.
- ☐ The thread of a story.
- ☐ To embroider the truth.
- ☐ A knotty problem.
- ☐ To be on pins and needles.
- ☐ A crosspatch.
- ☐ To be pinned down.
- ☐ To be in stitches.

CHAPTER EIGHT

Earth and Sky, Water and Fire

Background Reading for the Teacher

Speakers learn the extended meanings of the words in this chapter both from actual experience and from seeing how other people use the words. For example, one of the worst things a person who lives in an area filled with mountains and canyons can imagine is falling over a cliff. As a way of stimulating excitement, western serial movies used to end with episodes showing a hero hanging by his fingertips from the edge of a cliff. This dramatic image would bring the viewers back the next week to see how the hero escaped his apparent fate. Today, many speakers who never saw such melodramatic movies still refer to suspenseful elections, contests, or court cases as *cliff-hangers.*

A less dramatic, but richer, example is the Latin word *terra,* meaning *earth.* English speakers use this root word in many combinations ranging from *territory, terrarium, terrace,* and *terrier* (dogs bred to dig) to the title of the movie *E.T.* about an *extraterrestrial* being—someone from beyond the earth. Another rich example is the word *plain* as in *The Great Plains.* From this image of a flat area of land that is relatively free from vegetation we get the word *plain* to refer to a person who is not physically attractive, as in the title of the book and TV movie, *Sarah Plain and Tall.* The *planes* that carpenters use to make boards flat are related, and so are *plane geometry* (the study of flat figures) and *airplanes* (which get their lift from level wings that are basically flat).

Students enjoyed working with real rocks and sand, and even a dust bunny—real lint gathered from a clothes dryer.

Notes to Help Teachers Elicit Ideas from Students

One way to introduce this chapter is to read aloud William Steig's prize-winning picture book *Sylvester and the Magic Pebble* (Windmill, 1969). Pay special attention to how Steig makes use in the plot of pebbles, rocks, and boulders,

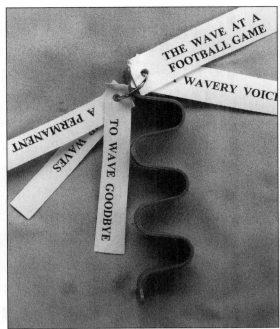

Thirteen-year-old Salua demonstrates the motion of waves using a taco holder and attached word strips reading *The wave at a football game, a wavery voice, to wave goodbye, a permanent wave,* and *The WAVES.*

including the part where Sylvester becomes "stone dumb." Also, point out how he uses the different shapes of the trees and the changing weather to illustrate the passage of time. Another good read-aloud book is *Cloudy with a Chance of Meatballs* by Judi and Ron Barrett (Atheneum, 1978, Aladdin paperback, 1982). It is a wonderfully funny picture book set in the town of *Chewandswallow* where rain comes in the form of soup and snow in the form of mashed potatoes. All is well, until the weather takes a turn for the worse. Another possibility is Dr. Seuss's *Bartholomew and the Oobleck* (Random House, 1949).

As a more specific introduction to the lessons on weather, you might share these sentences with students and ask them to tell you which ones are referring to real weather conditions and which to more metaphorical concepts.

1. A judge constantly faced with child custody issues has to take a *cold-hearted* approach to decisions. (metaphor)

2. Citrus growers suffered a loss when an unexpected *cold wave* hit southern California. (real weather)

3. Newcomers complain that our school has a *hostile climate.* (metaphor)

4. She was really *steamed* about having her reservation cancelled. (metaphor)

5. Samantha walks around with a *cloud hanging over her head.* (metaphor)

6. In the *Wizard of Oz,* Dorothy and Toto were caught in a *cyclone.* (real weather)

7. After marrying against her parents' wishes, she was *left out in the cold.* (metaphor)

8. The wind currents caused us to *drift way off course.* (real weather)

9. The bride's father kept his diagnosis of cancer secret because he did not want to *cast a shadow* over the festivities. (metaphor)

10. Despite her well-presented plan, the idea got only a *chilly reception.* (metaphor)

Notes to Help Teachers Elicit Ideas from Students

CHARMANDER

HE CAN BECOME CHARMELEON AND CHARIZARD

Second-graders could remember that *charcoal*, *chafe*, and *chauffeur* relate to heat because they connected them with the Pokémon "fire" creatures, *Charmander*, *Charmeleon*, and *Charizard*.

We have not taken the space to define all of the concepts in this chapter because they are so basic that most native speakers know them, even though they have not thought about their relationships to each other. Our ESL students, especially, profited from considerable discussion of weather-related words, which illustrated differences in size, power, or quantity. The final workshop about fire is the most complex, and so with younger students you may want to skip parts of it. And as with the other lessons, do much of the work orally and with pictures instead of through the written exercises.

For older or advanced students, add information about the Latin verb *to burn*, which is *flagrare*, as seen in *conflagration* for a large disastrous fire, or metaphorically for any conflict or war that causes heavy damage. You might also talk about *flammable*, meaning that something can burn. Such related terms as *inflame*, *inflammable*, and *inflammatory* are mostly used metaphorically as in these sentences.

- The speaker *inflamed* the crowd.
- His *inflammatory* remarks were based on exaggerations and distortions.
- It was such an *inflammatory* situation that a Riot Squad was called in.
- *Inflammation* is reserved for bodily conditions in which there is swelling, heat, and redness as with an infection from a cut or an insect bite, or with *inflammation of the joints* caused by arthritis.

People grew so accustomed to these words with the *in-* prefix that when tanker trucks started transporting gasoline to service stations, the word *INFLAMMABLE* was painted on their sides. Whether a cargo is likely to explode or burst into flames is crucial information when an accident occurs, so other truckers had *NONINFLAMMABLE* painted on their sides. However, this word is so long that it was hard to print in restricted spaces—and even harder to read at a glance. Finally, thoughtful people began pointing out that *flammable* already meant that something could burn; the *in-* was redundant. So today, most signs read either *FLAMMABLE* or *NOT FLAMMABLE*. Many trucks have fold-down signs so that the appropriate message can be displayed depending on the cargo.

Down to Earth

Name: _____ **Period:** _____ **Date:** _____

Earth is a very old Middle English word that names the planet on which we live. Lexical extensions include such terms as *earth science, earthquake,* and *earthworm.* The word for *potato* in both French and Farsi (modern Persian) translates to *apple of the earth. Earth tones* are various rich colors that contain at least some brown, while *earthworks* are human-made structures such as dams, dikes, and ramparts made from soil and rocks. *Earthshine* is the sun's light reflected from the earth to the moon. Although it is pale, it sometimes enables people to see the dark parts of the moon, those that are not receiving light directly from the sun.

Metaphorically, people talk about *Mother Earth* as a symbol for a divine source of life. If a woman is called an *earth mother*, she is being described as having maternal and nurturing characteristics. When an event is described as *earth shattering*, we hope the use is metaphorical rather than literal. And of course it is metaphorical when people say they will *move heaven and earth* for someone, or when they chide a friend who is day-dreaming with something like, "You've got to *come down to earth* and be a bit more practical." Being *down to earth* usually has positive connotations, as when a person is described as *the salt of the earth*. However, if someone is described as *earthy*, the meaning is probably that the person is vulgar or is not concerned with spiritual or heavenly matters. *Earthy* people tell *dirty* jokes.

PART I Here is an alphabetical list of names that speakers use for some of the smaller pieces of earth. Rewrite the list, arranging the items from small to big. Do not worry if you cannot decide between several terms in the middle. The point is to think about how size is incorporated in some words. If you are unsure of some of the meanings, you can look them up in a dictionary or talk to your classmates about them.

a boulder	**1.** _____
a grain of sand	**2.** _____
a lump of coal	**3.** _____
a pebble	**4.** _____
a piece of gravel	**5.** _____
a dust mote	**6.** _____
a stone	**7.** _____
a rock	**8.** _____

PART II From these words adapted from the above list, choose the appropriate ones to write in the blank spaces of these metaphorical sentences.

> Boulder   dust   gravelly   lump of coal   pebbled   Rocky   sand   stone

1. In his determination, he promises to leave no _____ unturned.

2. Her lectures are dry as _____.

3. My grandmother was told that if she were bad, Santa would leave a _____ in her Christmas stocking.

4. My aunt has a _____ voice—from smoking, I think.

5. When I used to rub my eyes because I was sleepy, my mother would tell me that the _____ man had come.

6. _____ boots and purses are made from fake leather with small bumps in it.

7. It is easy to see why Hoover Dam was first called _____ Dam.

8. _____ Road is my favorite flavor of ice cream.

Geological Formations

Name: _____ **Period:** _____ **Date:** _____

The earth's surface or *crust* is made up of a combination of solid stone formations and smaller pieces that have broken off or eroded. Because the smaller pieces are so common and the ones we come in contact with, we frequently base metaphors on them as when we describe a strong "hard" person as *a rock*, or when we describe someone who is on drugs as being *stoned*.

If we say someone is *caught between a rock and a hard place*, we mean the person has two equally bad choices. Earlier forms of this same metaphor alluded to being *between the devil and the deep blue sea* and *between Scylla and Charybdis,* two monsters in Greek mythology who lived on opposite sides of a strait through which Odysseus's ship had to pass.

If a drink is served *on the rocks*, it is served *on ice*, which is something almost as hard as a rock. But if someone's business or marriage is *on the rocks*, it is in a state of destruction. The allusion is to a ship that has foundered *on rocks* instead of making it to a safe harbor. The meaning is similar to something *hitting rock bottom*, meaning that things have gone as low as they can go. This is a negative when people are talking about their careers or their grades, but when store owners advertise that they have lost their lease and are being forced to sell merchandise at *rock-bottom prices*, customers are supposed to think that the situation is bad for the store owner but good for the customers.

Rock music gets its name not from a piece of *stone*, but from a different word, also pronounced and written *rock*. It comes from Middle English *rokken,* meaning to move back and forth as with *rocking chairs* and the *rocker arms* on engines. *Rock 'n' roll* music has a strong beat that makes people feel like moving their bodies. Whoever invented the term *hard rock* was making a pun on the two meanings of *rock*.

Read the following statements about these other earth-related words and then choose the appropriate words to go in the metaphorical sentences that follow. Talk about the relationships between the more metaphorical uses and the original meanings.

PART I Loose or Movable Pieces of the Earth

A. *Ground* originally referred to the sediment at the bottom of a body of water. Knowing this, makes it easy to see how *coffee grounds* were named. *Groundhogs* live in burrows under the earth, while in baseball a *grounder* is a hit in which the ball never gets very high in the air. When big new public buildings are begun, there is usually a *ground-breaking* ceremony where officials pose with shovels that they symbolically stick in the ground. A more abstract meaning of *ground-breaking* is any invention or development that is considered to be so revolutionary that it is some kind of a new start.

background	ground crew	grounded	groundless

1. Learning about someone's _____ usually helps you to become friends.

2. If your suspicions are _____, you have no firm evidence.

3. On "Malcolm in the Middle," the older brothers are always getting _____.

4. The _____ is as important to airplane safety as is the flight crew.

B. *Dirt* is something from the earth that happens to be in the wrong place. At your house, for example, it is fine to have dirt and mud where the hedge or the lawn is growing, but nobody wants you to track them inside the house. Synonyms include *filthy, foul, nasty,* and *squalid.*

dirt	dirt poor	dirty jokes

1. If an author describes a family as _____, they might live in a house with no floor.

2. _____ are sometimes described as earthy humor.

3. If someone does you _____, the person has treated you unfairly.

C. *Soil* is a synonym for *dirt*, but it is more likely to be used in relation to gardening and farming as when people talk about the *rich, black soil* in Kansas and Iowa.

soil	soil bank	soiled

1. The government has a _____ program to encourage farmers to let some fields "rest" for two or three years.

2. When she came home from camp, her suitcase was full of _____ and grubby clothes.

3. If you keep telling such lies, you will _____ your reputation.

D. *Sand* is finely ground stone. It will have been ground up by either water or wind, so the two most likely places to find it is on a beach or on a desert where there is nothing to stop the wind from constantly shifting and moving sand dunes.

sandals	sandpaper	Sandy

1. I don't like wearing _____ on the beach because more sand gets in than falls out.

2. His damaged skin felt like _____.

3. His name is Sanford, but everyone calls him _____ because of the color of his hair.

E. *Stones* are so much a part of life that it is not just *The Flintstones* who are given such names as *Pebbles* and *Barney Rubble*. An important period of prehistory is known as *The Stone Age* because archaeologists have found evidence that people were amazingly skilled at making tools from rocks and bones. Stones have long been an easily accessible weapon, and even today news stories show people in troubled areas *throwing stones* at people they view as enemies.

no stone unturned	stepping stone	stony

1. Police promise to leave _____ when they want to reassure crime victims.

2. In baseball, playing on a farm team is often a _____ to joining a major league team.

3. If someone gives you a _____ look, the person is expressing hostility.

PART II   Connected Geological Formations

A. *Hills* can be as small and inconsequential as an *anthill* or as large and important as *Capitol Hill* in Washington, DC. When people say something is not worth a *hill of beans*, they are referring to the small mounds that farmers make when planting bean seeds. Technically, the Great Smoky Mountains, the Appalachians, and the Cumberland Plateau qualify as mountains, but some call the people who live there *hillbillies*.

downhill	molehill	over the hill	uphill

1. School is an _____ struggle for kids who have a hard time reading.

2. Making a mountain out of a _____ is to be overly concerned about something trivial.

3. Being _____ usually means that someone has passed his or her peak.

4. After spring break, it seems _____ all the way to summer vacation.

B. *Mountains* are so big that speakers tend to exaggerate and complain about a friend bringing *mountains of luggage* or about a teacher assigning *mountains of homework*.

mountains	mountaintop	mounting	to mount

1. A _____ experience is something memorable and out of the ordinary.

2. Elderly cowboys have to stand on something _____ their horses.

3. The school is worried about _____ transportation expenses.

4. She's got to have _____ of emotional support or she won't make it through the year.

C. *Peaks* are the very tops of mountains and, metaphorically, anything that resembles the shape as with the *peak of a roof* or the *peak of a hat*.

peak	peak performances	peaked

I. Our school's test scores _____ three years ago and have gone down ever since.

2. Gymnasts often have their _____ when they are in their young teens.

3. The _____on his cap made him look almost like a clown.

D. *Valleys* are large, usually elongated areas surrounded by mountains or hills. Smaller areas are called *vales* or *dales*. Both are associated with sadness in such expressions as *a vale of tears* and *going down into the valley of death. Death Valley* in California got its name from this idea, while the paradise to which King Arthur is carried after his death is named *Avalon*.

avalanche	vail	valedictory	Valley girl	Valley of the Sun

I. In an _____ great quantities of snow and ice fall into valleys.

2. The word _____ is related to *valley* in the name of the famous ski resort in Colorado.

3. _____ speeches relate to sadness in that they are farewell speeches.

4. _____ and *Valley speak* allude to a particular California lifestyle.

5. In Arizona, the Phoenix area is called the _____.

Words from the Sky

Name: _____ **Period:** _____ **Date:** _____

In a way, the moon is more fascinating than the sun because it appears to change size and shape as illustrated in Vachel Lindsay's poem where he calls the moon the "North Wind's Cookie" that is continually being eaten up. Also, it is easier to look at the moon and to imagine that we can see its face or that it is made out of green cheese. And while we tend to take the sun for granted, on dark nights we are especially apprecia-tive if there is a *full moon* or a *harvest moon*, meaning one so bright that people could keep working at night to harvest their crops.

   Here are words taken from the objects we see in the sky. Use the meaning and the grammatical clues to figure out which phrase fits best in each blank space. After you write in the appropriate phrases, talk about how their meanings developed from the original concepts.

A. CLOUD   cloud nine   clouded   silver lining

1. In the movie, Stuart Little was always looking for the _____ that Mr. Little promised was part of every *cloud* that came his way.

2. She's been on _____ since she learned about the trip.

3. He has a pretty _____ history.

B. MOON   month   mooning around   moonlighting

1. A _____ job is an extra job, beyond one's usual hours of work.

2. People who are _____ are acting silly, as if they are affected by a full moon.

3. The word _____ comes from *moon* because 30 days is approximately the length of time between one full moon and the next.

C. LUNA (ROMAN GODDESS OF THE MOON)   looney   lunar   lunatic

1. I love to watch all the craziness on _____ *Toons* cartoons.

2. Millions of people watched on the Internet when NASA's _____ modules explored the moon.

3. A _____ is a crazy person based on the idea that full moons have strange effects on people.

D. Star   in the stars   movie stars   starfish

1. If you say something is _____, you are saying that it is predestined to happen.

2. If a _____ gets washed up on the beach, you can save its life by throwing it back into the ocean.

3. Lots of people look up to _____, but in a different way than we look up to real stars.

E. Stella (Latin for *STAR*)   constellations   Stella   stellar

1. A _____ performance is of star quality.

2. The _____ are made up of stars.

3. If your name is _____, your parents probably thought of you as a *star*.

F. Aster (Greek for *STAR*)   asterisk   Astrodome   astronauts

1. _____ are sailors among the stars.

2. The Houston _____ got its name because lots of astronauts live in Houston and work for NASA.

3. An _____ looks like a star and so do the flowers called *asters*.

Weather-Related Words

Name: _____ **Period:** _____ **Date:** _____

Thanks to modern technology, the old saying "Everybody talks about the weather but nobody does anything about it" is not quite as true as it used to be. Nevertheless, the saying reflects the role that weather plays in people's talk. Such sayings as, "It's always darkest before the dawn," and "Every cloud has a silver lining," might be literally true, but they are most often said as a way of reassuring people who are in a difficult situation that the future will be brighter. Similarly, while most people are interested in actually *clearing the air* of smog, few individuals are in a position to control such things. Thus, when they refer to *clearing the air,* they are probably recommending the opening up of lines of communication.

In the literal sense these words refer to weather conditions, but they can also refer to things quite different from the weather. Read the sentences and use the meaning and the grammatical clues to choose which phrases to write in the blank spaces. Talk about what the metaphorical meaning has in common with the weather-related meaning.

A. AIR	clear the air	hot air	walking on air

1. I don't take him seriously because he's so full of _____.

2. Let's talk about your suspicions and _____.

3. She's so excited about being chosen that she's _____.

B. BREEZE	a breeze	breeze through	breezeway

1. That test was _____.

2. Natural _____ often occur between steep hills.

3. Everyone was disappointed when all she did was _____.

C. WIND	whirlwind	wind	windbag	window

1. In houses an *eye for the wind* is called a _____.

2. He's such an old _____ that I don't bother to listen.

3. Don't decide until you see which way the _____ is blowing.

4. They had a _____ tour of New York City.

D. Cool   cool   coolers   your cool

1. So-called picnic _____don't really make things cool; they just keep them the same temperature.

2. It was a really a _____ concert.

3. Be careful not to lose _____.

E. Cold   cold   cold shoulder   cold water

1. I was surprised when he gave his dad the _____.

2. She threw _____ on the whole idea.

3. The reason it is so hard to cure the common_____ is that it is caused by dozens of different viruses.

F. Freeze   Freeze!   frozen   frozen out

1. His mistake was not stopping when the policeman yelled "_____"

2. She gave me a _____ smile.

3. My dad was _____ of the company when it reorganized.

G. Ice   iceberg   ice breaker   thin ice

1. What you found out is only the tip of the_____.

2. Literally, an _____ is a specially designed ship used to plow a path through icy waters, but at parties it is something to get people to relax and talk with each other.

3. You will be on _____ talking about that subject.

H. Warm   warm up   warmed over   warmly

1. She greeted him _____.

2. Our two cats are starting to _____ to each other.

3. I hope we don't get a _____ lecture.

I. Hot   heated   hot under the collar   hotdogging

1. Jeremy was _____ on his skateboard and broke his ankle.

2. The coaches had a _____ argument about the decision.

3. Our coach was especially _____.

Two Kinds of Light

Name: _____ **Period:** _____ **Date:** _____

English has two words that both happen to be spelled *light*. One of these words comes from the Germanic *leicht*, meaning the opposite of *heavy*. The other *light*, which we are more interested in for this workshop, comes from Middle English *liht* and is related to *lucere, lucid,* and *lumen,* all referring to the kind of *light* that is the opposite of *dark*.

Sometimes it is not easy to tell the difference between the two kinds of *light*. For example, if we hear someone talking about a *light wood* such as pine burning easily, we might think the allusion is to color because pine happens to be light in color. However, what makes pine burn easily is not its color, but its lack of density. We might be similarly confused if we hear someone say, "I expect a wedding cake to be light, so I was surprised when they used her grandmother's recipe for apple-sauce cake." In this instance, the wedding cake was both heavier and darker than the speaker expected. The ambiguity in these two examples is unusual.

As illustrated by the sentences below, there are usually enough clues that people will be able to figure out which kind of *light* is the source of a metaphorical use. Divide these italicized uses from the following sentences into the two different meanings. Near the light bulb, write the metaphors based on the idea of *light* being the opposite of *dark*. Near the scale, write the metaphors based on the idea of *light* being the opposite of *heavy*.

1. The *pilot light* on our water heater keeps going out.

2. For weighing over 200 pounds, he's unusually *light on his feet*.

3. *In light of* what I now know, I would not have voted for her.

4. It's the thunder, not the *lightning*, that scares me.

5. I love to see old *lighthouses* along the New England coast.

6. Manufacturers of diet foods have adopted a simplified spelling of *lite*.

7. He's really an intellectual *lightweight*.

8. Croissants are *lighter* than bagels.

9. It is easy to see how *lightning bugs* got their name.

Figure 8.1

Light as opposite of dark

Light as opposite of heavy

Water Words

Name: _____ **Period:** _____ **Date:** _____

Water is one of life's most dramatic and indispensable substances. When teacher Annie Sullivan came to work with the blind and deaf Helen Keller, she did finger-spelling in Helen's hand for several weeks. Helen learned to imitate the movements, but she did not understand that Miss Sullivan was spelling words for her until the eventful day that the teacher walked with Helen down to the wellhouse. Many years later, Helen wrote in her autobiography,

Someone was drawing water and my teacher placed my hand under the spout. As the cool stream gushed over one hand she spelled into the other the word *water*, first slowly, then rapidly. I stood still, my whole attention fixed upon the motions of her fingers. Suddenly I felt a misty conscious-ness as of something forgotten—a thrill of returning thought; and somehow the mystery of lan-guage was revealed to me. I knew then that *w-a-t-e-r* meant the wonderful cool something that was flowing over my hand. That living word awakened my soul, gave it light, hope, joy, set it free! There were barriers still, it is true, but barriers that could in time be swept away.

PART I   Here are six sets of words related to water. They are arranged from small to big. Talk about the differences in size and why we need such a variety of words.

1. creek	**2.** puddle	**3.** ditch	**4.** ripple	**5.** spring	**6.** drip
stream	pond	gully	wave	gush	trickle
river	lake	canyon	tidal wave	flood	flow

PART II   Choose the appropriate words and write them in the spaces below. Talk about what these metaphorical uses have in common with the water-related uses.

> | ditch | drip | flows | gushy | puddle | ripple | sprang |

1. I don't know why he acts like such a _____.

2. When the weather's good, kids like to _____ school.

3. She is so _____ that I cannot believe she's sincere.

4. In musical medleys, one piece _____ into the next.

5. Ideas _____ up all over the room.

6. That plane is nothing but a _____ jumper.

7. When the house lights dimmed, a _____ of excitement ran through the crowd.

More Water-Related Words

Name: _____ **Period:** _____ **Date:** _____

Standard desk dictionaries have nearly four columns of words that start with *water*. Most of them are lexical extensions simply naming things that have something to do with water as with *waterborne* germs, a *water cannon*, a *watering hole*, *waterless cooking*, *watermelon*, *water repellent*, and *watertight*. But among the metaphorical is the term *water cooler talk* to refer to casual gossip, the kind that people might share in an office when they meet around a coffee pot or a water cooler. Another figurative term is *watershed*. Literally, this is the area from which water gathers and runs into a river or gathers into a basin or lake. Metaphorically, a *watershed* might be anything that unexpectedly produces a wealth of information. For example, a set of records might be found in an investigation that would turn out to be a *watershed* of evidence.

If speakers say that something has been *watered down,* the literal meaning is that a person has added water to a beverage to make it go further, as with *watery soup.* The figurative meaning is that something is weaker or less potent than it should be, as when a teacher *waters down* a course to make it easier for students. *Watered stock* came into English to describe what old-time ranchers and cowboys did to the cattle that they drove miles and miles to market. The day before they would get to where the cattle would be sold, they would find a river and drive the thirsty and starved animals into it where they could drink and soak up gallons of water. In this way the cowboys could get more money because each animal would weigh more. Today the term *watered stock* is not quite so literal. It refers to the way unethical businesses dilute their stock and claim to have more assets than they have.

The following paragraphs illustrate other metaphorical uses of water-related words. Use the clues that are given and what you know about the real world to figure out which word should go in each sentence. Talk about the relationships between the literal and the extended meanings.

PART I

A. *Waves* seem to be connected at one end but to be free-flowing at the other. People living near oceans and lakes see *waves* in water, while people living in the middle of the country see *waves* as the wind moves across fields of grain, and people living in deserts see *heat waves* rising from hot surfaces. The first hair permanents for women were called *Marcel waves.*

to wave	wave	WAVES	waving

1. After September 11, flags were _____ across the United States.

2. The baby's parents were excited when he learned _____ goodbye.

3. Doing the _____ at football games keeps fans from getting bored.

4. Women serving in the Navy are called _____ from Women Accepted for Volunteer Emergency Service.

B. *Whirling water* is seen at home when water goes down a drain, but it is also seen in nature when currents come together to form *whirlpools*. Off the coast of Norway, there is a place where currents form a powerful and permanent whirlpool called a *maelstrom* (from *mill stream)*. Metaphorically, if a politician, for example, is described as being caught in a *maelstrom* of criticism, the idea is that he is in so much trouble that both his political career and his personal life will probably suffer. A similar situation, but one not quite so serious, would more likely be described as something like a *whirlpool of gossip and intrigue*.

whirl	whirlagigs	whirling

1. A kind of modern cottage industry is the making and selling of brightly painted _____.

2. Square dancing is fun to watch because of all the _____ skirts.

3. Customs surrounding U.S. weddings mean that families are caught up in a _____ of social activities.

C. *Hydro* is the Greek word for water and is used in several English words including *hydrophobia*, a condition in which the afflicted person is afraid of water. Especially in the summer time, runners and other athletes must be careful not to get *dehydrated*.

hydrants	hydrofoils	hydroplane

1. As part of the bicentennial celebration, many U.S. residents painted their fire _____ with patriotic or historical designs.

2. A _____ can take off and land on water.

3. _____ are smooth-riding boats because they float on a cushion of air between the water and the boat.

D. *Vapor* is a word borrowed from French to describe mist that is in the air. It is the root of *evaporate,* used to describe the concern that water is *evaporating* from artificial lakes in dry states.

evaporates	vaporized	vaporizing

1. When money gets tight, the support for community projects often _____.

2. In one of Tom Clancy's novels, the villains planned to spread a disease through the _____ (or misting) system at the Australian Olympics.

3. When there is terrible heat, as from a nuclear explosion, bodies will be _____.

E. *Raining cats and dogs* has been an English description of a big rainstorm since at least the 1700s. Some people think that it originated as a mistaken interpretation of a Latin phrase, while other people conjecture that after a big storm drowned cats and dogs would be seen floating down ditches or lying in gutters.

raining	a rainy day	to rain

1. Saving for _____ is a good idea.

2. Spoil-sports are the people who go around _____ on other people's parades.

3. When leaders make unpopular decisions, criticism is apt _____ down on them.

PART II These words are more common and so explanations of their basic meanings are not provided.

A. MIST	misters	mists	misty-eyed

1. Mothers are apt to grow _____ when people mention a child's illness.

2. The first time I saw _____ at a sidewalk cafe, I thought the restaurant was on fire.

3. The _____ of time make it hard to know what King Arthur's Court was really like.

B. FOG	fog	foggiest	foghorn

1. Some people always seem to be in a _____.

2. If you haven't the _____ notion of what someone said, you did not understand what they were talking about.

3. Coaches who have _____ voices can be heard clear across a gym.

C. Flood	flood	flooded	floodgates

1. The clearance sale was so well advertised that customers _____ through the doors as soon as they opened.

2. When there is a _____ of applicants, it is hard to make your offer stand out.

3. Companies hesitate to reimburse customers for fear it will open the _____ so that everyone will expect the same thing.

D. Spring	bed springs	sprang up	spring

1. _____ is the time of year when everything comes up out of the ground.

2. A month before elections, campaign signs _____ on all the neighbor's lawns.

3. Kids who treat beds like trampolines are in danger of breaking the _____.

E. Pool	carpools	pool table	pool your money

1. If you _____, you can sometimes get a better deal.

2. Some mothers suspect that _____ are more aggravating than helpful.

3. People better check the size of their doors before they buy a _____.

F. Stream	stream	streamers	streaming

1. Because of security checks, people no longer _____ into the stadium—they trickle in.

2. It is hard to know how to react to someone crying so hard that tears are _____ down.

3. Parade horses have to be well trained so they won't be frightened by balloons and _____.

Fire-Related Words

Name: _____ **Period:** _____ **Date:** _____

Read the following explanations of words related to fire and then choose the best terms to write in the blank spaces. Talk about the connections between the more literal uses that are explained and the more metaphorical ones that are illustrated in the sentences.

A. *Fire* has been a productive English word for centuries. As far back as the 1300s, towns and villages had *curfews* (*couvrir feu*) to tell people when to *cover their fires*. People were not allowed to keep their fires burning all night because they might set the house on fire, which in turn would probably set the neighbors' houses on fire. Another term with a long history is *being fired* from a job. In primitive societies the way to let people know that they were no longer wanted was to burn their houses and their belongings so that they would have to leave. A *firewall* is a fireproof wall designed to keep accidental fires from spreading throughout different sections of a building. In contrast, a *wall of fire* is a huge, moving fire, the kind that might occur in a forest fire. This could be part of a *firestorm*, which is such a big fire that the heat creates its own winds that circle around, *fanning the flames* so that the fire continues growing. A *fireball* results from an explosion of something like a bomb, an airplane, or a gas tank. Guns are called *firearms* because the first ones needed gunpowder that actually had to be *fired*. *Firing up* such things as furnaces and engines is getting them ready for some kind of combustion.

curfews	fired	fired up	firewalls

1. When towns establish _____, the purpose is usually to keep teenagers off the streets late at night.

2. If someone is _____ from a job, the person is dismissed or "let go."

3. Someone all_____ about something might also be called a *fireball* of enthusiasm.

4. _____in computers are put in to protect files from getting mixed up with each other.

B. *Flame* is almost as old as *fire* and can be traced back to Middle English and Old French. Lexical extensions include *flammable* and *nonflammable*, as well as the more metaphorical verb *to inflame*, as when someone *inflames* a situation or says something *inflammatory*. If a jet engine *flames out*, it unexpectedly quits working. More metaphorically, a person who *flames out* is someone who appears to be on the way to a big success and then falters. When computer users *flame* each other on e-mail, they are scolding each other for bad computer manners. Some people think that such *flaming* just *fans the flames of hostility*.

| flambé | flamboyant | flamingos | old flame |

1. A common plot on television sitcoms is to have an _____ (an old boyfriend or girlfriend) come to visit one of the members of a married couple.

2. If at a French restaurant you order something_____, it will usually be set on fire at your table.

3. A _____ person makes a striking first impression.

4. _____ are big tropical birds that are flame-colored.

C. *Charcoal* is only one of several fire-related words that begin with *ch*. In Middle English, the word *chafe* meant to warm something by rubbing it back and forth. At a restaurant *charred* means that something has been lightly burned as with *charbroiled* hamburgers or steaks, but when people talk about the *charred* remains of a building, it has been heavily damaged. The Pokémon characters *Charmander, Charmeleon,* and *Charizard* are the lizard-like Pokémon with flames coming out of their tails. The first *chauffeurs* were firemen on French trains. Trains were invented long before cars, so when people hired men to drive their cars, which in the early days belched steam and smoke and seemed like individualized trains, they transferred the name of *chauffeur* from someone tending the coal-burning engines of trains to someone tending the engines of cars. *Chafing dishes* are those fancy serving pots that have either little flames or electrical heating elements underneath to keep the food warm.

| chafe | chafed | chauffeuring |

1. If your skin gets _____, it might be from the kind of rubbing together that gives people prickly heat.

2. In a more metaphorical sense, people _____ under restrictions that they consider to be unreasonable.

3. Mothers who complain about _____ their children should be grateful that they seldom have to worry about tending fires in the engine.

D. *To burn* something is to set it on fire, or with food, to cook it too long or at too high a temperature. People purposely *burn* things they want to get rid of, as with brush cut in the yard. They also *burn* fuel (wood, gas, oil, etc.) to produce heat and the kinds of energy that will power engines and provide electricity. Almost every child has had the experience of *being burned* by touching something like a hot stove, a hot light bulb, or food that was too hot. Children have probably also been *sunburned.* Metaphorically, there are two senses of the word burn. One expresses excitement or enthusiasm, as when someone is *burning* to share a secret, while the other one expresses damage of some kind as when someone is *burned* in a business deal.

| burn their bridges | burning | porch light burning | slow burn |

1. "We'll leave the _____ " is a way to tell friends they will always be welcome to visit.

2. Army generals who _____ behind them have made troubles for themselves and their soldiers if they need to retreat.

3. Someone growing increasingly irritated about something can be described as doing a _____.

4. _____ the candle at both ends means to be taking chances by not getting enough sleep or by spending more money than one earns.

E. *Pyr* (Greek for *fire*) is an ancestor of the English word *fire*. It is seen in such English words as *iron pyrite*, a common mineral, sometimes called *fools gold*. If struck with flint, it will give off sparks and so is also called a *fire stone*. A more formal-sounding name for *fireworks* is *pyrotechnics*.

| funeral pyres | Pyrex® | pyromaniac |

1. A _____ is a person with an impulse to set fires.

2. _____ is the registered trademark for a company that patented glass that can be baked in an oven without breaking.

3. In India, it is customary to have _____ for the ceremonial burnings of the bodies of deceased people.

A Fiery Crossword Puzzle

Name: _____ **Period:** _____ **Date:** _____

Here are the clues to use for filling in the crossword puzzle.

ACROSS

2. A _____ was originally a fireman on a French train.

7. _____ on a computer is scolding another user.

8. _____ occurs when people lose their energy and enthusiasm.

9. Redheads are said to have _____ tempers.

DOWN

1. To _____ the flames of a controversy is to increase the problem.

3. A _____ of protest means lots of people are voicing strong objections.

4. In the *Harry Potter* books, Harry _____ under the restrictions that the Dursleys place on him.

5. When a plane or helicopter filled with fuel crashes, a _____ usually rises above it.

6. The sparks from iron _____ can be used to start fires.

7. It makes sense for firefighters to check for signs that identify something as _____ before they get close to a wrecked truck or train.

Workshop 8.1: Part I. 1. a dust mote, **2.** a grain of sand, **3.** a piece of gravel, **4.** a pebble, **5.** a rock, **6.** a lump of coal, **7.** a stone, **8.** a boulder. **Part II. 1.** stone, **2.** dust, **3.** lump of coal, **4.** gravelly, **5.** sand, **6.** pebbled, **7.** Boulder, **8.** Rocky

Workshop 8.2: Part I. A: 1. background, **2.** groundless, **3.** grounded, **4.** ground crew. **B: 1.** dirt poor, **2.** dirty jokes. **3.** dirt. **C: 1.** soil bank, **2.** soiled. **3.** soil. **D: 1.** sandals, **2.** sandpaper, **3.** sandy. **E: 1.** no stone unturned, **2.** stepping stone, **3.** stony. **Part II. A: 1.** uphill, **2.** molehill, **3.** over the hill, **4.** downhill. **B: 1.** mountaintop, **2.** to mount, **3.** mounting, **4.** mountains. **C: 1.** peaked, **2.** peak performances, **3.** peak. **D: 1.** avalanche, **2.** vail, **3.** valedictory, **4.** Valley Girl, **5.** Valley of the Sun.

Workshop 8.3: A. 1. silver lining, **2.** cloud nine, **3.** clouded. **B. 1.** moonlighting, **2.** mooning around, **3.** month. **C. 1.** looney, **2.** lunar, **3.** lunatic. **D. 1.** in the stars, **2.** starfish, **3.** movie stars. **E. 1.** stellar, **2.** constellations, **3.** Stella. **F. 1.** astronauts, **2.** Astrodome, **3.** asterisk.

Workshop 8.4: A. 1. hot air, **2.** clear the air, **3.** walking on air. **B: 1.** a breeze, **2.** breezeways, **3.** breeze through. **C: 1.** window, **2.** windbag, **3.** wind, **4.** whirlwind. **D: 1.** coolers, **2.** cool, **3.** your cool. **E: 1.** cold shoulder, **2.** cold water, **3.** cold. **F: 1.** Freeze!, **2.** frozen, **3.** frozen out. **G: 1.** iceberg, **2.** ice breaker, **3.** thin ice. **H: 1.** warmly, **2.** warm up, **3.** warmed over. **I: 1.** hotdogging, **2.** heated, **3.** hot under the collar.

Workshop 8.5: Opposite of dark: 1. pilot light, **3.** in light of, **4.** lightning, **5.** lighthouses, **9.** lightning bugs. **Opposite of heavy: 2.** light on his feet, **6.** lite, **7.** lightweight, **9.** made light, **8.** lighter.

Workshop 8.6: Part II. 1. drip, **2.** ditch, **3.** gushy, **4.** flows, **5.** sprang, **6.** puddle, **7.** ripple.

Workshop 8.7: Part I. A. 1. waving, **2.** to wave, **3.** wave, **4.** WAVES. **B. 1.** whirlagigs, **2.** whirling. **C. 1.** hydrants, **2.** hydroplane, **3.** hydrofoils. **D. 1.** evaporates, **2.** vaporizing, **3.** vaporized. **E. 1.** a rainy day, **2.** raining, **3.** to rain. **Part II. A. 1.** misty-eyed, **2.** misters, **3.** mists. **B. 1.** fog, **2.** foggiest, **3.** foghorn. **C. 1.** flooded, **2.** a flood, **3.** floodgates. **D. 1.** spring, **2.** sprang up, **3.** bed springs. **E. 1.** pool your money, **2.** carpools, **3.** pool table. **F. 1.** stream, **2.** streaming, **3.** streamers.

Workshop 8.8: A. 1. curfews, **2.** fired, **3.** fired up, **4.** firewalls. **B. 1.** old flame, **2.** flambé, **3.** flamboyant, **4.** flamingos. **C. 1.** chafed, **2.** chafe, **3.** chauffeuring. **D. 1.** porch light burning, **2.** burn their bridges, **3.** slow burn, **4.** burning. **E. 1.** pyromaniac, **2.** Pyrex®, **3.** funeral pyres.

Workshop 8.9: Across: 2. chauffeur, **7.** flaming, **8.** burnout, **9.** fiery. **Down: 1.** fan, **3.** firestorm, **4.** chafes, **5.** fireball, **6.** pyrite, **7.** flammable.

End-of-Chapter Activities

1. This chapter has focused on the most common parts of the earth, the things we all take for granted. Now that you see how speakers have extended the meanings of such common words as *rain, rocks, dirt, mud*, and *streams*, take a look at the names of less common things and see what metaphors you can find. While precious minerals and metals are less common than the things we have talked about, they will still be the source of metaphors. Come to class ready to tell either a small group or the whole class about one such item. Bring a visual aid if you can. For example, if you decide to look at the word *marble*, you might talk about playing the game of marbles. Bring in a *marble* to show how it feels and looks like the highly polished marble that might be part of a *marble statue*. If you really wanted to go all out, you could bring in a *chocolate marble cake* to share so that your classmates could see how the chocolate dough runs through the white dough to make the kind of design that appears in many types of *marble*.

Here are some geology-related words that have metaphorical extensions; perhaps you can think of others. The first step is to search through dictionaries, but also ask for ideas from friends and the people you live with.

☐ Brass: Metaphors include *military brass* (officers with lots of medals), to grab the *brass ring* on a carousel (to have good luck), and to get down to *brass tacks* (the practical details). The *brass section* of a band is the horns, while to be *brassy* or *brazen* is to be shamelessly bold as is a newly polished piece of brass.

☐ Copper: Police officers were called *coppers* and later *cops* because in the mid-1800s, they had *copper buttons* on their uniforms. *Copperhead snakes* are reddish-brown, especially on their heads.

☐ Diamond: A *diamond* shape (baseball *diamonds, diamondback* rattlesnakes, the jack of *diamonds* in cards, etc.) is so named because jewelers often cut diamonds in this shape to increase their shine.

☐ Gold: Metaphors include a *goldbricker*, a *gold digger,* a *golden* opportunity, the *Golden State Warriors*, a *golden wedding anniversary,* someone's *golden years*, and *good as gold*.

☐ Iron: Metaphors include a *cast-iron constitution*, a *cast-iron stomach*, the *iron curtain*, having *too many irons in the fire*, and *to rule with an iron fist*.

☐ Lead: Metaphors include getting the *lead* out of your feet and something going over like a *lead balloon*.

2. Choose one of these clichés or proverbs to illustrate and explain to your fellow students. Be ready to tell them if you have made a literal interpretation or a metaphorical one.

- ☐ People who live in glass houses should not throw stones.
- ☐ All that glitters is not gold.
- ☐ Having too many irons in the fire.
- ☐ Being born with a silver spoon in your mouth.
- ☐ Shoot for the moon.
- ☐ Hitch your wagon to a star.
- ☐ Don't burn your bridges behind you.
- ☐ Seeing stars.
- ☐ Burning the candle at both ends.
- ☐ A fountain of good ideas.
- ☐ It is raining cats and dogs.
- ☐ Being on Cloud Nine.

CHAPTER NINE

Tools, Jobs, and Equipment

Background Reading for the Teacher

A good way to begin this lesson is simply to go through your tool drawer and bring in whatever you can find to use as conversation starters. The surprise for students is how such common things as *hammers, nails, screws, drills,* and *bolts and nuts* have served as the basis for many meanings not at all related to construction.

Students are so familiar with various kinds of tools that they are eager to illustrate comparative meanings. You might want to download the words strips on our website to provide students with preprinted cards that they could illustrate for a "Toolbox" bulletin board.

With tools, it is sometimes hard to decide whether a name is a target of a metaphor or the source of a metaphor. Because most tools and pieces of equipment have been developed as part of the industrial revolution, their names are not as old as the names for items found in nature. When speakers need a name for some newly developed piece of equipment, they most likely focus on what the item does and then give it a related name. This means that with many tool-related words, the tools are not the first thing that people learned about or think about when they hear the name. For example, most speakers learned about *picking out* what they wanted to wear long before they learned how a miner can *pick* something from the ground with a *pick ax.* They also learned that it was a good

Seventh graders enjoyed illustrating preprinted cards (top) based on tool metaphors. On the bottom, a fourth grader made this picture showing the similarity in shape between the teeth of a saw and a mountain range. *Sierra* (related to *serrated*) is the Spanish word for *saw,* which is why Spanish explorers named one mountain range *Sierra Madres* (saw of the mother) and another *Sierra Nevada* (snow-covered saw).

White boards are good for working with partners. Pairs of students can figure out how to illustrate a literal and a metaphorical meaning. Here, the boy on the left is drawing a *hammerhead shark*, while the boy on the right draws a *hammer*.

idea not to *shove their friends around* before they learned that *shovels* are made for *shoving* dirt.

In these source-based lessons, we have included such words only when we found evidence of new usages that appear to have come from, or at least to have been influenced by, the names of the tools. This is why the tools and weapons that are studied in this chapter as metaphorical sources are relatively old inventions. One of the end-of-chapter activities that we suggest is to look at how such pieces of equipment as *tractors, road graders, pliers,* and *pencils* took their names from words that were already in the language. The same processes are at work with such items as *adding machines, typewriters, calculators, computers, word processors,* and *printers.*

Surnames related to occupations also relate to jobs that have been around for a long time. Margaret Thatcher's ancestors were probably roofers; Peter Sellers' ancestors were in marketing, and Russell Baker's ancestors made bread and cakes. In some countries where people adopted surnames only within the last century, families are named *Engineer* and *Contractor,* but in English-speaking countries it is rare for families to have surnames taken from such modern jobs as *Nurse, Doctor, Secretary, Teacher, Mechanic,* and *Waiter.* If you want to pursue this subject further, J. N. Hook's *Family Names: How Our Surnames Came to America* (Macmillan, 1982) is a good source for information.

Notes to Help Teachers Elicit Ideas from Students

A skill that is crucial to comprehending metaphors is the ability to recognize what feature of a source is being emphasized in the target word (the word that "inherits" a name from the source word). Talk with students about the following pairs of sentences. Help them decide whether the feature that is being stressed is one of action or of appearance, most likely shape.

Saddles

1. *Saddle shoes* were popular for teenagers of your grand-parents' generation. (Appearance. The white shoes look as if they have a brown or black saddle thrown across them.)

2. Ever since high school, she has been *saddled with the responsibility* of her younger brother. (Action. She has felt a burden much like a horse feels when carrying a saddle.)

Cables

1. If we get in trouble, we can ask my mother *to cable* some money. (Action. The mother actually sends a message over a cable or perhaps through some "wireless" communication, but she does not send the actual money, which is why we have included this as a metaphor.)

2. My new sweater has *cable stitching* on the sleeves. (Appearance. This particular kind of knitting stitch results in what looks like twisted cables.)

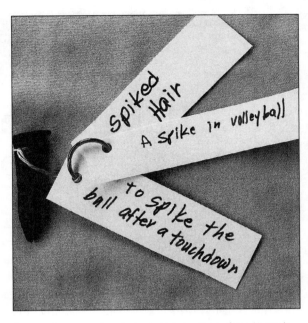

A way of encouraging students to bring items from home is to provide sets of empty cards on the same kinds of rings that we use for items we have brought. This is an old, rusty *spike* that allowed students to see how *spikes* differ from *nails*.

Hatchets

1. When the company got leaner and meaner, they hired my uncle as a *hatchet man*. (Action. The uncle had to cut jobs, that is, fire people. You might also talk about someone doing a *hatchet job* on someone's character.)

2. His birthday present was a bone-handled knife *hatched* with silver. (Appearance. *Hatch marks* are fine insets, close together as if something has been hit with a hatchet and then filled in. The word *hash* could have also been used here because it is related to the idea of something being chopped or *hatched up*.)

Spikes

1. Football players can be penalized for *spiking* the football after a touchdown. (Action. Slamming a football to the ground is similar to when a railroad worker would slam down a sledge hammer to drive a spike into the railroad tie or log.)

2. *Spiked* hair is a kind of fashion statement for teenagers. (Appearance. Hair that is really spiked looks like the wearer has spikes sticking out of his or her head.)

Hammers as Sources and Targets of Metaphors

Name: _____ **Period:** _____ **Date:** _____

Hammers are probably the first tool that people invented. Even toddlers have *pound-a-pegs* to play with, and if they don't have a toy hammer, they might use a toy truck or a shoe or a fist to pound on someone or something. The importance of hammers is seen in such things as the former Soviet Union's *hammer and sickle* flag, which was designed to symbolize the combining of industrial and agricultural strengths. Thor, the main god in Norse mythology, had a mighty hammer that he would fling across the sky, causing thunder and lightning. The symbol of Thor's twirling hammer, the *swastika*, is what Adolph Hitler adopted two thousand years later as the insignia of the Nazis.

Because hammers are so important, they have been both the receivers and the sources of metaphors. As you read the descriptions below, decide whether the hammer-related word is referring to a hammer that is metaphorically named from something else. If so, write the term and draw a picture in the right-hand box on page 155. If the term names something else that is in some way similar to a hammer, write its name in Figure 9.1 in the box labeled "Things that are like hammers." Talk about how the items relate to the word *hammer*.

- *Hammerhead sharks* have an advantage in seeing what might be coming after them because their eyes are located on a part of their heads that bulges out from both sides.
- *Jackhammers*, those heavy-duty hammers that have a power source to help them break up concrete and asphalt, are named after the men who work them. *Jack* is a common male name that is often used in association with work as with a *jackknife, a jacket,* and the *jack* that is used to lift cars.
- Mediators are hired to *hammer out* agreements so that there won't be so many lawsuits.
- The athletes with the biggest muscles at a track meet are probably the ones who are going to be in the *hammer throw*.
- *Claw hammers* are a good invention for carpenters because one side can be used for pounding in nails, while the other side can be used for taking them out.
- The name of a *sledge hammer* is related to an Old English word for *slay*. These are such big hammers that they require two hands and could very well slay either an animal or a person.
- Some people have *hammer toes*, which means that their middle toes are bent upwards. The condition may be inherited or it might develop from children wearing shoes that are too short.
- In the 1980s, thousands of family farms in the Midwest went under the auctioneer's *hammer*.

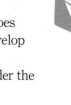

Figure 9.1

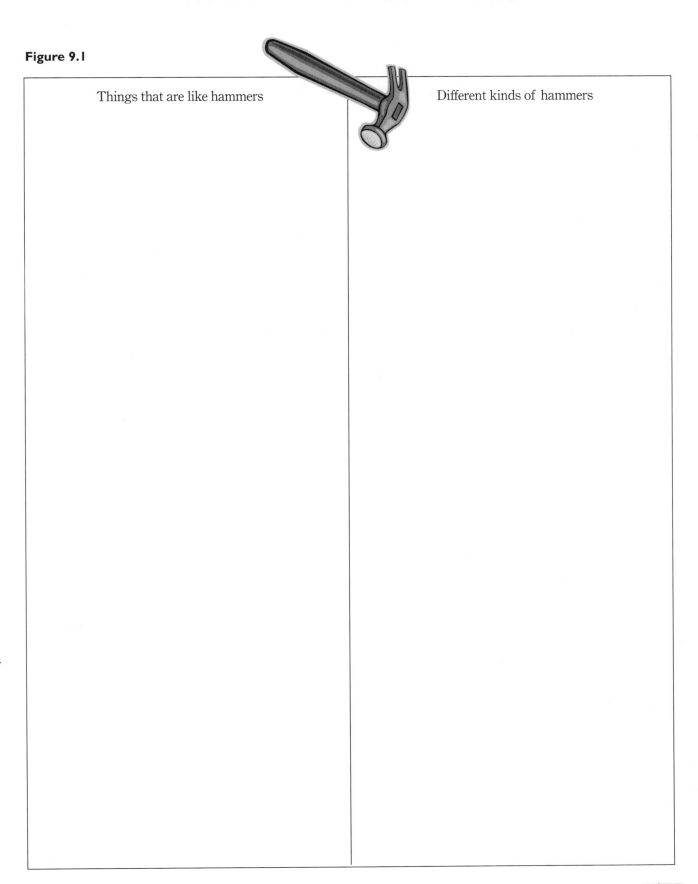

Things that are like hammers

Different kinds of hammers

Tools from Basic to Metaphorical

Name: _____ **Period:** _____ **Date:** _____

After reading about these various tool words, choose the most appropriate words or phrases and write them in the blank spaces. The sentences are devised to help you see the extended and metaphorical meanings of the names of tools with which you are probably already familiar. Talk about what the extended meanings have in common with the basic or tool-related meanings.

A. *Bolts* were originally short spears or arrows launched from bows or catapults during fighting or hunting. Their speed and danger in coming through the air is what these early bolts have in common with a *bolt of lightning*. Their straight and rounded shape is what they have in common with a *bolt of cloth* or the kind of bolts sold at hardware stores. The *nuts* that screw onto these kinds of *bolts* were named because of being small like the *nuts* that grow on trees. A *bolt-action rifle* differs from an automatic rifle. The shooter has to manually pull on a bolt to eject the old shell and put the new bullet in place.

> **a bolt**   **bolt out of the blue**   **bolted**   **deadbolts**   **nuts and bolts**

1. The news was a _____.

2. She insists on having _____ on all the outside doors.

3. When our papers were passed back, Eddie _____ from the room.

4. I would rather buy cloth from _____ than from a table of odds and ends.

5. Is the committee sure it has the _____ figured out?

B. *Chains* are made from rounded wires that are welded or soldered together. They can be as fine as those in gold necklaces or as heavy as those used to tow trucks and boats. For either kind, the old saying holds true, "A chain is no stronger than its weakest link."

chain link	chain-reaction	chain restaurants	chain stitched	chained

1. She is emotionally _____ to her childhood home.

2. The dust storm caused a _____ accident involving seventeen cars.

3. _____ fences are efficient but ugly.

4. I hate it when I pull on a thread and the whole thing comes loose because it was _____.

5. _____ have brought consistent food standards to the United States.

C. *Keys* are small metal pieces designed to match grooves in locks so that they can be opened. Because of the symbolism connected to opening doors or treasure chests, *key* has many extended meanings.

key	keyboarding	keyhole	keynote	keystone	latchkey

1. Computers are so important that most people are learning _____.

2. The _____ speaker was not as interesting as some of the lesser known participants.

3. _____ kids carry their keys on a string around their necks because they get home from school before their parents get home from work.

4. The sharps and flats in music determine the _____ signature.

5. Pennsylvania advertises itself as the _____ state, partly because of all the keystones in its arched bridges, but also to reflect is role in U.S. history.

6. Ordinary _____ saws aren't really small enough for sawing keyholes.

D. *Nails* are expected to be stronger than what surrounds them as shown by the metal nails that carpenters pound into wood and by the hardness of our *fingernails* and *toenails* as compared to the flesh of our fingers and toes.

fingernail	to nail down	nailed	toenail

1. Coming down Main Street, I got _____ for speeding.

2. It took a 16-hour session _____ the details of the new contract.

3. Even the ancient Egyptians used _____ polish.

4. When carpenters _____ a board, they to pound the nail in at a slant.

E. *Saws* made from steel are used for cutting wood and other substances. Their most distinctive feature is their jagged edges, that is, their *saw teeth*. *Sierra* is a Spanish word for *saw,* thus when Spanish explorers found the mountains they named the *Sierra Madre*, the name meant something like "the saw of the mother." When they named the *Sierra Nevada*, they were describing "a snow-covered saw." The English word *serrated* is related. When a knife is *serrated*, it has a jagged (saw-like) edge.

sawbucks	saw grass	sawhorses	saw-toothed	serrated

1. It is harder to sharpen _____ knives because of the jagged blade.

2. Sawbucks differ from _____ in that their side pieces are taller and are crossed in an X so that they look like the horns of a buck, a male deer.

3. Ten-dollar bills used to be called _____ because the 10 was shown with a big Roman numeral ten, which is X.

4. Currycombs for horses are _____.

5. _____ will cut your fingers if you grab onto it without realizing that the edges are jagged.

F. *Wrenches* are used by mechanics to grab onto things as when they need to tighten the bolts on a wheel or loosen a connection of some kind. One of their main features is how hard they can clamp onto something and hold it while it is pushed or pulled.

heart-wrenching	monkey wrenches	to wrench	wrenched

1. They had to make a _____ decision about removing the life support system.

2. Household wrenches are called _____ because when people use them they have to stretch and bend like monkeys to reach hard-to-get places.

3. The jaws of life _____ open the door on the wrecked car.

4. When he put an affectionate hand on her shoulder, she wanted _____ away, but she controlled herself.

On the Cutting Edge
with *s*, *c*, *sh*, and *ch*

Name: _____ **Period:** _____ **Date:** _____

The Latin word for *cut* is *caedere*, while the Latin word for *scissors* is *cisorium*. Dozens of modern English words that express an idea related to cutting can be traced back to these words as shown by the way they make use of the letters *s, c, sh,* and *ch*. Here are some of the most common. You have probably seen or heard most of these words, but you may not have thought of how they relate to each other. As you read the following paragraphs tying some of these words together, study this list and write the appropriate word in each of the blank spaces.

PART 1

| chisel | cutting out | pinking shears | scalpel | scissors | scythes | shears | sickles |

Clippers, 1. _____, and 2. _____ are written in the plural form because they are

made from two blades fastened together so that the blades work against each other for efficient cutting. The elec-

tric *clippers* that barbers use probably have more than two blades. *Scissors,* which are used for cutting things like

paper, cloth, and hair, are smaller and finer than are *shears.* 3. _____ have such thick blades that

they are made to cut jagged edges. Those used for *shearing* sheep have to be heavy enough that they can be

thrown around a corral and sharp enough that they can do the job of cutting away the wool before the sheep get

impatient and break loose.

Construction workers use either *tin snips* or *tin shears* for cutting different kinds of sheet metal. *Shard* relates to

shear in that it describes something that has been *sheared off.* The word is most commonly used to refer to the *pot-*

tery shards that anthropologists find among the remains of prehistoric home sites.

Even bigger and heavier cutting instruments are the 4. _____ and the 5. _____

that farmers use for harvesting crops. A *sickle* is like a long knife whose blade has been curved. It has a handle and

is used by one person to harvest grain or such standing crops as grass and alfalfa. The design on the old Soviet

flag of a *sickle* and a hammer symbolizes a partnership between industrial and agricultural strengths. *Scythes* are

bigger and not as curved. If you have seen pictures of *Father Time* celebrating the New Year, you might have

noticed the *scythe* that he carries over his shoulder to represent the harvesting of time.

Probably the heaviest of the listed cutting tools is the **6.** _____, which is used in combination with a hammer. Miners will use big, thick chisels that they will pound with sledge hammers. *Sculptors* use a variety of different sizes, depending on whether they are carving a delicate or a gross part of a statue.

In contrast to pieces of construction and farm equipment, a doctor's **7.** _____ is a *precision* instrument that comes in varying sizes. It must be sharp and able to be sterilized because surgeons use it for making *incisions* into people's bodies and for **8.** _____ diseased or damaged tissue. Words related to this kind of cutting include *incision, incisors* (your teeth that cut), *precision, precise,* and *concise.*

PART II This explanation of *cutting* instruments has been fairly literal. But in the following sentences, the *cutting* words are to be used in a more metaphorical sense. Choose from the following terms and write the appropriate words in the blank spaces. After you have made your choices, talk about the connections between literal and metaphorical uses of the words.

clipped scissor-tailed	concise shear off	cutters to chisel	incisive to cut	scissors hold

1. If you are going to make a _____ speech, you have to cut out all the extra words.

2. Because of the recession, the company had _____ its work force.

3. In wrestling a _____ is a powerful move because people's legs are stronger than their arms.

4. Her comments are always _____, even though not very supportive.

5. It isn't hard to imagine what a _____bird looks like.

6. Earthquakes sometimes _____ big cliffs and boulders.

7. Some sleek ships are called _____ because of the way they cut through the waves.

8. Her husband embarrasses her because he is always trying_____ down the price.

9. The new camp director _____ the gang's wings.

Bigger and Stronger

Name: _____   **Period:** _____   **Date:** _____

Read these paragraphs about particular kinds of tools and then look at the words and phrases below the paragraph and try to figure out the most appropriate ones to write in the blank spaces of the sentences that follow. While the paragraphs focus mainly on basic or literal senses of the words, the sentences focus more on metaphorical uses. After you choose the terms to write in the blank spaces, talk about the features that the metaphors have in common with the more literal uses of the terms.

PART I   ## Things That *Tie*: *Thread, String, Rope*

Thread is fine enough to be fitted through needles and used in sewing. It is fragile and breaks easily, which is why someone whose future is *hanging by a thread* is in a precarious situation. *String* is stronger because it is made from several strands of thread twisted together. Rope is even stronger because it is made from strands of string either braided or twisted together. All three of these items are common and fairly inexpensive, which is probably one of the reasons that half of the sentences below allude to poverty.

| at the end of her ropes | make ends meet | shoestring | |
| stringing | the ropes | threadbare | tie the knot |

1. I bet he is just _____ her along.

2. She thinks that any day now he is going to want to _____.

3. If they get married, they will have to live on a _____.

4. Already, everything they have is _____.

5. I doubt that they know _____ about renting an apartment or getting jobs.

6. Her mother is _____.

7. She will be surprised if the kids figure out how to _____.

PART II   ## Things That *Hold*: *Clips, Hooks, Rivets*

The kind of *clips* that hold things probably got their name from the *clips* that cut things because they are both two-sided tools that clamp or clinch onto something. The one that cuts goes on through (as with *fingernail clippers*), while the one that holds just clinches something as with *paper clips, hair clips, clip-on ties,* and *clip-on earrings.*

Both meanings apply to people who *clip* coupons because they *clip* them out and then *clip* them together to take to the store. When things go *at a fast clip*, the meaning has been taken from the sound of horses' hooves *clip-clopping* along on a hard surface, such as a road.

Fish hooks are probably the oldest forms of hooks, but today people hang their clothes on *coat hooks*, firemen rely on *hook and ladder* trucks to fight fires and rescue people in tall buildings, hockey players get called for *hooking* penalties, and both boxers and basketball players make *hook shots*. The backs of many women's dresses and the fronts of many men's pants are fastened with *hooks and eyes*. When *high-button* shoes and *tightly buttoned* long sleeves were fashionable, people had to have *buttonhooks* to help them get dressed. And probably because of the way that both animals and people can be surreptitiously caught by *hooks*, the word sometimes has unsavory connotations.

Rivets are small metal pins or bolts. One side is pushed through something and fitted into the head on the other side. The two parts are then pounded together to make a permanent connection. These rivets are seen on the bodies of airplanes, tanks, and other pieces of equipment too big to be made from single sheets of metal. During World War II, *Rosie the Riveter* was a "poster girl" encouraging women to take the kinds of heavy-duty factory jobs that used to be held by the men who were now off fighting. In the mid-1800s, an enterprising young man, Levi Strauss, made himself a fortune by using tent cloth to make heavy-duty pants for the California gold miners, who were tired of their pockets and their crotches splitting out. He used *rivets* at these points of stress, and for more than a hundred years, copper rivets identified *Levis* as pants made by his company. For the most part, the *rivets* are left off today, especially on back pockets, because they scratched people's chairs.

| by hook or by crook | clipboard | clip-on | hook shot | play hooky | riveted |

1. Twenty-five years after Elvis Presley's death, people are still _____ to his image and his music.

2. I like a computer program that lets you save lots of material on the _____ for later use.

3. That boxer's _____ is both deceptive and powerful.

4. To to do something _____ means the person is willing to cheat.

5. The kids planned to _____ on the day their papers were due.

6. He's a politician with a _____ smile.

PART III Things That *Stick: Tacks, Nails, Spikes*

*Tack*s are used for fastening lightweight and relatively thin items, as when *thumb tacks* are used to fasten paper to bulletin boards or *upholstery tacks* are used to fasten cloth to the wood frame of a chair or a couch. Because *tacking* is a relatively simple process, it is used to describe teachers *tacking on* extra homework or students *tacking* their projects together in a hasty and careless fashion. This probably contributed to the practice of referring to low-class and shabby things as *tacky*.

Tack is related to the word *attack*, which comes from a Middle French word meaning "to attach" oneself to something. If you have ever been out in a desert and been *attacked* by the *stickers* on a cactus, you can understand the connection. When sailors *tack*, they are changing the direction of their boat by going directly into (*attacking*) the wind and altering their sails so that they go in a zigzag pattern, which has the overall effect of moving them in the intended direction. Tailors use this same zigzag pattern when they use thread to *tack* linings inside wool jackets and coats.

Nails are used for fastening pieces of lumber together. Carpenters would have a hard time building houses without nails. Speakers have empathy for the way nails are continually pounded on. The phrase, *dumb as a doornail*, really alludes to a door knocker that is continually being pounded on. If, in sports, you *nail* an opposing team, you have beaten them mercilessly. The losers probably feel much the same as does a driver who gets *nailed* (gets a ticket) by a police officer for speeding.

Spikes are bigger and heavier than nails. They are used for holding heavy things together as when the rails on a track are pounded into the log ties underneath. The most famous spike in the United States is the *golden spike* that was used to join the eastern and western railroad lines on May 10, 1869 at Promontory Point in Utah. The size and more dramatic nature of a *spike* is the reason that the word is used when a volleyball player hits a ball down with unusual force or when someone surreptitiously throws alcohol into a bowl of punch so that it is *spiked*. Some plants have *spikes* and so do protective walls around castles. The sharpness of *spiked heels* on women's high-fashion shoes have caused them to be outlawed in historic buildings and other places where the floors and carpets could be damaged.

---

brass tacks   dead as a doornail   hit the nail on the head   spiked   spiking   tacky

---

1. When varnish or paint is not quite dry, it is called _____ because of the way it will stick to your fingers if you touch it.

2. The School Board said the idea of all-day kindergarten was _____.

3. _____ hairstyles require lots of mousse.

4. Jenny got a volleyball scholarship because she was to good at _____ the ball.

5. What Ernesto said really _____.

6. Getting down to _____ means getting down to the basics.

PART IV Things That Make Holes: *Drills, Spades, Shovels, Screws*

Drills can be as fine as a dentist's drill that grinds out tiny bits of a damaged tooth or as gigantic as the *auger* that in August 2002 broke through the stone mountainside and enabled rescuers to successfully bring up ten coal miners who had been trapped 200 feet underground. Because the *bits* in *drills* turn around and around in a rather boring fashion, speakers often use *drill* to describe actions that have to be repeated over and over as *drills*.

Spades and *shovels* are both used for digging dirt. *Spades* are usually thought of as being smaller and often pointed, as shown on the *spades* in a deck of cards. Garden *spades* are fairly small and usually pointed so that a person kneeling down can dig around tender plants without accidentally damaging them. *Shovels* (related to *shove*) have long handles and are used for work that does not have to be so fine. *Shoveling* snow off your driveway with a *spade* would be almost impossible, but it is fairly easy with a *snow shovel*, and even easier with a *snow plow*. The first machine-powered shovels were *steam shovels*. While these big pieces of equipment might still be referred to as *steam shovels*, they now operate with gas engines.

Screws work like miniature drills, but they are left in place. They are sturdier than nails, and because they are ridged instead of smooth they will not pull out as easily. They are often alluded to in a negative sense as when a person with strange behavior is described as having *a screw loose*.

drilled	drilling	screwball	screwy	shovel	spade

1. When Civil War soldiers, who did not know the meaning of *right* and *left,* were _____ in marching, the commander tied hay to soldiers' right feet and straw to their left feet and made them chant "Hayfoot, strawfoot!"

2. If you are asked to do the _____ work for a detective, you go out and dig up whatever evidence you can find.

3. Our teacher says she will just keep _____ us on prepositions until we learn what they are.

4. His flattery was so thick, we could _____ it out.

5. A man who hangs around our neighborhood acts a bit _____.

6. The Diamondbacks won the game because of their pitcher's _____.

Job-Related Surnames

Name: _____ **Period:** _____ **Date:** _____

The use of family surnames developed during the Middle Ages. Until then most people were known by a single name, but as cities became larger and people began to trade beyond their own neighborhoods, there was a need for more identification.

About one-fourth of the names that families took came from the work that the family did. This is easy to see in such family names as *Hunter, Farmer, Mason* (a stone worker or bricklayer), and *Smith* (from blacksmith or coppersmith). People who made clothing were named *Taylor* or *Tailor*, or in Germany *Snyder* or *Schneider* (related to *scissors* and cutting). Here are some other job-related surnames that we might not recognize because we do not know the older meanings of the words:

Murphy = seafighter	Roger = famous spear	William = resolute protector
Ryan = little king	Walter = ruler of the army	Ward = guard

When we know the meanings, it is possible to see some relationships. For example, a *resolute protector* would of course need a strong *will*, and in modern English the words *warranty* and *guarantee* both *guard* the interests of a purchaser.

Because most people keep the family names that their family has had as far back as anyone can remember, the names come from professions and jobs that have been in the language a long time. Ponder on these two columns of surnames and try to figure out which families had ancestors involved in the same line of work. Write the family's name from the alphabetical list on the right in the space by the family name with a similar meaning in the column on the left.

_____ **1.** The Cantors   The Arrowsmiths
(A *cantor* sings or chants.)

_____ **2.** The Chandlers   The Barkers
(*Chandlers* made candles.)

_____ **3.** The Joiners   The Carpenters
(British carpenters were called *joiners.*)

_____ **4.** The Forresters   The Carriers

_____ **5.** Mr. and Mrs. Tanner   The Merchants
(*Tannen* for working with leather comes from tree bark.)

_____ **6.** Mr. and Mrs. Carter   The Parkers
(Deliverers worked from *carts*.)

_____ **7.** Mr. and Mrs. Sellers   The Singers

_____ **8.** Mr. and Mrs. Fuller   The Weavers
(*Fullers* worked with new cloth by adding starch-like finishes.)

_____ **9.** Mr. and Mrs. Fletcher   The Wickmans
(*Fletchers* made bows and arrows.)

Jobs with Expanded Names

Name: _____ Period: _____ Date: _____

The professions discussed in this lesson are those that have been around so long that their names are now used in a variety of ways. Brief explanations are given followed by a list of words from which you are to choose the most appropriate terms to write in the more metaphorical sentences that follow.

A. ***Scribes*** were the old fashioned equivalent of today's *secretaries*, a group of people who got their name because they are "the keeper of the *secrets*." Before there were typewriters or carbon paper or photocopy machines, *scribes* had the job of copying other people's handwriting. The name of their profession relates to *script*, so it is hard to know whether the following examples are based on *scribe* or on *script*, but either way the allusion is to something written.

| description | postscript | prescription | scribble | script |

1. Drugstores must receive a _____ written by a doctor before they sell specified drugs.

2. We expect 3-year-olds to _____, but it is a surprise when a 10-year-old does it.

3. When I'm doing a hard assignment, I like to have a written _____ of what I am to do.

4. A *P.S.* added to a letter is a _____.

5. If the comedian's joke _____ doesn't get laughs, she will change it.

B. ***Cleaners*** work in all kinds of places. Their main job is one of sorting things out. Dirt is fine when it is outside in a garden, but people do not want it on their kitchen counter or on the couch in the living room. *House cleaners* use brooms, mops, vacuum cleaners, and rags, while *dry cleaners* use chemicals to clean your clothes without the water that might make them shrink or fade.

| clean sweep | cleaned out | the cleaners |

1. Tiger Woods made a _____ in the last three golf tournaments.

2. Through some kind of computer foul-up, his bank account was _____.

3. He was surprised when his old poker partners took him to _____.

C. Millers were unusually important in the days when people had to take their grain to be ground into smaller pieces suitable for eating. One piece of evidence supporting this idea is how many people are named *Miller* or *Mueller* (German for *miller*). As alluded to in the famous song, "Down by the Old *Millstream*," *mills* were usually located by rivers so that their water could turn the wheels that turned *millstones*, which would crush the grain. Waterpower was also used when people figured out how to weave cloth in factories, thus these factories were also called *mills*. Something described as *run of the mill* means that it was made in a factory without the care that goes into custom-made products. *Molé* is Spanish for something that has been *milled* or *ground up*, while *moulin* is the French word for windmill.

| guacamole | mill | millstone | molars | Moulin Rouge |

1. During the trial, he was put through the _____.

2. _____ is made from smashed up avocados.

3. Having a _____ around your neck is to be carrying a burden.

4. Your _____ are the teeth that grind your food.

5. The _____ in Paris is a famous nightclub that for a hundred years has been identified by the red windmill on its roof.

D. Hunters, especially in preindustrial times, had a huge responsibility for finding and killing animals to provide people with meat. Today's *hunters* are more likely to be sportsmen because farmers and ranchers grow the animals that will provide meat for people to eat. Common English words that relate to hunting as a sport include *hunting lodge, hunter's stew*, and *hunter green*. Speakers use the verb *hunt* to describe looking for things as different as lost contact lenses and missing pets.

| headhunters | hunt-and-peck | hunter-gatherers |

1. Primitive people who did not farm are labeled _____.

2. It used to be that in movies men always used a _____ method of typing to make them look "tougher" than secretaries.

3. Modern _____ are companies that go looking for smart people to fill all sorts of jobs, such as CEOs (Corporate Executive Officers), presidents of universities, or managers.

E. Laborers are people who *labor* or work in a variety of settings. *Common laborers* do work that requires more muscles and energy than education and training. *Labor Day*, held on the first Monday of September, is meant to honor people who do both skilled and unskilled *labor. Travail*, related to *travel*, is one of the synonyms for *labor*. This shows us that for centuries traveling has been considered more *laborious* than fun.

labor	laboratories	labored	laborious

I. Scientists work in their _____.

2. When people have pneumonia, their breathing is apt to be _____.

3. The process that mothers go through in giving birth is called _____.

4. Any job can be _____ if the working conditions are poor.

F. *Wrights* were *workers*. A *wheelwright* was a person who made or repaired *wheels*, a *cartwright* made or repaired carts, a *shipwright* made ships, and a *playwright* made or wrote plays. Modern speakers mostly rely on the word *work* in such expressions as *the world of work, a working man*, and *to rework* something like a script for a television show. When we refer to *wrought iron*, we are referring to iron that has been worked into a design, and when we talk about a person being emotionally *wrought up*, we are saying that person is *worked up*.

work	worked	the works	to work out

I. I want _____ on my hamburger.

2. If you are serious about body building, you have _____.

3. The horse_____ itself into a lather.

4. The doctor said he had to stay quiet or the stitches would _____ themselves loose.

G. *Builders* might also be called *contractors* because they sign agreements to be responsible for a *building*. Modern buildings are so complicated that a builder has to coordinate the work of *architects, engineers, steel workers, concrete workers, masons, carpenters, plumbers, electricians, painters, finishers,* and many others. Because *to build* is a basic term, it is the one that has been extended the most. It can refer to something as concrete as *built-in cupboards* and to something as abstract as *the building up of stress*.

body building	build	build up	building blocks	is building

I. He won't do anything unless you _____ a fire under him.

2. Learning responsibility is one of the _____ of success.

3. Pressure _____ on the coach to resign.

4. Stacy thinks it is a girl's job to _____ her boyfriend's confidence.

5. Boys who go out for _____ are tempted to take steroids.

A Tool Crossword Puzzle

Name: _____   **Period:** _____   **Date:** _____

Use these clues to fill in the crossword puzzle.

ACROSS

2. A saw-tooth knife is _____.

5. If sheep are _____ when the weather is too cold, they can get pneumonia.

6. A miner would have a hard time without a shovel and a _____.

9. _____ children come home before their parents get off work.

10. For a _____ kick, a swimmer keeps her knees straight.

11. Modern medicine brings about some heart-_____ decisions.

DOWN

1. A wrestler doing a _____ is bending his opponent's arm behind his back.

2 A _____ is a sawhorse with horns.

3. A fire_____ is less painful than a dentist's drill.

4. _____ letters that ask for money are illegal.

7. Your _____ teeth are the ones that cut.

8. Knowing the _____ and bolts of a project is understanding the nitty gritty or the basics.

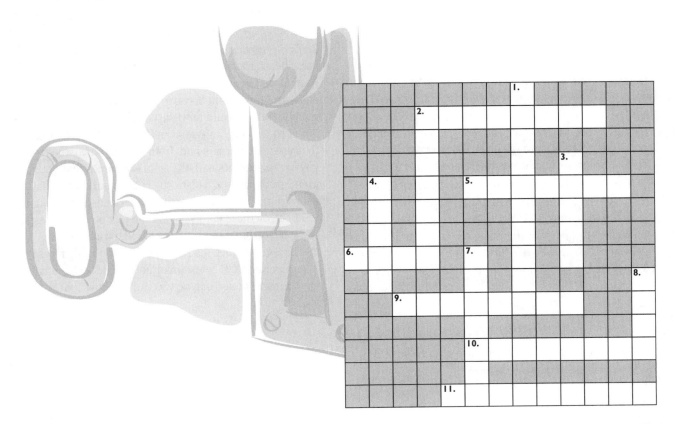

Workshop 9.1: Things that are like hammers: Hammerhead sharks, to hammer out, hammer toes. **Different kinds of hammers:** Jackhammers, hammer throw, claw hammers, sledge hammer, auctioneer's hammer.

Workshop 9.2: A. 1. bolt out of the blue, **2.** deadbolts, **3.** bolted, **4.** bolts, **5.** nuts and bolts. **B. 1.** chained, **2.** chain-reaction, **3.** chain link, **4.** chain stitched, **5.** chain restaurants. **C. 1.** keyboarding, **2.** keynote, **3.** latchkey, **4.** key, **5.** keystone, **6.** keyhole. **D. 1.** nailed, **2.** to nail down, **3.** fingernail, **4.** toenail. **E. 1.** serrated, **2.** sawhorses, **3.** sawbucks, **4.** saw-toothed, **5.** sawgrass. **F. 1.** heart-wrenching, **2.** monkey wrenches, **3.** wrenched, **4.** to wrench.

Workshop 9.3: Part I: 1. scissors (or shears), **2.** shears (or scissors), **3.** pinking shears, **4.** sickles (or scythes), **5.** scythes (or sickles), **6.** chisel, **7.** scalpel, **8.** cutting out. **Part II: 1.** concise, **2.** to cut, **3.** scissors hold, **4.** incisive, **5.** scissor-tailed, **6.** shear off, **7.** cutters, **8.** to chisel, **9.** clipped.

Workshop 9.4: Part I: 1. stringing , **2.** tie the knot, **3.** shoestring, **4.** threadbare, **5.** the ropes, **6.** at the end of her rope, **7.** make ends meet. **Part II: 1.** riveted, **2.** clipboard, **3.** hook shot, **4.** by hook or by crook, **5.** play hooky, **6.** clip-on. **Part III: 1.** tacky, **2.** dead as a doornail, **3.** spiked, **4.** spiking, **5.** hit the nail on the head, **6.** brass tacks. **Part IV: 1.** drilled, **2.** spade, **3.** drilling, **4.** shovel, **5.** screwy, **6.** screwball.

Workshop 9.5: 1. Singers, **2.** Wickmans, **3.** Carpenters, **4.** Parkers, **5.** Barkers, **6.** Carriers, **7.** Merchants, **8.** Weavers, **9.** Arrowsmiths.

Workshop 9.6: A. 1. prescription, **2.** scribble, **3.** description, **4.** postscript, **5.** script. **B. 1.** clean sweep, **2.** cleaned out, **3.** the cleaners. **C. 1.** mill, **2.** guacamole, **3.** millstone, **4.** molars, **5.** Moulin Rouge. **D. 1.** hunter-gatherers, **2.** hunt-and-peck, **3.** headhunters. **E. 1.** laboratories, **2.** labored, **3.** labor, **4.** laborious. **F. 1.** the works, **2.** to work out, **3.** worked, **4.** worked. **G. 1.** build, **2.** building blocks, **3.** is building, **4.** build up, **5.** body building.

Workshop 9.7: Across: 2. serrated, **5.** sheared, **6.** pick, **9.** latchkey, **10.** scissors, **11.** wrenching. **Down: 1.** hammerlock, **2.** sawbuck, **3.** drill, **4.** chain, **7.** incisor, **8.** nuts.

End-of-Chapter Activities

1. Choose a tool that has been a rich source of metaphors and make a picture of it. List three words that are related to the name of the tool and explain what they have in common with the tool.

2. In this chapter we have studied how tools and jobs that have existed for a long time have given their names to other items and concepts. However, the process also works the other way around. Newer tools are more likely to be named because of what they do. Here are some descriptions of pieces of equipment that have been developed more recently than the ones discussed in this chapter. See if you can guess their names.

☐ This piece of farm equipment usually leaves *tracks* because it is used to drag plows and harrows through fields. (tractors)

☐ This piece of road equipment smoothes out the *gradations* on unpaved roads. (graders)

☐ A French word that means "to bend" has given us such English words as *pliable, compliant,* and *complicate*. What common household tool has a related name? (pliers)

☐ *Pens* have been around for centuries, but something that is smaller and does not write so permanently was given a related name. (pencils)

Now do some brainstorming and see how many other pieces of equipment you can think of that were given names related to words already in English. In most cases, such names will simply describe what the tool does.

3. Find a surname in your family and write an imagined story about the first person who had this name. You will need to talk to your relatives to find out where your ancestors came from because that will influence the naming patterns and how the name was written and pronounced. You can choose from the two different surnames that your two parents had, from the four surnames that your grandparents had, the eight surnames that your great-grandparents had, or the sixteen surnames that your great, great grandparents had. Chances are that at least one of these names will relate to a profession, especially if you have someone to help you translate the meanings of names that have come into English from other languages. If you cannot find a work-related name in your own family, maybe you can "borrow" one from a friend.

CHAPTER TEN

Sports, Games, and Travel

Background Reading for the Teacher

In today's world, the entertainment and travel industries portray the subjects of this chapter as the pleasures of life and the rewards for hard work. While for some people this may be true, for others sports and travel are their work. Historically, these activities were very serious. Hunting and fighting are the ancestors of games, while foraging for food and shelter is the ancestor of travel.

English lends support to the idea that sports are good practice for the *game of life* through such related words as *compete, competent, competition,* and *competitive.* To *know the score* in life is to be generally knowledgeable, while *being a good sport* and *being a winner* refer to more than playing games.

Metaphors connected to both sports and travel have an unusual power to communicate with speakers, probably because they can allude to a whole process (e.g., "Life is a journey!") rather than just to a single feature of the source word. *The Domino Theory* is a metaphor that deserves capital letters because of how U.S. political leaders used it to explain their reasoning in support of the Vietnam War. The idea was that if Vietnam fell to the Communists, all of Southeast Asia, and maybe the world, would follow suit.

Some sports metaphors have outlasted the sports from which they were coined. The phrase *from pillar to post,* now defined in the Webster's Tenth as "from one place or one predicament to another," comes from a kind of indoor tennis game. In the days before architects and engineers could create free-standing roofs, it was mostly a game of frustration because the ball was always hitting a pillar or a post, if not the ceiling. In the 1300s, *Hazard* was a dice game that by the 1500s

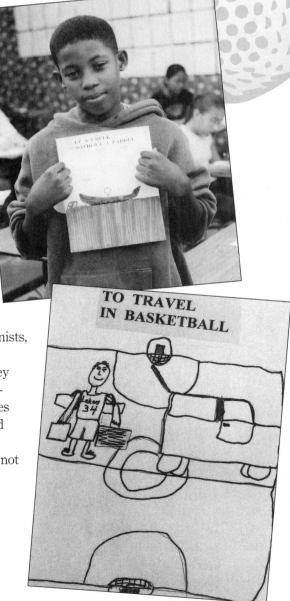

Twelve-year-old Keenen shows his interpretation of "Up a creek without a paddle." On the right is 12-year-old Chris's interpretation of "To travel in basketball."

Seventh-grade girls were amused at the difference between a *triple-decker* ice cream cone and a *triple-decker* ship and at the idea of *shipping* things across the Arizona desert.

had been extended to refer to the *game of chance* that is life itself. And today when we *bandy something about*, we are using a verb taken from the name of a game that in the 1600s was a forerunner to hockey.

Words connected with traveling are another good illustration of how slow language is to catch up to cultural and technological changes. Today, many more things are *shipped* by trucks, trains, and airplanes than by ships, and many more people launch their journeys from *airports* than from *seaports*. And long before there were airplane *pilots*, Mark Twain was writing about wanting to be a *steamboat pilot* on the Mississippi River.

The original *cockpits* were holes dug in the ground where two roosters or cocks would be placed for fighting. From this the name came to be used for confined scenes of violent and bloody conflicts. On battleships, the *cockpits* were small compartments used by junior officers and as treatment centers for sailors wounded in battle. The term was then transferred to any small, confined area in such vehicles as race cars or airplanes where drivers have to work hard to maintain control. Recent terrorist attacks on airplanes and the authorization of pilots to carry guns have brought the name back to its original meaning of a small, confined scene of violent conflict.

The first *boards* (as in *to go aboard*) that people stood on for traveling were those laid out on the decks of boats and ships. Today, even though trains and airplanes are both made from metal, train conductors call, *All aboard!* and at the airport people cannot get on a plane until they have obtained their *boarding passes*. While some people have passes to sit in *First Class*, most people are seated in *coach*, an allusion to the kind of travel experienced by our ancestors on *stagecoaches*.

In another example, the first *cars* were probably *carts*, soon followed by *carriages* and *chariots*. The word goes back to Middle English *carre*, which is related to Latin *currere* meaning to run or move, as with a *current* of water or electricity. Railroad *cars* were in existence long before either *automotive cars* (self-moving) or *elevator cars* (ones that go up and down) were invented. The first automotive cars were in fact called *horseless carriages*.

Another thing we can learn from travel-related words is how speakers prefer short and simple words to longer, more complex words. For example, people more frequently say *plane* than *airplane*, *car* than *automobile*, and *train* than *railway locomotive*. The first buses were called *omnibuses* (*omni* from Latin *all* alluding to how many people they would carry), but speakers soon shortened the word to *bus*. In a similar situation, the first *taxis* were called *taxi cabriolets*, which speakers soon shortened to either *taxi* or *cab*.

Notes to Help Teachers Elicit Ideas from Students

In the history of the world, organized sports are a fairly recent development, at least when compared to nature's creations and to such human activities as obtaining food, clothing, and shelter. This, plus the fact that the metaphors are spread thinly over various sports, means that metaphors related to the less common sports are fairly limited. You might talk about the following examples to get students ready for the workshops that focus on sports played by more people. See if someone in the class can identify the sport or the game and tell what the meaning is both literally and figuratively. Point out to students how efficient the metaphors are as compared to the fuller descriptions of the situations that you and students give as explanations.

1. **He is *up a creek without a paddle*.** (From canoeing; someone is in a bad situation because of not having what is needed.)

2. **It is time to *cut to the chase*.** (From hunting; it is time to end such preliminaries as planning and scouting and *go for it*. It is *make-or-break* time.)

3. **She is always finding herself *behind the 8-ball*.** (From pool; in *8-ball*, the number 8 ball has to be the last one to go into the pocket. A ball that is in the way is in the wrong place at the wrong time.)

4. **Don't worry; that's *par for the course*.** (From golf, where *par* is the expected number of shots that it should take a good player to make a particular hole.)

5. ***Hockey-puck locks* are a new invention to prevent mail theft.** (This kind of a lock on community mailboxes is hard to break or cut through because it as almost as big and heavy as is a *hockey puck*.)

6. **Did you make the cake from *scratch?*** (Before people were affluent enough to build special facilities for sports, such events as racing and boxing were held outdoors. The manager would simply *scratch* a line in the dirt, so that *doing something from scratch* meant starting from the beginning.)

7. **Don't just sit there; either *fish or cut bait*.** (The idea is that someone out fishing should be doing more than daydreaming. People who are not fishing should at least be getting ready to fish by preparing the bait for the hooks. In other situations, the message is something like, "Get to work," or "Get busy!")

8. **It was *dirty pool* for them to pull out at the last minute.** (The allusion is to someone cheating while playing pool. The phrase has been extended to refer to people not playing fairly in any aspect of life.)

9. **He acts like such a *big wheel!*** (Someone on a vehicle with big wheels is advantaged in the same way as is a walker who has extra long legs. For each rotation, the vehicle moves further than does a vehicle with smaller wheels. From this, a person called *a big wheel* is someone who expects to get extra mileage for his or her efforts.)

As you move from sports to the subject of travel, you might start with this old riddle, which illustrates how natural it is for people to talk metaphorically about travel:

 Where does this road go?

 It doesn't go anywhere; it just sits here. But if you get on it, you can go to Memphis (or Chicago, or Los Angeles, or wherever).

To get students thinking about metaphorical extensions connected to travel, you might ask them to work with you to figure out the origins of the following names or idioms:

- One of the strong images from western movies is of people climbing down from or up into *stagecoaches* and of drivers whipping the horses to make them go faster. Why were these called *stagecoaches*, instead of just *coaches* or *carriages*? (The term did not originate in the U.S. frontier West, but it is forever associated with that time and period because the distances were so great and the land so barren that this method of travel was especially dramatic. The *stage* part of the name refers to the scheduled segments or stages of each journey. While the passengers stayed on, the horses and sometimes the drivers were changed at each *stage* of the trip.)

- When someone declines doing something that is generally viewed as a pleasure by saying "No, thanks it would be a *busman's holiday*," the activity is being described as too similar to what the person does everyday. (This phrase became popular when people's idea of a holiday was to take long car trips. Of course, a bus driver would not want to embark on a two-week trip driving the family car three or four hundred miles a day.)

- If people *barge into a party* uninvited, they are being compared to a river barge, those long flat boats that are either pushed or pulled by tugboats. (Barges are almost like trains in that several sections might be connected. However, they do not run on tracks or have their own power source. This means that they sometimes bump up against other boats or the support pillars of bridges. A pleasure barge is different in having its own power source.)

- Allusions to *decks* illustrate different generations of metaphors. For example, you can work with students to decide which of these metaphors allude to the *deck of a ship* and which to a *deck of cards*, a metaphor that itself is based on a comparison to the way cards are stacked up just as the decks of ships are stacked one on top of the other.

  1. *Double-decker buses* are part of the charm of London.

  2. From the beginning, *the deck was stacked against him.*

  3. In baseball, the person *next on deck* is the next one to bat.

  4. He's not *playing with a full deck.*

  5. Fancy clubs were the first ones to make *triple-decker sandwiches*, commonly called *club sandwiches.*

(Numbers 1, 3, and 5—*double-decker buses, next on deck*, and *triple-decker sandwiches*—allude to the decks of a ship, while numbers 2 and 4—*a stacked deck* and not *play with a full deck*—allude directly to a *deck* of cards and indirectly or historically to the *decks* of a ship.)

Play Ball

Name: _____ **Period:** _____ **Date:** _____

In prehistoric compounds, anthropologists have found evidence of pits that were used for ball games, which means that ball games are among the oldest of sports. Another way to judge how old ball games are is to look at how many metaphors they have provided for English speakers. Look at the following examples and decide which game they are most likely based on. One of them could refer to either baseball, basketball, or football, but the others are more specific. Write the phrases near the appropriate ball (or balls). Talk about their literal meanings, that is, what they describe in the game they allude to. Then talk about their extended or metaphorical meanings. Try to think of different sentences that will also illustrate the metaphorical meanings.

1. She only hinted that Jerry did it, but *right off the bat* he said he was sorry.

2. That boy has always been *out in left field*.

3. Of course she was elected; it was a *slam dunk*.

4. To *kick off* the fundraising campaign, the automobile dealer donated a pickup to be raffled off.

5. Child welfare workers find it hard to *cover all bases*.

6. When Todd left, he told Jesse that the *ball was in his court now*.

7. The director of our steel drum band is *on the ball*.

8. Don't feel bad; that's *how the ball bounces*.

9. What your neighbor said was *way off base*.

10 That is such a problem, I hardly know how *to tackle it*.

Figure 10.1

Football

Basketball

Baseball

A Variety of Sports and Games

Name: _____ Period: _____ Date: _____

The metaphors in each of these sets are taken from the identified sport or game. Read the sentences and choose the appropriate terms to write in the blank spaces. Read the sentences aloud and talk about the relationships between the sports or game-related meanings and the extended meanings in these sentences.

A. BOXING   on the ropes   pull any punches   throw in the towel

1. Having run out of money, the third candidate has decided to _____.

2. The attorneys did not _____ when they went after the tobacco companies.

3. I'm not optimistic about that new restaurant; it looks like it's _____.

B. SWIMMING   against the current   jump off the deep end   out of my depth

1. Having swum _____ all his life, he has self-confidence.

2. She is probably going to _____ when she finds out that she lost.

3. I'm _____ in this class.

C. RACING   down to the wire   hurdles   jumped the gun
                  play catch-up   the inside track   the long run

1. She has _____ on getting a good part in the play because her aunt is the director.

2. He _____ in April by inviting Suzie to a fourth of July picnic.

3. It's _____ if you wait to study until the night before the test.

4. In _____, you will be glad you came back.

5. I had to _____ all year because I started school a month late.

6. They have cleared away all the _____, so I think we can go.

D. TARGET SHOOTING   aim high   hit the spot   targeted

1. A cold soda would really _____ right now.

2. If you don't _____, you won't get very far in life.

3. People are worried about who gets _____ for extra security checks at airports.

E. ARCHERY   arch   archer fish   straight arrow

1. John is known as a _____.

2. Babies _____ their backs when they do not want to be cuddled.

3. _____ catch insects by squirting them with drops of water.

F. BASEBALL   ball park   curve ball   hard ball

1. She threw him a _____ when she said she never had liked him.

2. The contractor for the school says all he can give is a _____ figure.

3. That gang prides itself on playing _____.

G. PLAYING CARDS   an ace up his sleeve   raw deal   shuffled

1. Don't count him out; he's always got _____.

2. The CEO had _____ money into secret accounts.

3. She thinks she got a _____.

H. GAMBLING   no dice   poker face   wheeler-dealer

1. My uncle is a real _____.

2. She said _____ to my idea.

3. Kyle would be a good one to tell her because he has a _____.

Check, Game, and *Play*

Name: _____ Period: _____ Date: _____

The longer words have been in a language the more meanings they develop. The three words in this workshop are good illustrations of how words develop different meanings. Read the explanations and the sample sentences. Then sort out the sample sentences by copying the italicized phrases near the appropriate drawings.

A. Check comes from the game of chess, as seen in *checkmate*. In Persian and Arabic, the term was something like *shah mat*, to refer to the death of the *shah* (Persian for *king*), but as often happens, English speakers changed the pronunciation to something that they could remember and pronounce more easily. Today speakers use *check* in many different ways. Some refer to the *checkered* design of a chessboard, while others refer to the actions of some kind of authority. This "authority" can be as informal as a classmate *checking* your homework answers, as powerful as a hockey player hitting an opponent with a *body check,* or as legalistic as a bank making sure you have signed a *check* authorizing the bank to disburse some of your money. Read the following sentences and, to the right of the picture of a crown symbolizing authority, copy the italicized phrases that were used in sentences illustrating authority. Under the chessboard, copy the phrases alluding to a checkered design.

1. England has a *Chancellor of the Exchequer* while the United States has a Treasurer.

2. Did you get a *claim check* when you left your jacket?

3. Pizza parlors often have red-and-white *checkered* tablecloths.

4. Some airports already X-ray *checked bags.*

5. *Chinese checkers* did not come from China.

6. A person with a *checkered past* usually tries to avoid publicity.

7. Do you have your own *checking account*?

A checkered design

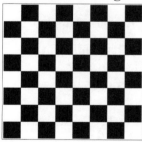

Figure 10.2

A symbol of authority

B. *Game* began as a word related to hunting. In fact, hunting animals or *game* was probably the first competition that people engaged in, and the first place where they saw the benefit of forming teams so that they could *win*. Because of the similarities between hunting and sports, it is easy to see how the term developed additional meanings related to sports. Read the following sentences. If the allusion is to animals as *game,* copy the italicized phrase near the picture of the deer. If the allusion is to some kind of competitive play (including metaphorical allusions), copy the italicized phrase near the board game.

1. A *game warden* has the authority to examine people's hunting licenses.

2. He wouldn't agree to join our group until we explained the *game plan*.

3. Someone stole his Nintendo *Game Boy*®.

4. Children cannot be near the *gaming tables* in Las Vegas.

5. There is a *gamey smell* in here.

6. It is dangerous to have a *game preserve* near the airport.

C. *Play* has two major meanings. One relates to pretending that something is true as when children *play house* or *play doctor* or when grownups *put on a play*. The other meaning relates to a more organized kind of play as when people *play* a musical instrument or a game. With the following sentence, copy the italicized phrases near the stage for the sentences about a pretense of some kind. Copy the italicized phrases near the ball for the sentences about an organized game or sport.

1. Susie *plays possum* when she is supposed to be napping.

2. She *plays second violin* in our city's youth orchestra.

3. The coach was mad when we lost a copy of his *play book*.

4. We are going to perform *the play* for three different audiences.

5. I get to *play the part* of a villain.

6. It is surprising how many kids *can play chess* better than their parents.

Figure 10.3

Game as in to play

Game as in animals

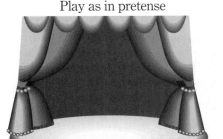

Figure 10.4

Play as in organized game or skill

Play as in pretense

Earth, Water, or Air

Name: _____ **Period:** _____ **Date:** _____

Because traveling is so common, speakers use it to make many different metaphors. Read the following sentences, each of which is based on an allusion to some kind of travel. Figure out if it is *earth-, water-,* or *air*-based. Write the italicized phrases near the boat if the allusion is to water travel. Write them near the bus if the allusion is to earth-based travel and near the airplane if the allusion is to air travel. If something could be either air or water, put it both places. There are fewer allusions to air travel, because people have been traveling through the air for a much shorter time than they have been walking, riding, or sailing. This means there has been less time for metaphorical uses to develop. After you figure out the answers, talk about what the italicized phrases mean and how the meanings are connected to something in the source word.

Air

1. Every *float* in the Rose Bowl parade must be covered with flowers.

2. She goes *overboard* on whatever she is asked to do.

3. He has been *spinning his wheels* ever since he was dropped from the football team.

4. She *sailed through* the statewide tests that are given every March.

5. He's a *middle-of-the-road* kind of guy.

6. Now that Wendy moved back, Jefferson is *flying high.*

7. Sadly, she was left *high and dry* by the company's collapse.

8. I hope he doesn't do anything *to rock the boat.*

9. We got off on *the wrong track*, and it's hard to start over now.

10. Janella set such *a fast pace* for our group that I had to do part of my work at home.

Earth

Figure 10.5 Different kinds of travel

Water

Drivers, Pilots, Helmsmen, and Engineers

Name: _____ **Period:** _____ **Date:** _____

Today's speakers naturally think of *drivers* in relation to cars, buses, and trucks, while we think of pilots in relation to airplanes because that is where we see them the most often. However, long before people drove cars, they *drove* animals both in herds and in harnesses where the animals supplied the power to pull wagons, plows, and carriages. Since the 1500s, *pilots* have been directing the routes taken by riverboats and ships. They are the navigators or the *helmsmen*. Metaphorically, a *pilot* goes in front and clears the way as when someone who wants to produce a television show prepares *a pilot* to convince network officials that the show will be a success.

The *pilot house* on a ship is a *deckhouse* for the *helmsman*. It contains a steering wheel, a compass, and other navigational equipment. For practical reasons, the *helmsman* stands near the rudder or *helm* so as to steer the passengers and the cargo away from harm. *Helmets* are "little protectors," named after these *helmsmen* and designed to fit the specific needs of someone wearing a *bicycle helmet,* a *space helmet,* a *football helmet,* a *fireman's helmet,* or a *soldier's helmet.*

When your great-grandparents heard the word *engineer*, they probably thought of a man who wore gray-and-white striped coveralls and drove a train. He had tremendous prestige and power because he was in charge of the most impressive piece of machinery that many people would see in their lifetimes. Today, trains are still awe-inspiring, but the *engineers* are not as visible because they do not sit up front nor do they wave to people along their routes. Also, today's trains must compete for people's attention with cars, trucks, buses, airplanes, and even rockets to the moon. There are also many more kinds of engineers who work to solve problems ranging from computer malfunctions to the controlling of floods and traffic. Someone who works to organize services offered by government and religious agencies might be referred to as a *social engineer*.

The following sentences illustrate more metaphorical uses of these terms. Choose the most appropriate and write them in the blank spaces of the following sentences. Talk about the relationships between the travel-related meanings of these terms and the more metaphorical meanings illustrated in these sentences.

autopilot	driven	drivers	drove	drover
helm	pilot light	pilot study	search engine	

1. The wall of flames _____ the rescue team back.

2. Our class is going to be part of a _____ (a trial run) before the whole district adopts the plan.

3. Being at the _____ of a school the year it opens is challenging.

4. In the old West a _____ was someone who worked on long cattle drives.

5. Judging from the glazed look on his face, I think he's been on _____ and won't remember a thing you've said.

6. You need to have a good _____ if you hope to get the most out of the Internet.

7. My father's golf game is not as good since my little brother ruined his _____.

8. She has always felt _____ by her parents' ambitious plans for her.

9. The _____ on the furnace went out.

The Paths You Take

Name: _____ **Period:** _____ **Date:** _____

Roads, streets, pathways, walkways, sidewalks, lanes, trails, tracks, highways, freeways, and *turnpikes* all make it easier for people to travel whether *on foot* or in a vehicle. *Turnpikes* were the first toll roads, probably made from logs laid over swampy areas. The entrances were guarded by a pole mounted on a turnstile. An attendant stood by to collect the fee and turn away the *pikers* (those who were too poor to pay).

Way comes from Middle English *weg* meaning "to move." It relates to *wiggle*, which is what a lot of people do if they are stuck in the back seat of a car or squeezed into an airplane seat for hours at a time. But in its modern form, *way* has a surprising variety of meanings as shown by these sentences:

- The *Ways and Means* committee is responsible for getting us the resources we need.
- *By the way*, did you hear that we're going to have split sessions at school next year?
- People are worried that there may be *no way out* of the conflict.
- *Way to go!* Three cheers for Shaneela!
- The *Interstate Highway System* means that a lot of people now miss the *byways* of the United States.
- While *freeways* may be free of competing traffic, most of them cost money.
- While *highways* may be higher than the drainage ditches that run alongside them, they nevertheless go through valleys and canyons and sometimes pass under other roads.

In mountainous logging areas, a *skid road* was a rough path that lumbermen used to push or slide (to *skid*) logs down to the mill. A *skid road* then became the name for any really rough roadway. As the metaphor moved away from logging areas and from the people who understood the original allusion, the pronunciation changed to *skid row* and to a metaphorical kind of rough place. In inner cities, *skid rows* are the rough parts of town where people *on the skids* hang out.

There are so many metaphors based on roads and paths that we don't have space to write about them all. However, you probably know many of them already as when you describe a friend as having *street smarts* or your mother as being on the *warpath*. Since medieval times, French and English speakers have interacted with each other, thus it is to be expected that they would have contributed to each other's words in relation to travel. The latest example of a new French/English travel word is *The Chunnel*. This is the name given to the tunnel that opened in the late 1990s under the English Channel. The Chunnel makes it possible for people to travel by train (or in their car carried on a train) between France and England without seeing a drop of ocean water.

PART I Here are some older travel words that English speakers borrowed from French speakers:

channel = a long body of water
jour = day

depot = a storage place
rivus = stream

As usually happens, the words have undergone some changes, but they still have related meanings. See if you can figure out which word to write in the following blank spaces. Talk about how the terms relate to their French roots as well as to the meanings in these sentences.

| canals | channel | channels | deposit | journal | journey | rivals |

1. Having so many _____ on television does not seem to make watching any more enjoyable.

2. I like to keep a _____, but I do not have the discipline to write in it every day.

3. California and Arizona are _____ because they both want the water from the Colorado River.

4. Even though _____ are made by humans, the engineers try to find places where nature has done most of the work.

5. It makes sense to _____ your anger or jealousy into something productive.

6. People who are on a _____ have something new to write about each day.

7. When traveling, it feels good to _____ your luggage at the depot.

PART II The following terms hint at a variety of other metaphorical usages. Read the sentences and write in the appropriate terms. Then talk about their extended or metaphorical meanings as compared to their more literal meanings.

| fast lane | hitting the road | on track | road to ruin | Rocky Road |
| runways | trail blazer | wayward | | |

1. There's an old saying about the _____ being paved with good intentions, meaning that success takes more than daydreaming.

2. If you live in the _____, you better be prepared for sudden changes.

3. He's _____ for a college scholarship.

4. My favorite flavor of ice cream is _____.

5. "I'm out of here!" is another way of saying you are _____.

6. There's a big difference in size, if not in shape, between the _____ at an airport and at a fashion show.

7. Jackie Robinson was a _____ in being the first African American baseball player to play in the major leagues.

8. A _____ child has gotten off the straight and narrow.

The Conveyances You Use

Name: _____ **Period:** _____ **Date:** _____

Conveyances are whatever people use to carry themselves or other things from one place to another. If you are on an airplane and look out the window either before takeoff or after landing, you will see *conveyor belts* at work helping to transfer your luggage from the plane to little *wagons*. These *wagons* or *carts* (a word related to *carry*) will take your luggage to other *conveyor belts* so that you can pick it up in the *Baggage Claim* area.

Other conveyances can be as simple as a skateboard or as complicated and big as an aircraft carrier. However, the *conveyances* that people have interacted the most with and are therefore the most likely to have inspired additional meanings include *cars, trucks, bicycles, trains, ships,* and *airplanes.*

Wheels play an important role in all of these conveyances. Airplanes could not get onto runways if they did not have wheels, and ships could not be built or loaded without the use of hundreds of *wheeled* conveyances. The ancestors of families named *Wainwright, Wheeler, Wagner,* and *Wagoner* worked either in making wheels or wagons. When people talk about someone being a *fifth wheel*, the implication is that the person is an extra tag-along. However, some chariots used to have a *fifth wheel* that was placed horizontally in front of the chariot. If the chariot started to tip over, it would help set it upright. Today some trailers and trucks are called *fifth-wheelers* because a large wheel-like connector is placed in the back of a truck where it supports a connection to an oversized trailer.

Trains and ships have been around the longest and so have provided the most metaphors. When people lose their *train of thought* or when they *train* their dog, they are alluding to the orderly way in which the cars of a train follow the engine. Assertive people are described as *railroading* their ideas through a committee, while someone who gives up might be described as *abandoning the ship*. An expression of hope for a better future has long been the phrase, "When our ship comes in...." The image, taken from the days before communication at sea was possible, is of seaside merchants scanning the horizon for any sign of the ship that months, or even years earlier, they had sent off with all their money and with high hopes of treasures being brought back from India, China, or Europe.

Jeter is an old French word that means *to throw*. Being thrown through the air is an extremely fast way to travel, so when *jet-propelled airplanes* were developed in the 1940s, *jet* was a good choice of a name because the rearward discharge of fluid, in effect, throws the airplane forward. In connection with jet airplanes, English acquired such words as *jetliner, jet set, jet-propelled,* and *jet lag*. The *jet stream* is a long current of high-speed winds that meander in a generally westward direction, sometimes going 250 miles an hour.

These newer words contrast with such older words as *jettison*, which is the action of throwing things away or sacrificing them as when a boat is overloaded and the cargo has to be *jettisoned. Flotsam and jetsam* (related to *float*) is a term describing trash floating in an ocean, while a *jetty* is a structure such as a wall or a wharf that has been "thrown" into a body of water to protect a harbor or a beach.

Other metaphorical uses are illustrated in the sentences below. Try to figure out the appropriate terms and write them in the blank spaces. Talk about the extended or metaphorical meanings as compared to the more literal meanings.

conveyed	jet-setter	one-track	pedal uphill	sailing
shipshape	train	train of thought	trim their sails	wheelie

1. Popping a _____ is easier on a bicycle than on a motorcycle.

2. His body language _____ more than his words.

3. Her bridal _____ is so long that two little girls will have to hold it up.

4. Mrs. Larson insists on having the room _____ before we leave.

5. From here on out, it should be smooth _____.

6. It is hard to get along with people if you have a _____ mind.

7. Having to row upstream is saying almost the same thing as having to _____.

8. They have to _____ if they want to stay out of bankruptcy.

9. She is such a _____ that I doubt she will be happy staying home with her new twins.

10. When you lose your _____, you get off track.

The Long Reach of *Tele*

Name: _____ **Period:** _____ **Date:** _____

Tele, the Greek root word for *far off* or *distant*, is seen in dozens of common English words. Galileo, a great astronomer, invented what is now called the *telescope*, which literally means *far seeing.* He first used the names *instrumentum* and *perspicillum*, but in 1611, he began using the word *telescope*, a name that had been invented by Prince Cesi, head of the Italian Academy.

PART I The human drive to reach out and extend our powers and our abilities is reflected in many new words connected to modern technology. See if you can figure out which of the following *tele-* words that describe fairly recent developments you should put in the following sentences.

> telecommuting   Telecopier®   telegenic   telemarketers   TelePrompTer®

1. A _____ is a piece of equipment that enables people to send facsimile copies of documents over telephone lines.

2. People are described as _____ if they use their computers to work from home.

3. The _____ is a device that unrolls a script in the enlarged type so that a television performer can appear to be looking at the audience while reading.

4. There are probably going to be new laws to control_____ because people are so tired of getting unwanted phone calls from salespeople.

5. People or types of programs that are _____ are inherently well suited to being on television.

PART II Look at the following fairly basic English words and talk about their meanings. Then see if you can think of how the underlined parts might be combined with *tele-* to make a new word that has something to do with distance.

> broad<u>cast</u>   em<u>pathy</u>   <u>graph</u>   mara<u>thon</u>   <u>phon</u>ics   <u>photo</u>   <u>type</u>writer   <u>vision</u>

These sentences will give you hints because each one can be completed with a *tele-* word related to the above concepts. Write your newly created words in the appropriate blanks.

1. Before e-mail and fax machines, newspapers received the latest breaking news on _____ machines that constantly printed news from the wire services.

2. In 1876 when Alexander Graham Bell invented the _____,
he used a name that had been in the language for 200 years to name anything that could carry sound.

3. People who claim skills in mental _____ say they can tell what people
are thinking or feeling even at a distance.

4. Spies who want to take pictures from a distance have_____ lenses on their cameras.

5. While a *broadcast* could be either on TV or radio, a _____ is specifically on television.

6. For practically two decades, Jerry Lewis conducted a _____ on
Labor Day weekend to raise money for Muscular Dystrophy victims.

7. When _____ was invented, people thought the radio was doomed to extinction.

8. If you need a written record, it is better to _____ a message than to telephone it.

PART III The oldest and the most commonly used *tele-* words have been given additional meanings. Read the following sentences and see if you can figure out which of
these terms to write in the blank spaces of these more metaphorical sentences.

telegraph	telegraphic	telephoto	telescope	telescope bag

I. Any contest that is really close might be described as a _____ finish, meaning
that people have to look carefully at the evidence to see who won.

2. Some baseball pitchers do not realize that their faces _____ the kind of pitch
they intend to throw.

3. A _____ is a suitcase that can be stretched out to hold more things.

4. In complicated books, authors often _____ time and events when relaying information from the past.

5. _____ speech is short and choppy based on the messages people send
when they have to pay by the word.

A Sports-Related Crossword Puzzle

Name: _____ **Period:** _____ **Date:** _____

Use these clues to fill in the crossword puzzle. After you have chosen the words, talk about the connections between the sports-related meanings of the words and the more metaphorical meanings in these sentences.

ACROSS

6. Grandparents make good _____ for kids.

8. The sun _____ across the ripples on the water.

9. The tutors in the Writing Center are now called _____.

DOWN:

1. There are _____ and losers in all aspects of life.

2. The kindergarteners were good _____ when the bus driver forgot to come for their field trip.

3. The Thanksgiving Day Parade is the _____ for Christmas shopping.

4. They decided to have one person _____ all the questions.

5. Sheila had to play _____ because she joined the choir just one week before the concert.

7. A book called *The* _____ *People Play* shows how friends insult each other.

Workshop 10.1: 1. baseball, **2.** baseball, **3.** basketball, **4.** football, **5.** baseball, **6.** basketball, **7.** could be all three, **8.** football, **9.** baseball, **10.** football.

Workshop 10.2: A: 1. throw in the towel, **2.** pull any punches, **3.** on the ropes. **B: 1.** against the current, **2.** jump off the deep end, **3.** out of my depth. **C: 1.** the inside track, **2.** jumped the gun, **3.** down to the wire, **4.** the long run, **5.** play catch-up, **6.** hurdles. **D: 1.** hit the spot, **2.** aim high, **3.** targeted. **E: 1.** straight arrow, **2.** arched, **3.** archer fish. **F: 1.** curve ball, **2.** ball park, **3.** hard ball. **G: 1.** an ace up his sleeve, **2.** shuffled, **3.** raw deal. **H: 1.** wheeler-dealer, **2.** no dice, **3.** poker face.

Workshop 10.3: A. Crown: Chancellor of the Exchequer, claim check, checked bags, checking account. **Checkered design:** checkered, Chinese checkers, checkered past. **B. Deer:** game warden, fair game, gamey smell, game preserve. **Board game:** game plan, Game Boy®, gaming tables. **C. Stage:** plays possum, the play, play the part. **Ball:** plays second violin, play book, can play chess.

Workshop 10.4: Air travel: flying high. **Water travel:** float, overboard, sailed through, float, high and dry, rock the boat.

Earth-based bravel: spinning his wheels, middle-of-the-road, on the wrong track, a fast pace.

Workshop 10.5: 1. drove, **2.** pilot study, **3.** helm, **4.** drover, **5.** autopilot, **6.** search engine, **7.** drivers, **8.** driven, **9.** pilot light.

Workshop 10.6: Part I: 1. channels, 2. journal, 3. rivals, 4. canals, 5. channel, 6. journey, 7. deposit. **Part II: 1.** road to ruin, **2.** fast lane, **3.** on track, **4.** Rocky Road, **5.** hitting the road, **6.** runways, **7.** trailblazer, **8.** runaway, **9.** wayward.

Workshop 10.7: 1. wheelie, **2.** conveyed, **3.** train, **4.** shipshape, **5.** sailing, **6.** one-track, **7.** pedal uphill, **8.** trim their sails, **9.** jet-setter, **10.** train of thought.

Workshop 10.8: Part I. 1. telecopier, **2.** telecommuting, **3.** TelePrompTer®, **4.** telemarketers, **5.** telegenic. **Part II: 1.** teletpe, **2.** telephone, **3.** telepathy, **4.** telephoto, **5.** telecast, **6.** telethon, **7.** television, **8.** telegraph. **Part III. 1.** telephoto, **2.** telegraph, **3.** telescope bag, **4.** telescope, **5.** telegraphic.

Workshop 10.9: Across: 6. cheerleaders, **8.** played, **9.** coaches. **Down: 1.** winners, **2.** sports, **3.** kickoff, **4.** field, **5.** catch up, **7.** games.

End-of-Chapter Activities

1. Choose a hobby or a sport that you enjoy playing, doing, or watching. Do you play chess or a musical instrument or take lessons in martial arts, gymnastics, cheerleading, dancing, or swimming? Maybe you are good at skateboarding or bicycle riding, or you play on a Little League team or a soccer team, or in some other sport. If so, ask yourself what words you know that people not in your activity might not know. Choose one term that your classmates probably do not know and figure out a way to explain it to either a small group or to the whole class. Try to think of a visual aid that you could use to help students remember what you teach them.

2. This chapter shows how sports have served as a source for words that refer to other things. However, many sports have also been the receivers of words taken from items or actions that were well known before the particular sport was developed. There were *baskets* before anyone thought of calling a game *basketball*; there were *bases* before people thought of calling a game *baseball*, and certainly people did many things with their feet before the game of *football* was named. Jot down several words that are used in relation to various games or sports and see if you can figure out the history of two or three of them. For example, look up the word *volley* in a dictionary and figure out how a *volleyball* got its name. What

about the *birdie* that is used in badminton and the *fly ball* in baseball or the *sack* in football?

3. Authors like to write stories about people going on trips because they have new adventures and meet different people. Here are the names of a few well-loved books that involve trips. Your classmates or your librarian could probably offer other ideas. Read a book about a trip. After you finish, go back and look for words relating to travel. Make a list of a half-dozen such terms. Try to find one that is used in an unusual or a metaphorical sense or one that you can use as the basis for a metaphor. Be prepared to tell your teacher and your classmates about the word.

Books for Older Readers

Abel's Island by William Steig. Farrar, Straus, 1976. Abel is a gentleman mouse who sets out to retrieve the scarf that blew away from his lovely fiancée. He was gone for more than a year.

Out of the Dust by Karen Hesse. Scholastic, 1996. It is the 1930s and Billie Jo lives in a dried-out part of Oklahoma. When her mother is killed in a terrible accident and her father is too consumed with grief to help Billie Jo, she decides to leave.

The Phantom Toll Booth by Norton Juster, illus. by Jules Feiffer. Random House. 1961. A mysterious package left in Milo's room turns out to contain a turnpike tollbooth. When Milo drives his miniature electric car through, he finds himself in a land that has enough wordplay to satisfy even the most ambitious reader.

Walk Two Moons by Sharon Creech. HarperCollins, 1994. During the course of an automobile trip across the United States, readers grow close to 13-year-old Sal and the grandparents, who have a special reason for taking her on a cross-country automobile trip.

The Watsons Go to Birmingham—1963 by Christopher Paul Curtis. Delacorte, 1995. A family from Michigan drives to their relatives in the South, only to get there in time to be part of the infamous church bombing.

Books for Younger Readers

The Gardener by Sarah Steward, illus. by David Small. Farrar, Straus & Giroux, 1997. A girl figures out a way to make life better when she is sent to live with an uncle who is less than cheerful.

Immigrants by Martin W. Sandler. HarperCollins, 1995. This nonfiction book uses Library of Congress photographs to tell the true stories of many travelers.

The Polar Express by Chris Van Allsburg. Houghton Mifflin, 1985. Christmas magic is at work in this travel story.

Tar Beach by Faith Ringgold. Crown, 1991. Eight-year-old Cassie Lightfoot lives in Harlem during the 1930s and magically flies from the roof of her apartment house over the George Washington Bridge and the Union Building.

CHAPTER ELEVEN

Sounds and Music

Background Reading for the Teacher

Because human and animal voices make many of the same sounds, it is not always easy to know whether particular words referred first to animal noises and later to human noises or the other way around. But speakers probably described pigs as *squealing* before they described girls as *squealing* over a rock star, roosters as *crowing* before they described boys as *crowing* over their athletic accomplishments, and wolves as *howling* before they described people as *howling* over funny jokes. It is also likely that people learned to *whistle* and to *sing* by imitating the sounds made by birds, and we know for sure that geese *honked* long before anyone invented cars and trucks with their *honking* horns.

With older or advanced students, you may want to also teach the Latin root *sonare* and the English word *sound*. *Sonar* is at the root

Twelve-year-old Kami brought in her saxophone when she made a class presentation talking about the naming of such fairly recent musical instruments as the saxophone, the sousaphone, the clarinet, and the tuba. On the left is a picture of various *bell*-metaphors made by 13-year-old June. This is a good chapter for shape-based posters illustrating metaphors based on such musical instruments as *drums, fiddles, pipes,* and *lyres.*

of such words as *supersonic* (faster than sound), *sonic boom, sonorous, sonata,* and *resonate.* English speakers use *sound* in such expressions as a *resounding success, a sounding board, sounding out* someone, and *to sound off.* In Workshop 11.1, where we are talking about a bell, we say "sound waves go back and forth from side to side." You could show advanced students how *reverberate* would be a more efficient word.

To keep the workshops fairly short, we treated *bells* and *whistles* separately, but in your discussion you might want to tie them together because they are among the oldest noisemakers that people have devised. They are easy to make and with surprisingly little effort can produce sounds that carry a long way. Because they are so common, the two were tied together in a metaphor that became popular in the 1970s. When something is described as having *bells and whistles*, it means that it is equipped with lots of frills or extras. If a family buys a new car and friends ask "What are the *bells and whistles*?" they are asking about the accessories. Does the car have a video player for passengers? Is there a computer that will print out maps when they are needed? Is there separate air conditioning for the different passengers? Does the car "speak" to the driver if it is left unlocked?

In addition to this metaphorical joining, bells and whistles are closer to each other in construction than most of us realize. A referee's whistle contains a *ball* inside that works like the *clapper* of a bell. As this ball clangs against the metal sides of the whistle, it changes the consistency of the sound so that it is more noticeable. If you have a plain whistle and one with a ball inside, you might bring them in and let students hear the difference in sound. When you talk about the *clapper* in a bell, lead students to see the relationship to people clapping their hands. *Bell* is thought to be related to the Old English word for *bellows*, the kind of bag that is used to blow air onto a fire to help it burn more quickly. A person *bellowing orders* is blowing out air, which is similar to the action of whistles.

Another *bell*-related term that you might want to teach to older or more mature students is *bellwether*. Many speakers think the term is somehow connected to weather forecasts. Actually, the word *wether* refers to the castrated sheep or goat that is acting as a leader of a flock. A bell would be tied to this leader, and by listening for the bell the sheepherder would know where the flock was going. As a comparison to this, people metaphorically allude to events or to individuals as *bellwethers* of things to come. For example, "We all hope that the events of September 11th are not a *bellwether* for the future."

When we taught this lesson, we took in lots of props, including the items that June drew on her poster and the *bell-bottom* pants that Arena is posing with. In relation to the end-of-chapter activity where we suggest that students make posters illustrating either the fable "The Boy Who Cried Wolf" or "The Belling of the Cat," we took in scraps of fur purchased at a remnant store. We also brought in some miniature bells. Our idea was that those who chose to illustrate "The Boy Who Cried Wolf" could use bits of wool and other fur, while those who illustrated "The Belling of the Cat" could each have a bell to tie into their picture. While the latter group did not mind having a bell to use, all the children wanted to glue on scraps of fur, so we ended up with pictures of

Nine-year old Arena had fun posing with bell-bottom pants as part of a discussion on whistles and bells. The picture at the top made by 13-year-old Salua illustrates the parable of "The Boy Who Cried Wolf."

monstrous-sized mice. This probably did not matter since the goal of helping the children remember the stories was undoubtedly achieved.

Because these stories are so easily remembered, this activity might be a good opportunity for students to practice their storytelling while using their posters as visual aids. It would be ideal if you could arrange for your students to go in pairs to retell the two stories to groups of three or four children in younger classrooms. The younger students could in turn choose short stories to read to your students.

Notes to Help Teachers Elicit Ideas from Students

The following sentences use sound-related metaphors. Lead students in talking about the meanings and then deciding what the sources are. Were the names originally used for sounds made by human voices? Or by animal "voices"? Or by something else such as a sound in nature or something that people made? Sample sentences are given here. If you make word strips of the italicized phrases, you can have students create other sentences. Talk about whether the sounds come from a HUMAN VOICE, an ANIMAL VOICE, or SOMETHING ELSE. Encourage students to make up alternate sentences using the terms in either their literal or metaphorical senses. Students might be more comfortable working with partners. When they share their sentences, talk about whether the usage is literal or metaphorical. As you move on to Workshop 11.1, you will probably want to continue to lead students to do the work out loud, as well as in writing, so they will get to hear the expressions several times.

1. Because of the *thunderous applause*, the group sang three encores.

2. Nearly every morning we hear the baby *babbling and gurgling* to herself.

3. She could *talk her grandparents out of anything*.

4. She was the victim of a *whispering campaign*.

5. He had such a funny look on his face that we *howled* with laughter.

6. She got to be a cheerleader without even knowing *the school yells*.

7. Ambitious young actors answer every *cast call* they learn about.

8. The crowd *roared its disappointment* when the concert was cancelled for fear of lightning.

9. The trip was *such a blast*, I hope we get to go next year.

10. "Don't come any closer!" *growled the angry man*.

11. The *Big Bang theory* is a fairly new idea about the origin of the earth.

12. We could hear the *grinding of the gears* as the trucks labored up the hill.

Bells

Name: _____ **Period:** _____ **Date:** _____

Read this information about bells carefully enough that you can figure out which of the following terms to write in the blank spaces. As you read, watch for metaphorical usages so that at the end you can write in the bell the names of five things that are not bells but are named for bells because of their shape.

PART I

| bell-bottom | bell captain | bell peppers | clapper | dumbbells |

Bells are made from an outside cover, usually made from metal, that is fitted with a loosely hanging piece, called a

(1.) _____. The cover is closed at the top and flares out at the bottom.

When the bell is moved so that the *clapper* hits or clangs against the sides, sound waves go back and forth from

side to side and then flow out the bigger bottom. Wind chimes are similar to bells except that the *clappers* hit each

other instead of the sides of a bell.

Some bells (*jingle bells* and *harness bells*) are shaped more like balls with holes in them. These may be the kinds

of bells from which **(2.)** _____ are named, or maybe the metaphor is based

on the fact that such peppers are empty and sometimes have little round pieces inside that resemble *clappers*.

In general, most things that are named after the shape of bells are flared out at the bottom as with

(3.) _____ *trousers*, *bell jars*, *bell flowers*, and even *thimbles*, which were

originally *bells* to be worn on people's thumbs and used to push dull needles through leather and heavy cloth. The

(4.) _____ that people use for lifting weights are heavy like iron bells, and

because of the way the different weights are added, they are also shaped somewhat like bells. However, unlike real

bells, they do not make a sound and hence are called *dumb*, meaning silent.

Bell-shaped curves are rounded on top and flared out at the bottom. If all the sixth-graders in your school take a

standardized test and the scores are shown on a chart, chances are that the scores will make a *bell-shaped* curve.

There will be a few people at one end who have earned really high scores and a few people at the other end who

have earned really low scores. The other scores will go gradually up to a middle rounded-off point.

Other uses of *bell* are based on actions related to bells. At hotels, *bellhops* come to help people with their luggage

when the **(5.)** _____ dings the little bell on his or her desk. Students might think that the cliché of being *saved by the bell* refers to a situation when the school bell rings just before the teacher assigns homework or asks a hard question. While the phrase works for such a situation, it originally came from boxing where each round lasts an exact number of minutes. Even if a boxer has been knocked out, if the bell rings before the referee has counted to ten, the knockout does not count.

PART II Look back through this information and find five things that are named because their shape is similar to that of a bell. Either write their names or draw a picture of them on the bell.

Figure 11.1 Bell-shaped items

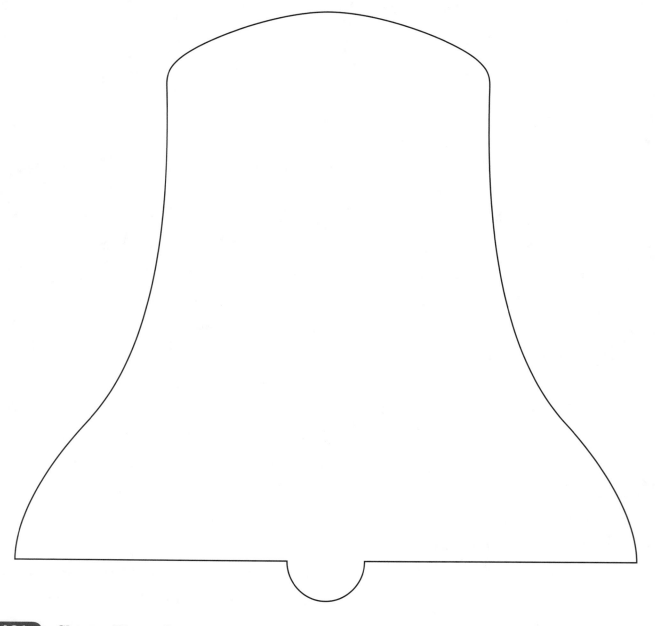

Whistles

Name: _____ **Period:** _____ **Date:** _____

Read this information about *whistles* carefully enough that you can figure out which of the following terms to write in the blank spaces. Afterwards talk about which ones are metaphors and which ones are referring to actual whistling. Also talk about the differences in the volume of sound made by such whistles as a bird whistle, a referee's whistle, a factory whistle, and a whistle made to warm a town of danger.

PART I

> **clean as a whistle**   **whistle**   **whistle in the dark**   **whistleblower**   **whistles**

To *whistle* is to make a shrill, clear sound by blowing or drawing air through puckered lips. People probably learned

to whistle by imitating the sounds of birds and the sound that the wind makes when on a stormy night it

(1.) _____ around buildings or through trees. Human-made whistles

range from simple wooden whistles carved from willows to the huge whistles that warn people of approaching trains

or that let people know that it is time to change shifts at a factory. Even bigger whistles are posted on the tops of fire

stations or on hills overlooking towns. They are there to sound out fire calls and warn people in a town of such dangers

as tornados or floods.

The small whistles that people used to carve from willows gave English such terms as *slick as a whistle* and

(2.) _____. The allusion is to the way that the bark on cut willows

slips free from the inner part of the branch so that the maker can cut out the part where the sound will resonate.

If you live in a town that is described as a *whistle stop*, you live in a town so small that a train would stop for passen-

gers only when it was signaled. Otherwise, it would just **(3.)** _____ and go on through.

Whistling is usually associated with good feelings as when in Walt Disney's *Snow White* movie, the seven

dwarfs *whistle while they work*. From this idea that *whistling* represents good feelings comes the expression to

(4.) _____meaning to keep up your courage by pretending to be brave even if you are afraid.

Newspaper headlines often refer to *whistleblowers*. These people do not really blow a whistle. They are being com-

pared to a referee or an umpire in a game who blows a whistle to stop play because someone has broken a rule. In a

company, a **(5.)** _____ is a person who alerts authorities or the press to the fact that

rules are being broken. Laws have been passed to protect such people from being punished or fired from their jobs.

The Human Voice

Name: _____ **Period:** _____ **Date:** _____

Voice is one of the oldest words we have in English. It has been traced clear back to the Sanskrit *vak*, which is the root word for *vocal, vocabulary, vocalize,* and *vociferous*. Our *vocation*, or our *calling* in life, is what we feel compelled to do. If you have *no voice* in matters, it means that you are unimportant, while if a group speaks *with one voice*, the people are showing their strength and their agreement. All of these words reflect on the importance that people ascribe to their voices.

Here are some other basic terms describing what people can do with their voices. Read the basic definitions and then choose the most appropriate terms to write in the blank spaces of the more metaphorical sentences. Read the completed sentences aloud and talk about what the extended meanings have in common with the basic meanings.

A. *To scream* is to produce a sudden high and sharp sound.

kicking and screaming	a scream	screamed to a halt

1. They were dragged _____ into the computer age.

2. The ferris wheel _____ when the manager saw the boy stand up.

3. The new Austin Powers movie is _____.

B. *To cry* is to call out loudly and sharply. It sometimes includes weeping and sobbing.

cried wolf	cries out	a crybaby

1. The story about the boy who _____ still teaches a good lesson.

2. The problem of homelessness _____ for a solution.

3. No child likes to be called _____.

C. *To sing* is to produce musical tones by using one's voice. People probably learned to sing from imitating birds.

to sing	sing-along	sing the praises

1. Having _____ movies is a new innovation.

2. Parents often _____ of their children.

3. It is against their code for criminals _____ on each other.

D. *To shout* is to utter a loud cry.

shout out	shout song	shouting distance

1. We're within _____ of each other—practically neighbors.

2. His clothes and hairstyle absolutely _____ for attention.

3. A _____ includes back-and-forth chanting between a preacher and the congregation.

E. *To talk* is to use one's voice for uttering words and communicating with others.

sweet talk	talk down	talked the man down	to talk it up

1. The police _____ from his perch on the bridge.

2. I hate to have teachers _____ to me.

3. You have got _____ or we won't get enough signatures.

4. She is so good at _____ that she can get anything she wants.

F. *To hum* is to make a continuous sound in the throat that more or less resembles the sounds that insects and some modern machinery make. Hearing *the dishwasher humming in the kitchen* could refer to either a person or an automatic dishwasher. The phrase that people pronounce as *hemming and hawing* is really *humming and hawing*, to mean that a speaker is stammering around instead of speaking forthrightly.

humdrum	humming with activity	hummingbirds

1. When _____ fly into our garage, we have to guide them out or they stay there and die.

2. So far, the program is pretty _____; we better get some new ideas.

3. Just before school starts every year, the mall is _____.

G. *To speak* is to use the vocal chords to talk. All normal humans are *speakers*, but some people get special titles if they speak for a group as does the *Speaker of the House* in Congress and the *spokesperson* or media representative for companies or institutions.

a loudspeaker	on speaking terms	speakers

1. They haven't been _____ for years.

2. Most cars now come equipped with stereophonic _____.

3. We need to set up _____ if we expect more than fifty people.

H. *Tone* is a word that could go either in this workshop or the next one because it is used to talk about both the human voice and the sounds of instruments. It comes from a Greek word meaning "to stretch," which is why people talk about *muscle tone*. In connection to talking or singing, people's tone is determined by how tightly they stretch their vocal chords. *Monotonous* speakers are those who go on and on in the same *tone*. If this is meant literally, such speakers do not raise or lower intonation patterns. If it is meant figuratively, they may have "an ax to grind" so they are always *harping* about the same old thing, or they might just never say anything interesting. *Tone* has been extended to refer to colors and emotions as well as to sounds.

baritone	tone	toner	tonettes

1. A _____ singer has a deep voice between bass and tenor.

2. In kindergarten we played _____.

3. The president is establishing a no-nonsense _____.

4. The copy machine needs some new _____.

I. *To call* is to talk loudly or to shout. It comes from an Old English word *hildecalla*, which was a call to battle. The term continues to have some of those same connotations. When we *call* people on the telephone, we are communicating over a distance, and when someone *calls out an alarm*, people quickly take action to protect themselves from whatever danger is at hand.

call the shots	call-in	call time-out	called on

1. Eugene always wants to _____.

2. In sports, people have to use body language to _____.

3. Some radio stations provide hours and hours of _____ talk shows.

4. The President _____ all Americans to make sacrifices.

Bands and Orchestras

Name: _____ **Period:** _____ **Date:** _____

There were probably *bands of robbers* before there were *bands of musicians;* nevertheless, when modern people hear the word *band* they are more likely to think of musicians than of robbers. *Band* is related to the word *bind,* and it refers to people *banding* or *bonding* together for a common purpose. It is the same root as used in such words as *headband, bandage,* and *bondage.* It came to be used in relation to music because before people knew how to amplify sound, it took many instruments and many people to make music loud enough to be heard by a crowd. The members of a *band* are bound together for an agreed-upon purpose.

   Orchestras are similar to bands except that they do not march, which means they can have more fragile instruments. The *conductor* of an orchestra is responsible for keeping the players together. From this comes the metaphorical use of the word *orchestrate,* which is used in such sentences as, "It is up to her manager to *orchestrate* a successful campaign," and "If they had planned it, they couldn't have *orchestrated* such confusion."

PART I The following terms are related to music as played by orchestras and bands. Read the basic definitions and then choose the most appropriate terms to write in the blank spaces of the more metaphorical sentences. Read the completed sentences aloud and talk about what the extended meanings have in common with the basic meanings.

A. *Phon* is the Latin and Greek root word for *voice* or *sound.* In English we use words made from *phon* to allude to many different kinds of sounds as when we talk on the *telephone* or play music on a *phonograph.*

> | phonics | saxophone | sousaphone | symphony |

1. John Philip Sousa's invention of the _____ helped him become known as "King of the March."

2. With the best _____ orchestras, the sounds blend so that the audience does not hear individual players, except when they have solos.

3. Antoine Sax was a Belgian instrument maker who in 1851 invented the _____.

4. When children study _____, they learn what sounds are represented by what letters.

B. *A concert* is a musical performance presented by a group of musicians. When the term is used metaphorically, the idea usually refers to people acting in harmony or in unison with each other.

> **concert grand**   **concerted**   **in concert**

1. They made the decision _____ with their relatives.

2. Counselors and teachers made a _____ effort to help those who were injured.

3. My uncle traded in his baby grand piano for a _____ and then couldn't get it through the door of his house.

C. *Harmony* is a word that is used in its most basic sense to describe the combination of musical notes that make up a chord. Its broader meaning, which has been extended to many aspects of life, is that of a pleasing combination of sounds, actions, beliefs, or things. In the mid-1800s, when groups of Americans began experimenting with communal styles of living, their hopes were shown in such names as New Harmony and Harmony Farms.

> **harmonica**   **harmonious**   **harmonize**   **harmony**

1. The meeting was far from _____ .

2. Paul Janeczko achieves _____ in his books because of the way he arranges the poems.

3. My mother tries to _____ the wall coverings and the drapes throughout our whole house.

4. I'm not very good at it, but I think it is fun to play a _____ .

D. *A drum* is a hollow container usually with a cover that resonates sound when it is hit. Players hit some drums with their hands, but more commonly they use sticks that range in size from large pencils to short baseball bats. The human *eardrum* works in much the same way as a musical drum, but most other uses of the word relate either to the shape of a drum or to the sound. If someone sets out *to drum up business,* the allusion is to the way that members of a circus band would parade through small towns beating a drum and announcing that a circus was coming to town. If someone is *drummed out* of a business or an organization, the allusion is to the old military custom of having a drum play while a disgraced soldier is expelled from the ranks.

beating the drum	brake drums	drum major	to drum

1. My _____ need new linings.

2. Our teacher tries in vain _____ grammar into our heads.

3. Our neighbor is always _____ for some cause.

4. The _____ is the leader of a marching band.

E. *Fiddles* are the common person's violin. They were to earlier generations what guitars are to today's young people. The cliché about *Rome burning while Nero fiddled* shows how long speakers have referred to *fiddling* as a kind of frivolous pastime. When people say *Oh fiddlesticks!* to imply that something is not worthy of serious consideration, they are making a similar comparison. Violins are harder to play and have more respect so that speakers do not use them in connection with trivial matters.

fiddler crabs	fiddles away	fiddling

1. Suzie just _____ her time.

2. _____ look like one arm is raised to play a violin.

3. I hate it when someone starts _____ with my hair.

F. *Pipes* and *flutes* have a similar kind of difference in connotation. *Pipes* are simpler instruments, while *flutes* are more complex because of their keys. They are associated with gracefully curved things. *Flute glasses* are tall, slender wineglasses. *Fluting* sewed onto clothing is gathered or pleated as with the big collars that were popular in the Middle Ages. *Piping*, on the other hand, is a straight piece of rolled cloth used to finish off edges as on men's tailored pajamas or cushions on a couch.

fluted	flutey	Pied Piper	piping

1. _____ columns are more graceful than plain columns.

2. If someone has a _____ voice, it is wavery in a musical way.

3. Our cheerleaders' costumes have contrasting _____ around the necks and the sleeves.

4. People worry that the Internet is a _____ leading young people astray.

G. *Lyres* are those symmetrical harps that are shown in pictures illustrating Biblical stories. This illustrates how old the *lyre* is. Another bit of evidence is how many lyre-based words English has as when the horns of impalas are described as *lyrate,* meaning they are shaped like a *lyre.*

| lyrebirds | lyrical | lyricist | lyrics |

1. A _____ is a person who composes song lyrics.

2. Karen Hesse's book *Out of the Dust* is written in a _____ style.

3. _____ have graceful tail feathers that remind people of the shape of a lyre.

4. A lot of people are upset about the _____ in today's rock music.

PART II Each of these sentences uses a word adapted from a musical instrument. Figure out what the instrument is and write its name on the blank space and then explain whether the metaphor is based on a similarity in shape or sound.

1. *Concertina wire* is barbed wire spread out in loose rolls to serve as a fortification.

_____

2. *Organ Pipe National Monument* is located in southern Arizona.

_____

3. If you have ever heard a *trumpeting elephant*, you won't forget it.

_____

4. The comic book store uses surplus *oil drums* as counters and dividers.

_____

5. Impalas have *lyrate* horns.

_____

6. At Mexican restaurants, *flautas* are one of my favorite foods.

_____

7. I wish people would quit *harping* about the dangers of body jewelry.

_____

8. I've never known anyone so quick to *blow her own horn.*

_____

A Musical Crossword Puzzle

Name: _____ **Period:** _____ **Date:** _____

Use these clues to fill in the crossword puzzle.

ACROSS

3. Most people don't like to listen to their friends _____ on the same old things.

5. Before music became popular on radio, people listened to music on _____.

9. The _____ of a meeting can be either social or business-like.

11. Nervous people sometimes have a habit of _____ their fingers on their desks.

12. _____ glasses are gently tapered out at the ends like the end of a flute.

DOWN

1. In early history, small groups of musicians would _____ together and travel from town to town to entertain people.

2. In 1846, Adolphe Sax invented the _____.

4. The _____ is the biggest instrument in a band. It is made from a long brass tube that winds around and flares out at the end.

6. To _____ something, a leader has to get people to work together and cooperate almost as if they are in an orchestra.

7. When your grandparents were young, they probably listened to music mostly on the _____.

8. If you have a feeling of _____ in a group, people are getting along and working well together.

10. People, motors, and some kinds of birds all _____.

Human voices: talk her grandparents out of anything, whispering campaign, the school yells, cast call. **Animal voices:** howled with laughter, roared its disappointment, growled the angry man. **Something else:** thunderous applause, babbling and gurgling, a blast, Big Bang theory, grinding of the gears.

Workshop 11.1: Part I: 1. clapper, 2. bell peppers, 3. bell-bottom, 4. dumbbells, 5. bell captain. **Part II:** bell peppers, bell jars, bell-shaped curves, bell flowers, thimbles, dumbbell weights.

Workshop 11.2: 1. whistles, 2. clean as a whistle, 3. whistle, 4. whistle in the dark, 5. whistleblower. The metaphors are #2 *clean as a whistle* and probably #4 *whistle in the dark*.

Workshop 11.3: A: 1. kicking and screaming, 2. screamed to a halt, 3. a scream. **B:** 1. cried wolf, 2. cries out, 3. a crybaby. **C:** 1. sing-along, 2. sing the praises, 3. to sing. **D:** 1. shouting distance, 2. shout out, 3. shout song. **E:** 1. talked the man down, 2. talk down, 3. to talk it up, 4. sweet talk. **F:** 1. hummingbirds, 2. humdrum, 3. humming with activity. **G:** 1. on speaking terms, 2. speakers, 3. a loudspeaker. **H:** 1. baritone, 2. tonettes, 3. tone, 4. toner. **I:** 1. call the shots, 2. call time-out, 3. call-in, 4. called on.

Workshop 11.4: Part I. A: 1. sousaphone, 2. symphony, 3. saxophone, 4. phonics. **B:** 1. in concert, 2. concerted, 3. concert grand. **C:** 1. harmonious, 2. harmony, 3. harmonize, 4. harmonica. **D:** 1. brake drums, 2. to drum, 3. beating the drum, 4. drum major. **E:** 1. fiddles away, 2. fiddler crabs, 3. fiddling. **F:** 1. Fluted, 2. flutey, 3. piping, 4. Pied Piper. **G:** 1. lyricist, 2. lyrical, 3. lyrebirds, 4. lyrics. **Part II.** 1. Concertina wire is SHAPED like the edges of the bellows part of a concertina (small round accordion). 2. Organ pipe cactuses grow straight up in a group SHAPED like organ pipes. 3. Trumpeting elephants SOUND like trumpets, only louder. 4. Oil drums are big containers SHAPED like drums. Steel drums from the Caribbean, are bringing the name full circle. 5. Lyrate horns are SHAPED like the edges of a lyre. 6. *Flauta* is Spanish for *flute*. Flautas are tortillas rolled and fried in the SHAPE of a flute. 7. When people are harping on something, they SOUND like a harp being played poorly. 8. Horns include trumpets, cornets, tubas, trombones, etc. SOUND is the basis for the metaphor.

Workshop 11.5: Across: 3. harping, 5. phonographs, 9. tone, 11. drumming, 12. flute. **Down:** 1. band, 2. saxophone, 4. tuba, 6. orchestrate, 7. radio, 8. harmony, 10. hum.

End-of-Chapter Activities

1. Choose one of the musical items talked about in this chapter and make a poster illustrating various metaphors that have come from it. A fairly easy way to make your point is to cut a piece of tag board into the shape of something like a bell, a whistle, a fiddle, a horn, a drum, or a lyre and then draw little pictures that you label or explain to show the metaphors.

2. If you play a musical instrument, make a report to the class on words that you know that other people probably do not know. Or you could take the opposite approach to the one we took in this chapter and make a report on how musical instruments were named from other sources. You could start with *horns*, which of course got their name from the horns of animals, which were among the first musical instruments people had. *Woodwind* instruments have wooden reeds that air goes through, while *stringed* instruments are equipped with special kinds of strings.

3. If you enjoy popular music, perhaps you could teach your classmates about words connected to electronic instruments, or you could do a study of the names of singing groups or bands. Many of them compete to see how unusual their names can be. They also invent unique spellings so that they can register their name as a trademark that no one else can use. John Lennon started the idea of unique spellings when he chose the name of *Bee-tles* to compete with *The Crickets*, a group that was already famous. He decided to spell *Beetles* as *Beatles* to make a pun on the *beat* in music. See if you can figure out the reason behind some modern names of groups.

4. Two of Aesop's fables are found on page 207. They have to do with the subjects of crying or calling out for help and using a bell or a whistle as a warning system. The stories are so well known that people often use just the titles to communicate the moral or lessons that the stories teach. Read the fables and talk about the lessons. Can you think of other ways that the same ideas could be expressed? Choose one of the stories on which to base a poster. Maybe you can use your poster to retell the story to a group of younger students or to someone at home.

Two Sound-Related Fables

THE BOY WHO CRIED WOLF

A young boy had the job of taking care of the sheep from his village. Every day he took them out into the hills where they could find fresh grass to eat. He generally enjoyed his job because there were many hours in which he could sit on a smooth rock and play his pipe or day-dream while he ate the good lunch his mother sent with him. But one day he grew bored and so he shouted as loudly as he could, "Wolf! Wolf!"

All the people from the village came running to help. The farmers brought pitchforks and axes, the housewives brought butcher knives and brooms. When they came running up to attack the wolf, the shepherd boy laughed with pleasure and said, "I fooled you!"

They scolded the boy and went back home disgusted. A few days later the boy pulled the same trick. Again, everyone came to help, only to be met by the laughing boy.

The very next day, a wolf really did come and begin to attack the sheep. The boy shouted "Wolf! Wolf!" No one came. The boy shouted again and again, but still no one came because they thought it was another of his tricks. The village lost many of its sheep that day and the boy lost his job.

Moral: Liars will not be believed even when they tell the truth.

THE BELLING OF THE CAT

A colony of mice was having a very hard time of it because they lived in the same house as a big and capable cat. The cat would sneak up on them so quietly that they would never know she was there until she had grabbed one of them and eaten it.

They gathered together in a great council to decide what to do. No one could think of a solution, until one young mouse had such a good idea that all the other mice clapped their paws for joy. The clever little mouse suggested that they tie a bell around the cat's neck. That way they would hear her coming and could run away before she had time to cause harm.

Amidst the general rejoicing at the solution to their problem, one very old mouse cleared his throat. When they all turned to listen to him, the wise old mouse complimented the young mouse for his suggestion. Then he solemnly asked, "Which one of us will tie the bell around the cat's neck?"

Moral: Before you offer a plan, think carefully as to whether it can be carried out.

CHAPTER TWELVE

Mythology and Names

Background Reading for the Teacher

Some of the world's most fascinating stories are the myths that have come down to us from ancient cultures. The myths from Africa, Australia, and the Americas are just as interesting as are the Norse, Greek, and Roman myths, but the latter ones have contributed the most words to English, so they are the ones we talk about in this chapter. Your school librarian will probably be able to loan you three or four books that can flesh out the stories we only hint at in this chapter. Books that we have found useful include Thomas Bulfinch's *Myths of Greece and Rome* (Penguin, 1981), the *D'Aulaires'* (Ingri and Edgar) *Book of Greek Myths* (Doubleday, 1962, paperback, 1989), and Leonard Fisher's *The Olympians: Great Gods and Goddesses of Ancient Greece* (Holiday, 1984). For the Norse stories, Mary Pope Osborne's *Favorite Norse Myths* (Scholastic, 1996) and Neil Philip's *Odin's Family: Myths of the Vikings* (Orchard, 1996) are good. Most dictionaries include basic information on the Greek and Roman names, but an overall guidebook would also be helpful. We used David Kravitz's *Who's Who in Greek and Roman Mythology* (Potter, 1976), but have also heard good things about two paperbacks: *Words from the Myths* by Isaac Asimov and illustrated by William Barss (Houghton Mifflin, 1961, paperback, 1989) and *Mini-Myths and Maxi-Words: English Vocabulary from Classical Mythology* by Susan K. Weiler (Longman Group, United Kingdom, 1991).

Students might wonder about the differences in the spellings of the various names of different gods. This presents an opportunity to discuss how in the days before the printing press was developed, writers had more freedom in how they spelled words because there were no dictionaries and no one to standardize spelling. In fact, the standardization of spelling was one of the first reasons that people made dictionaries.

PANDORA'S BOX

ATLAS

Seven-year-old Lauren and 10-year-old David enjoyed posing as Pandora and Atlas. Roman costumes are easy to put together if you have a supply of long shoelaces and lots of cloth.

Because myths were mostly shared orally by travelers who went from one country to another, it is to be expected that there are many different versions of them. And even when we try to match up the Greek gods to the Roman gods, we are oversimplifying because when stories are adapted into another culture, the nature of the characters changes along with the names. And in a "pure" sense, not all of the gods and goddesses are the sources of the words they are credited with because at least some of them (e.g., *Libertas* and *Psyche*) were probably given names that already had a meaning that fit with their personalities. Nevertheless, the fame of the stories and the vivid pictures they leave in people's minds have spread their names around the world.

Two or three generations ago, young people studied Latin and Greek and, as part of their studies, read the Roman and Greek myths in school. As a result, they were more familiar with the characters than are today's generation of young people. This meant they were likely to understand the allusions made to mythology in such brand names as *Argus* cameras (from the hundred-eyed giant) and *Mercury* cars (named after the messenger god and the ease with which he travels). They could relate more intimately with the silhouette of *Pegasus*, the winged horse that appears on Mobil gas stations, and with the name of the *Apollo* Space Mission, whose name NASA chose to make Americans think of handsome and heroic young men flying through the skies.

With these words, the problem of knowing whether to capitalize them is especially troubling. Of course, they are capitalized when they are used as the name of a planet, a day, a month, a trademark, or the name of something like the space program. But in other situations, they will be capitalized only when the source of the metaphor is widely recognized. For example, *erotic* and *matinee* are not capitalized, but *Herculean* and *Achilles' heel* will probably be capitalized. As with other eponyms, dictionaries can give you some guidance, but the opinions of editors also differ.

This is a good opportunity for art and drama. You might make word strips and let children choose which ones they want to illustrate and explain to the class. One of our student teachers did a wonderful mythology unit in which she let her sixth graders share a word-related story with their classmates. Some chose to draw a poster, while others told their story as a page from a comic book or a graphic novel. When we worked with one group, we brought in a small bag of feathers, which inspired students to focus on characters who fly including Hermes and Mercury, Pegasus, and Daedalus and Icarus.

Younger students enjoyed posing with props (see the photos on p. 208). Stories students seemed to remember the best included Iris sliding down a rainbow, Pandora opening the box, Sisyphus pushing his boulder up a hill, Hercules cleaning out the stables, Atlas holding the world on his shoulders, Achilles' mother holding him by his heel, and Tantalus standing in the water under the grapes.

As an end-of-chapter activity, we suggest that students look in the *Harry Potter* books for J. K. Rowling's allusions to Greek and Roman mythology. We point them to the following names, but they may find others. Various Websites also include information on names in the Potter books.

- Draco Malfoy's mother is named *NARCISSA* because she is almost as self-centered as was Narcissus, the young man who drowned because he was so enchanted with his own reflection.
- Percy named his owl *HERMES*, the Greek name of *Mercury*, the messenger god.
- *MINERVA McGonagall* is the smartest woman faculty member and assistant headmistress, so it is appropriate that she be named after *Minerva* (also *Athena*), the goddess of wisdom and the liberal arts.

When we taught a mythology unit to one group, we took in a bag of feathers from a craft shop. This tipped the popularity scales toward characters who flew including Pegasus, Mercury, Daedalus, Icarus, Apollo, and even Hermes, the messenger owl from the *Harry Potter* books.

• *Madame MAXIME OLYMPE,* the headmistress from Beauxbaton, like Hagrid, is half giant. Her name appropriately alludes to her size and to Mt. Olympus, the home of the gods.

• *SIRIUS Black* is the animage of Harry's godfather, who appears as a giant black dog. *Sirius* is the hunting dog of Orion, the brightest star in the sky, as seen in the *Canis Major* constellation.

Gifted students, who have read the books several times, might also point out that Rowling has included such characters from the myths as a *centaur*, a *chimaera*, a *hippocampus,* and a *griffin* as in the name of *Gryffindor House*. For other ideas about teaching vocabulary related to the *Harry Potter* books, see our article, "Lessons in the Teaching of Vocabulary from September 11 and Harry Potter" in the *Journal of Adolescent and Adult Literacy* 46:3 (November, 2002).

Toward the end of this chapter, we added two workshops on eponyms: one about words taken from the names of real people and one about words taken from the names of places. Our purpose was to show the continuing nature of the eponymic process. To be even more current, you could mention such coined terms as the Los Angeles police being accused of having a *John Wayne* syndrome (for shooting suspects), of people undergoing *trial-by-Oprah* (being judged in the media as if on a talk show), and of belligerent men being called *Rambo* (after the hero of the movies starring Sylvester Stallone). Only time will tell whether such coinages will find their way into dictionaries.

The area or the person who is "honored" with an eponym is not always the one who deserves it. King James was not the one who did the work or even had the idea of translating the *King James Bible*, nor did Pope Gregory XIII figure out the astronomy and the mathematics for the *Gregorian calendar,* which corrected the inaccuracies of the *Julian calendar*. Another unfairness is that people do not get to choose what their names will be remembered for. Dr. Joseph Lister (1827–1912), who developed the concept and the methodology of antiseptic surgery, wanted to go down in history as the founder of the Lister Institute of Preventive Medicine. Instead, his name is most often spoken when people talk about *Listerine* mouthwash, a commercial product, which he was unsuccessful in keeping from using his name.

Another example of how people lose control over their own names is what happened to General Ambrose Burnside of Civil War fame. He is the man who made cheek whiskers fashionable. The style was first referred to as *Burnsides*, but since the whiskers are on the sides of people's faces, speakers not familiar with General Burnside turned the word around and made *sideburns* a part of the English language.

Notes to Help Teachers Elicit Ideas from Students

Americans are, in general, more familiar with the stories from Greek and Roman mythology than from Norse mythology. Nevertheless, the Danish Vikings who invaded England in 789 brought with them many of their beliefs and customs; one of these was a system of counting by *twelves*. English speakers most likely adapted the Old Frisian word *twelf* into English *twelve* and also borrowed such customs as *twelve* inches to a foot, *twelve* items in a dozen, and *twelve* men to a jury from these northerners. Old English speakers also took the names of four days of the week from Old

Norse. While *Saturday* honors Saturn, the Roman god of harvest, and *Sunday* and *Monday* honor the Sun and the Moon, the other four days of the week honor the following Norse gods.

Tiu (sometimes spelled *Tiw* or *Ty)* is a son of Odin and a great warrior.
Woden (sometimes spelled *Odin*) is the highest of the Norse gods, sometimes called "The Father of the Universe."
Thor (sometimes spelled *Tor*) is the Norse God of Thunder. He drives a chariot pulled by two giant billygoats across the sky, thus causing thunder.
Freya is a highly revered goddess in Norse mythology. She was allowed to choose for herself half of all the warriors who were killed in battles.

Write the names on the board and help students match the names of the gods to "their" days, perhaps by writing the names of the gods and a little description of *Tiu* by Tuesday, of *Woden* by Wednesday, of *Thor* by Thursday, and of *Freya* by Friday. This is a good place to talk about how speakers "round off" or simplify pronunciation to match their own kind of speaking. For example, it is easier for English speakers to pronounce the fewer syllables in *Wednesday* than in *Woden'sday* and in *Friday* than in *Freya'sday*.

You might also talk about how all the planets except the earth are named for various gods as in this list, which goes from the closest to the farthest from the sun:

Mercury is named for the Roman messenger god, whose Greek name is *Hermes*.
Venus is named for the Roman goddess of love, who is also "honored" by having her name in *venereal disease*. Her Greek counterpart, *Aphrodite*, has her name in *aphrodisiac*.
Mars is the "red planet," and so was named for the god of war, whose name is also seen in such terms as *martial law* and *martial arts*.
Jupiter is the largest planet and so is named for the chief Roman god.
Saturn is named for the Roman god of agriculture, who was the father of Jupiter.
Uranus, the seventh planet out from the sun, is named for a god who was personified as the sky and was the father of the *Titans*.
Neptune, the eighth planet, is named for the god of the sea, who was also known as *Poseidon*.
Pluto, the farthest planet out from the sun was given one of the names of *Hades*, the god of the underworld. A few other minor characters also had the name of Pluto, but the Pluto that most U.S. children know is the dog with the funny tail in Disney cartoons.

Place names are another interesting possibility for talking. *Pomona*, California is named after the Roman goddess of fruit trees, while both *Athens*, Greece and *Athens*, Ohio are named for Athena, the Greek goddess of wisdom and the liberal arts. *The Olympics* are named for *Mt. Olympus*, which was the home of the gods, and the *Capitol* buildings that are the pride of each U.S. state are named for the famous Roman temple that was dedicated to Jupiter. It is because of this heritage that it is spelled with an *o* instead of an *a* as in such terms as *capital punishment, capital expenses,* and *decapitation*, which all refer to the kind of *capital* that means "chief" or "head."

Words from the Myths

Name: _____   **Period:** _____   **Date:** _____

Read these descriptions about some of the Greek or Roman gods and goddesses. Look at the derived words and the sentences that follow each set. Choose the appropriate words to write in the blank spaces. Talk about the relationships between the characters and show what the words taken from the mythological names now mean.

PART I

Achilles was a baby god whose mother dipped his body into the River Styx because the water of this river was supposed to provide lifelong protection. However, because she held him by his heel, this part of his body was not protected. And as any good storyteller would predict, Achilles was killed in battle when an arrow pierced his heel.

Eros is the Greek name for the god the Romans called *Cupid*. These gods are credited with shooting arrows of love to make people fall in love.

Hercules was one of the great heroes—half god and half human. To prove his worthiness, he was given some very demanding tasks, including cleaning out the Aegian stables.

Matuta is the Roman goddess of the morning. French speakers adapted her name to *matin*, for morning. English speakers use a related name to describe something that happens during the day instead of at night.

| **Achilles heel** | **erotic** | **Herculean** | **matinee** |

1. Vanity is her _____; she can be flattered into doing anything.

2. We can save money by going to the _____.

3. We thought the movie was going to be a comedy, but it turned out to be an _____ love story.

4. It is a _____ task to pick up all the trash after the college football games.

PART II

Pandora was the first mortal woman. She was fashioned by clay and each of the gods gave her a present such as beauty, music, homemaking skills, and charm. Zeus, however, gave her a box that she was forbidden to open. She was so curious about it that she opened it anyway and out came all the plagues of the world including sickness, discouragement, jealousy, and cruelty. All that was left in the box to help humankind was hope.

Arachne was a mortal who was so skilled at weaving that she challenged Athena to a contest. People expected that she would be put to death for her lack of humility, but Athena was so impressed with her skill that, instead of killing her, she changed her into a spider so that she and all her descendants could go on weaving. Ever since, spiders have been known as *arachnids*.

Atlas led the Titans in a fight against Zeus and was punished by having to hold up the earth. Pictures of him holding the world above his head were so often shown on books of maps that his name became intimately connected with maps.

Ceres is the Roman goddess of agriculture and so her name is connected with food made from grains.

Tantalus was one of Zeus's sons who, for a variety of misdeeds, was punished by having to stand in water up to his neck, from which he could not drink. A beautiful clump of grapes hung over his head, but the minute he would reach for them with his mouth, they would retreat.

arachnids	atlas	cereal	Pandora's box	tantalizing

1. Going to the mall instead of to soccer practice was a _____ proposition.

2. Zoologists classify spiders, scorpions, mites, and ticks as _____.

3. On summer vacations, I am the one in charge of the family's road _____.

4. The committee refused to tell because they did not want to open a _____.

5. What would breakfast be like if we didn't have _____?

PART III

Narcissus was a beautiful young man who loved himself so much that when he saw his reflection in a pool he leaned over to hug himself and thereby drowned. In his memory, a beautiful flower called the *narcissus* sprang up by the pond. It grows from a bulb, which means it comes up year after year.

Echo is the name of a beautiful young maiden who loved Narcissus. Once when Hera thought that Echo was telling a lie, she took away her ability to speak so that Echo can only repeat what others say. When Narcissus drowned, Echo was so sad that she stayed out in the wilderness where if you listen carefully you can still hear her voice.

Juno Moneta (more commonly called just *Juno*) was the wife of Jupiter and Queen of the heavens. The Temple of Moneta, named in her honor, was later changed to a place where money was made, and she was called the Goddess of Finance. Coins were called *moneta*, which the French changed to *moneai* and the English to *money*.

| echo | June | money | narcissism |

1. In northern hemispheres, _____ is such a pleasant month that it seems appropriate for it to be named after the wife of Zeus.

2. I love yelling my name in canyons and then hearing it _____ back.

3. Psychiatrists use the term _____ for people who are self-centered.

4. I'm not sure I believe the old saying that the love of _____ is the root of all evil.

PART IV

Gemini was the name given to Castor and Pollux, the twins, who have a constellation named after them. People used to swear "By Gemini," meaning they were swearing double.

Pan was a Greek satyr who was part man and part goat. When young maidens were out in the woods, he would chase them and cause great confusion and fright.

Orpheus was the god of the underworld who loved music and so is honored in Jacques Offenbach's opera, *Orpheus and the Underworld*.

Midas was a mythical Greek king who was granted his wish that whatever he touched would turn to gold.

| Gemini 6 and 7 | Midas touch | Orpheum | panic |

1. In 1938, widespread _____ set in when people mistook a radio broadcast of Orson Welles' science fiction thriller "The War of the Worlds" for a true news account.

2. In 1965, _____ space crafts (which each held two astronauts) were the first to rendezvous in space.

3. In the 1990s, some corporation executives mistakenly thought that they had the _____.

4. In the early days of movie theaters, nearly every town had an _____ theater.

Multiple Words

Name: _____ **Period:** _____ **Date:** _____

The names of these gods are even more productive than the ones in the last workshop. As you will see, they each gave us multiple words. Use the meanings and the grammatical clues to choose the best words to write in each space.

A. *Vulcan* is the Greek god of blacksmiths and is always shown working at his forge, which includes a hot fire to use when he shapes iron. It is easy to see why people thought of a god and his powerful forge when they saw *volcanoes*.

volcanic	volcano	vulcanized	vulcanology

1. The study of volcanoes is known as _____.

2. It was a big surprise when in 1980 Mt. St. Helens spewed out _____ ash.

3. The automobile industry would not have been such a success without _____ rubber.

4. A person with a _____ personality is unpredictable.

B. *Eos* was the Greek goddess of the dawn. A celebration called *Easter* was held for her every spring.

east	Easter	easterly

1. _____ was already a Greek holiday before the Christians developed a spring holiday to honor the resurrection of Jesus Christ.

2. All around the world the sun rises in the _____.

3. Ships that want to go in an_____ direction need to watch for where the sun rises.

C. *Iris* is the Roman messenger goddess who slides down to earth on a rainbow. Because rainbows are so colorful, her name is often associated with colorful things as when Spanish speakers call a rainbow *arco iris*.

iridescent	iris	irises

1. A new kind of contact lens changes the color of people's _____.

2. Something that is _____ reflects different shades of color, almost like a rainbow.

3. An _____ is a large showy and colorful flower that blooms in the spring.

D. *Libertas* was the goddess of liberty for all Roman people.

liberation	libertarian	liberty

1. A _____ is a person who believes that governments should be smaller.

2. The women's _____ movement has worked to give women more freedoms.

3. A democracy tries to provide _____ for all.

E. *Mercury* is the Roman messenger of the gods. He is usually pictured wearing a winged hat and winged sandals. His Greek names is *Hermes*.

mercurial	Mercury	mercury

1. _____ is a well-chosen logo for flower shops that promise immediate long distance delivery.

2. Because _____ clings together and goes sliding across smooth surfaces, it is informally called *quicksilver*.

3. A person with a _____ personality jumps from one mood to another.

F. *Janus* is the Greek god of doors, meaning that he is in charge of entering and exiting places. In this way he represents beginnings and endings and is often shown with two faces, one looking backwards and one looking forwards.

janitor	January	Janus-faced

1. At your school the _____ carries the keys and is in charge of locking the doors.

2. Someone accused of being _____ is insincere or two-faced.

3. The holiday when we "ring out the old and ring in the new" comes at the first of _____.

G. *The Sirens* were sea nymphs, part bird and part human, who with their beautiful singing would lure sailors to their deaths. Odysseus and his men had been warned about them and so did not succumb.

air raid sirens	siren	sirenians

1. Biologists classify sea mammals including sea cows and dugongs as _____.

2. A _____ song is sung in a seductive manner, probably by a beautiful woman.

3. Police sirens and _____ warn people away from danger.

H. *Saturn* was the Roman god of agriculture and for a while was ruler of the earth.

Saturday	Saturn	Saturnalia

1. _____ is the only day of the week named after a Roman god.

2. _____ is an ancient holiday in which the workers get to be bosses.

3. In 1969, the giant U. S. _____ V rocket launched the *Apollo ll* command module to the moon.

I. *Morpheus* was the Greek god of form, shapes, and dreams.

amorphous	morphine	morphology	to morph

1. Characters are able _____ in the *Animorph* books and in "The Mighty Morphin Power Rangers" cartoons.

2. Something _____ is without form.

3. _____ is what this book is about; it is the study of how words change their forms.

4. People suffering from pain are given _____ to help them sleep and have better dreams.

J. *The Muses* are the Roman goddesses of the fine arts. Some stories talk about nine muses while other stories talk about three.

amusement	amusing	museums	music	to muse

1. Disneyland has forever changed the concept of _____ parks.

2. The _____ of the world are treasure houses of what people value.

3. It is easy to understand why lonely shepherds liked to have flutes to play their own _____.

4. It seems easier _____ on a problem if you are in a natural and peaceful setting.

5. The movie wasn't anything special, but it was _____.

Eponyms from Real People

Name: _____ **Period:** _____ **Date:** _____

Even though the myths provide one of the fullest examples of how speakers take names that they happen to know and apply them to other concepts, something similar happens with the names of real people. Sometimes these names are so old that modern speakers do not recognize a connection. For example, Godfrey Derrick was an executioner in England in the late 1500s. He took pride in the building of elaborate wooden towers from which he is said to have hung thousands of people. Today, the tall structures that are used to hoist heavy loads and to support the drilling of oil wells are called *derricks* "in honor" of this infamous hangman.

The contributions made by the people described below have been more positive. Read the descriptions and then think about these people's names and see if you can figure out the eponym that is based on each name. If you are stumped on any of them, talk to your classmates. All of the items except number 4 are common, and you can probably guess what people would prefer to call this disease as opposed to the three hard-to-pronounce words that are in medical dictionaries. Write what you think the words are in the blank spaces.

1. *Sylvester Graham*, a young U.S. Presbyterian minister, frequently spoke out during the 1830s on the health benefits of using whole wheat flour. _____

2. *Louis Pasteur* was a French chemist who in the 1880s invented a process to destroy living organisms in milk and other foods. _____

3. *Jules Leotard* was a famous French acrobat who in the early 1900s wore tight-fitting one-piece costumes. _____

4. *Lou Gehrig* was a beloved baseball player who in 1941 died from a kind of spinal paralysis officially known as amyotrophic lateral sclerosis. _____

5. *Jean Nicot* was a French diplomat and scholar who died in 1600. *Nicot's herb* was the first name for several kinds of tobacco. _____

6. *Dr. Henry Heimlich* still lives in Cincinnati where he is a medical doctor. When he was in his mid-fifties, he designed and publicized a method of saving people from choking. His name has become famous around the world. _____

Eponyms from Places

Name: _____ Period: _____ Date: _____

PART I The names of items that hundreds of years ago were durable enough to be shipped across oceans are naturally the ones that made their way into various languages. Cloth was one of these items as were some kinds of food and drink. See if you can choose from this list the names of the cities or regions that supplied the following items to the world. Write them in the blank spaces. You will notice that as English speakers around the world began using the words, they simplified spelling and pronunciation so that the names you write in the blank spaces will not be exactly the same as the name of the item.

> **Calcutta, India**   **Champagne, France**   **China**
> **Madras, India**   **Oporto, Portugal**   **Parma, Italy**

1. For centuries exquisitely fine pottery has been shipped around the world from _____.

2. *Calico cloth* is inexpensive cotton made in _____ since the 1500s. It was often decorated with bright designs, so that plants and animals that are mostly white but splotched with colors are called *calico* as in the famous children's poem about *the gingham dog and the calico cat*. Black crappie fish are called *calico bass* while a kind of mountain laurel is called *calico bush*.

3. *Port wine* has been shipped from _____ since the 1600s. It is a dark red wine, so the kinds of red birthmarks that some people have are called *port wine stains*. The most famous is the mark that Russia's former leader Mikhail Gorbachev had on his forehead.

4. Since the 1500s, *parmesan cheese* has been shipped from _____. It is harder than most kinds of cheese and so does not mold or spoil on long ocean voyages.

5. _____ is the home of *madras* cloth, which is soft cotton with plaids of stripes woven in. Because of its deep colors, it has been popular for bedspreads and tablecloths.

6. Farmers from the province of _____ protested when a perfume company named one of its fragrances *champagne*. The company had to change the name of its perfume because that name can only be used for champagne produced in that place.

PART II The eponyms in these examples relate not so much to the actual items being shipped as to recipes or designs from one place being adopted into other places. Read the sentences and then choose the appropriate name to write in the blank spaces. Talk about which ones are fairly recent as opposed to being centuries old. Also talk about which ones are related to items that originally came from the geographical area being mentioned as opposed to being simply an idea associated with the region.

Alaska	Bermuda	Bikini	Denver	Dutch
Hamburg	Harvard	Milan	Scotch	Swiss

1. This ethnic group is known for being thrifty and so a _____ treat is one in which each person pays his or her own bill.

2. A _____ swimsuit is named for one of the Marshall Islands. The people living in the area, which played a crucial part in World War II in the 1940s, probably swam with little clothing, but it is doubtful that their suits resembled today's carefully manufactured swimsuits.

3. Dotted _____ cloth is lightweight (almost see-through) except for the little flecks that are put on in such a way that they reminded speakers of Swiss cheese.

4. Baked _____ is hard-frozen ice cream covered in meringue (whipped egg whites) and quickly toasted in a hot oven. When it is served, the outside is browned but the inside is still frozen.

5. A _____ omelet might also be called a *western omelet*. It will be spiced with tomatoes, green peppers, cheese, and maybe picante sauce.

6. This is another group with a reputation for being thrifty and so the 3M company chose _____ *Tape* as the name for a product they planned to advertise as a bargain.

7. _____ shorts are so fashionable in this part of the world that men wear them even for such formal events as weddings.

8. _____ is a city in Italy that was such a center of high fashion during the 1500s that it gave its name to *milliners*, people who make hats.

9. _____-ers do not contain ham. Instead they are made from meat that has been ground in a manner made famous by German butchers.

10. _____ beets got their name because the chef who figured out the recipe thought they were the same color as the uniforms worn by the band and the football team at this famous university.

A Mythological Crossword Puzzle

Name: _____ **Period:** _____ **Date:** _____

Use these clues to fill in the crossword puzzle.

ACROSS

2. People would probably rather live in a town named for _____, the goddess of wisdom and homemaking arts, than in a town named after the god of war.

3. The _____ was named for powerful giants called Titans.

6. Out in mountains and canyons, people can still hear the voice of _____, who can only repeat what other people have just said.

7. _____ was the supreme Roman God; the Greeks called him Zeus.

9. The other name for Eros is _____.

10. The U.S. _____ space program sent twelve astronauts to the moon.

DOWN

1. The god of war is _____, as alluded to in the phrase martial arts.

2. Spiders are called arachnids after _____.

4. Ceres is the goddess of grains who is honored by having_____ named after her.

5. A _____ looks like a gigantic forge for Vulcan, the god of fire and metalworking.

7. A modern day_____ is the keeper of the keys much like Janus was for the gods.

8. The _____ of the eye is the most colorful part of our bodies, so it reminds people of this goddess who slides to earth on a rainbow.

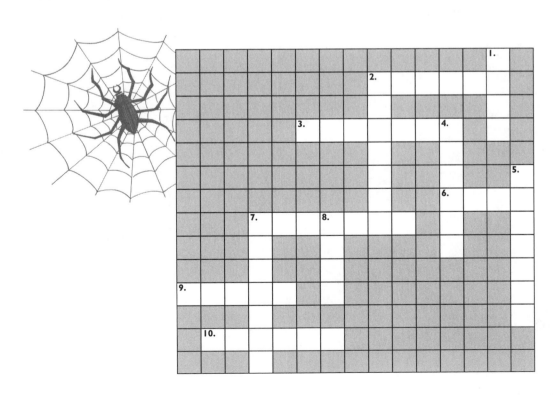

Workshop 12.1: Part I. 1. Achilles heel, **2.** matinee, **3.** erotic, **4.** Herculean. **Part II. 1.** tantalizing, **2.** Arachnids, **3.** atlas, **4.** Pandora's box, **5.** cereal. **Part III. 1.** June, **2.** echo, **3.** narcissism, **4.** money. **Part IV. 1.** panic, **2.** Gemini 6 and 7, **3.** Midas touch, **4.** Orpheum.

Workshop 12.2: A. 1. vulcanology, **2.** volcanic or volcano, **3.** vulcanized, **4.** volcanic. **B. 1.** Easter, **2.** east, **3.** easterly. **C. 1.** irises, **2.** iridescent, **3.** iris. **D. 1.** libertarian, **2.** liberation, **3.** liberty. **E. 1.** Mercury, **2.** mercury, **3.** mercurial. **F. 1.** janitor, **2.** Janus-faced, **3.** January. **G. 1.** sirenians, **2.** siren, **3.** air-raid sirens. **H. 1.** Saturday, **2.** Saturnalia, **3.** Saturn. **I. 1.** to morph, **2.** amorphous, **3.** morphology, **4.** morphine. **J. 1.** amusement, **2.** museums, **3.** music, **4.** to muse, **5.** amusing.

Workshop 12.3: 1. graham crackers, **2.** pasteurization, **3.** leotards, **4.** Lou Gehrig's disease, **5.** nicotine, **6.** the Heimlich maneuver.

Workshop 12.4: Part I: 1. China, **2.** Calcutta, India, **3.** Oporto, Portugal, **4.** Parma, Italy, **5.** Madras, India, **6.** Champagne, France. **Part II: 1.** Dutch, **2.** Bikini, **3.** Swiss, **4.** Alaska, **5.** Denver, **6.** Scotch, **7.** Bermuda, **8.** milliners, **9.** Hamburg, **10.** Harvard. **The newest names** are Bikini swimsuit, Baked Alaska, Denver omelet, Scotch Tape, and Harvard beets. The only items that are actually products of the areas that appear in the names are Bermuda shorts and Denver omelets.

Workshop 12.5: Across: 2. Athena, **3.** Titanic, **6.** Echo, **7.** Jupiter, **9.** Cupid, **10.** Apollo. **Down: 1.** Mars, **2.** Arachne, **4.** cereal, **5.** volcano, **7.** janitor, **8.** iris.

End-of-Chapter Activities

1. If you have read the *Harry Potter* books, you might enjoy looking for the way J. K. Rowling has named some of her characters with words from the myths. The giant spider that Hagrid cares for is named *Aragog*. This is probably a combination from *Arachne* and *gog*, a word meaning giant. Other puzzlers for you to try to figure out include why she named Draco Malfoy's mother *Narcissa*, why she had Percy name his messenger owl *Hermes,* and why Professor McGonagall's first name is *Minerva*. What is behind the names of Madame *Maxime Olympe*, the headmistress at the Beauxbatons school, and *Sirius Black*, the animage of Harry's godfather?

2. The book that won the 2001 Newbery Medal is *A Single Shard* by Linda Sue Park (Clarion/Houghton Mifflin, 2000). You would probably enjoy reading this exciting story about the making of fine pottery in Korea. It relates to the concept of eponyms by illustrating how they are often a matter of luck. Judging from the pottery-making skills of these ancient Koreans, today we could as easily be eating off from *Korea* as off from *China*.

3. Figure out a way to teach the meanings of one of the words from the myths to your classmates. You might do it through storytelling or by making a poster or bringing a visual aid or a costume from home.

Bibliography

Agee, Jon. *Who Ordered the Jumbo Shrimp? and Other Oxymorons*. New York: Harper Collins, 1998.

Allen, Janet. *Words, Words, Words: Teaching Vocabulary in Grades 4-12*. York, ME: Stenhouse, 1999.

Amende, Coral. *Famous Name Finder: Concise Biographies of Over 10,000 Legendary People*. New York: Random House, 1999.

Ammer, Christine. *Fruitcakes and Couch Potatoes and Other Delicious Expressions*. New York: Penguin, 1995.

Barnette, Martha. *Ladyfingers and Nun's Tummies: A Lighthearted Look at How Foods Got Their Names*. New York: Random House, 1997.

Braham, Carol, et al. *The Maven's Word of the Day Collection: Word and Phrase Origins from "Akimbo" to "Zydeco."* New York: Random House, 2002.

Carnicelli, Thomas. *Words Work: Activities for Developing Vocabulary, Style, and Critical Thinking*. Portsmouth, NH: Boynton/Cook/Heinemann, 2001.

Chase, Morgan. *Word Smart: A Visual Vocabulary Builder*. New York: Random House, 2001.

Claiborne, Robert. *Loose Cannons, Red Herrings, and Other Lost Metaphors*. New York: W. W. Norton, 1988.

Ehrlich, Eugene. *You've Got Ketchup on Your Muumuu: An A-to-Z Guide to English Words from Around the World*. New York: Henry Holt, 2000.

Evans, Cheryl, and Anne Millard. *Greek Myths and Legends*. London, England: Usborne Books, 1985.

Falletta, Nicholas. *The Paradoxicon*. New York: John Wiley, 1983.

Fromkin, Victoria, and Robert Rodman. *An Introduction to Language*. 3rd ed. New York: Holt, Rinehart and Winston, 1983.

Frye, Northrop. *Anatomy of Criticism: Four Essays*. 10th ed. Princeton, NJ: Princeton University Press, 1990.

Funk, Charles Earle. *"A Hog on Ice" and Other Curious Expressions*. New York: Harper and Row, 1948.

———. *"Heavens to Betsy" and Other Curious Expressions*. New York: Harper and Row, 1955.

Gwynne, Fred. *A Chocolate Moose for Dinner*. New York: Aladdin/Simon and Schuster, 1976.

———. *The King Who Rained*. New York: Aladdin/Simon and Schuster, 1970.

———. *A Little Pigeon Toad*. New York: Aladdin/Simon and Schuster, 1988.

Hendrickson, Robert. *The Henry Holt Encyclopedia of Word and Phrase Origins*. New York: Henry Holt/Owl Book, 1990.

Hofstadter, Douglas R. *Gödel, Escher, Bach: An Eternal Golden Braid*. New York: Vintage, 1980.

Holman, C. Hugh, and William Harmon. *A Handbook to Literature*. 6th ed. New York: Macmillan, 1992.

Hook, J. N. *Family Names: How Our Surnames Came to America*. New York: Macmillan, 1982.

Johnson, Dale D. *Vocabulary in the Elementary and Middle School*. Boston: Allyn and Bacon, 2001.

Jones, Charlotte Foltz. *Eat Your Words: A Fascinating Look at the Language of Food*. New York: Delacorte, 1999.

Jung, Carl G. *Four Archetypes: Mother, Rebirth, Spirit, Trickster*. Princeton, NJ: Princeton University Press, 1959.

Kirkpatrick, Betty. *Clichés: Over 1500 Phrases Explored and Explained*. New York: St. Martin's Press, 1996.

Knowles, Elizabeth. *The Oxford Dictionary of Phrase, Saying, and Quotation*. Oxford, England: Oxford University Press, 1998.,

Lakoff, George. *Women, Fire, and Dangerous Things: What Categories Reveal about the Mind*. Chicago, IL: University of Chicago Press, 1987.

Lakoff, George, and Mark Johnson. *Metaphors We Live By*. Chicago, IL: University of Chicago Press, 1980.

———. *Philosophy in the Flesh: The Embodied Mind and Its Challenge to Western Thought*. New York: Basic Books/Prometheus, 1999.

Lederer, Richard. *Word Circus*. Springfield, MA: Merriam-Webster, 1998.

Levin, Samuel R. *The Semantics of Metaphor*. Baltimore, MD: Johns Hopkins University Press, 1977.

Lodwig, Richard R., and Eugene F. Barrett. *Words, Words, Words: Vocabularies and Dictionaries*. Rochelle Park, NJ: Hayden Book Co., 1973.

Meltzer, Tom. *Illustrated Word Smart: A Visual Vocabulary Builder*. New York: Random House, 1999.

Nilsen, Alleen Pace. *Living Language: Reading, Thinking and Writing*. Boston: Allyn and Bacon, 1999.

———. "Of Ladybugs and Billy Goats: What Animal Species Names Tell About Human Perceptions of Gender." *Metaphor and Symbolic Activity* 11.4 (1996): 257-272.

Nilsen, Alleen Pace, and Don L. F. Nilsen. "Language Play in Y2K: Morphology Brought to You by Pokémon." *Voices from the Middle* 7.4 (May 2000): 32-37.

———. "Lessons in the Teaching of Vocabulary from September 11 and Harry Potter." *Journal of Adolescent and Adult Literacy* 46.3 (November, 2002): 2-8.

———. "Metaphor." *Encyclopedia of 20th Century American Humor*. Phoenix, AZ: Oryx Press, 2000. 199-200.

———. "A New Spin on Teaching Vocabulary: A Source-Based Approach." *The Reading Teacher* (February 2003): 436-439.

———. "Vocabulary Development: Teaching vs. Testing." *English Journal* 92-3 (January 2003): 31-37.

Nilsen, Don L. F. "Creativity, Metaphor, and Poetry." *Humor Scholarship: A Research Bibliography*. Westport, CT: Greenwood, 1993 84-92.

———. "The Grounding of Metaphors: An Exercise in Computer-Aided Writing." *Editors' Notes* 4.1 (1985): 16-20.

———. "Live, Dead, and Terminally Ill Metaphors in Computer Terminology." *Educational Technology Magazine* 24.2 (1984): 27-29.

———. "The Nature of Ground in Farfetched Metaphors." *Metaphor and Symbolic Activity*. 1.2 (1986): 127-38.

———. "A Note on the Process of Synesthesia." *Humor Scholarship: A Research Bibliography*. Westport, CT: Greenwood, 1993, 257-258.

Nilsen, Don L. F., and Alleen Pace Nilsen. *Language Play: An Introduction to Linguistics*. Rowley, MA: Newbury House Publishers, 1978.

———. "Out of the Frying Pan and into the Hot Water: How to Mix a Metaphor from Scratch." *Arizona English Bulletin* 23.2 (1981): 1-6.

O'Brien, Conan. "What I'll Miss about Bill Clinton." *Time Magazine* 157.1 (January 9, 2001): 80.

Orgel, Doris. *We Goddesses: Athena, Aphrodite, and Hera*. New York: DK Publishing, 1999.

Osborne, Mary Pope. *Favorite Greek Myths*. New York: Scholastic, 1989.

Panati, Charles. *Extraordinary Origins of Everyday Things*. New York: Harper and Row, 1987.

Parish, Herman. *Amelia Bedelia 4 Mayor*. New York: HarperCollins, 1999.

———. *Bravo, Amelia Bedelia*. New York: HarperCollins, 1997.

———. *Calling Doctor Amelia Bedelia*. New York: Greenwillow/HarperCollins, 2002.

Parish, Peggy. *Amelia Bedelia*. New York: HarperCollins, 1963.

———. *Amelia Bedelia and the Baby*. New York: Avon, 1981.

———. *Amelia Bedelia Goes Camping*. New York: Avon, 1985.

———. *Amelia Bedelia and the Surprise Shower*. New York: HarperCollins, 1966.

———. *Come Back, Amelia Bedelia*. New York: HarperCollins, 1971.

Prelutsky, Jack. *Monday's Troll*. New York: Greenwillow Books, 1996.

Pryle, Marilyn Bogusch. "Peek, Peak, Pique: Using Homophones to Teach Vocabulary (and Spelling!)." *Voices from the Middle* 7.4 (May 2000): 38–43.

Pugh, Sharon L., Jean Wolph Hicks, and Marcia Davis. *Metaphorical Ways of Knowing: The Imaginative Nature of Thought and Expression*. Urbana, IL: National Council of Teachers of English, 1997.

Scarry, Richard. *Best Word Book Ever*. Racine, WI: Western Publishing Company, 1980.

Soukhanov, Anne H. *Word Watch: The Stories Behind the Words of Our Lives*. New York: Henry Holt, 1995.

Stockwell, Robert, and Donka Minkova. *English Words: History and Structure*. New York: Cambridge University Press, 2001.

Terban, Marvin. *Scholastic Dictionary of Idioms, Phrases, Sayings, and Expressions*. New York: Scholastic, 1996.

Walker, Barbara G. *The Woman's Dictionary of Symbols and Sacred Objects*. New York: HarperCollins, 1988.

———. *The Woman's Encyclopedia of Myths and Secrets*. New York: HarperCollins, 1983.

Index

Air, 137, 180
Airplanes, 172, 185–186
Alphabet letters, 54–59, 73
    background reading, 54–55
    notes for eliciting ideas, 55–56
    shapes, 57–58
    shapes vs. initials or rankings, 59
Analogies, 18, 44
Angles, 62
Animals, 16–18, 26–32
    background reading, 16
    crossword puzzle, 31
    features, 26–28, 30
    heads, 29
    metaphorical idioms, 32
    notes for eliciting ideas, 17–18
    shelters, 108
    tails, 29
Apples, 78
Archery, 177
Aster, 136
Attack, 48

Bags, 96, 99, 109
Balls, 175
Bananas, 79
Bands, 201–205
Barges, 174
Baseball, 177
Baskets, 97
Beans, 77
Bears, 26–31
Beds, 107
Beef, 84, 87–89
Bees, 26–31
Bells, 192–193, 195–196
Bi, 68
Bloom, 23–25
Bloomers, 113
Boards, 172
Bobby sox, 114
Body actions, 33–36, 44–51
Body parts, 33–51
Bolts, 156
Bones, 9
Bonnets, 116
Bottles, 98, 99, 109
Bowler hats, 113
Bowls, 103

Boxes, 103, 109
Boxing, 176
Branches, 23, 25
Bread, 80, 87–88
Breezes, 137
Brows, 35
Buds, 23–25
Bugs, 26–31
Bulbs, 17, 25
Builders, 168
Burn, 125, 147–148
Bus, 172
Busman's holiday, 174

Cabins, 104
Cabinets, 101, 109
Cables, 153
Cakes, 81
Call, 200
Cans, 98, 99
Caps, 115–116
Capes, 117–118
Cars, 172
Carpets, 107
Cases, 97, 99
Caves, 104
Ceilings, 105
Centum, 69
Chains, 156–157, 169
Chairs, 107
Channels, 183–184
Char, 128, 146
Check, 178
Cheeks, 35
Cherries, 79
Chisels, 159–160
Circles, 60–61
Circum, 61
Cleaners, 166
Clips, 161–162
Clippers, 159–160
Closets, 105–106
Clothing, 111–125
    background reading, 111
    crossword puzzle, 124
    eponyms, 218–220
    hats, 115–116
    metaphorical idioms, 125
    metaphorical targets, 113–114

    notes for eliciting ideas, 112
    rags to riches, 117–118
    sewing, 119–123
Clouds, 135
Coats, 117–118
Cockpits, 172
Cold, 138
College instructors, notes for, 13–15
Concerts, 202, 204
Conscious action, 50–51
Containers, 93–103, 109
    background reading, 93–94
    crossword puzzle, 109
    food, 102–103
    household, 100–101
    metaphorical sources, 96–99
    notes for eliciting ideas, 94–95
    proverbs, 110
Conveyances, 185–186
Cooked food, 80–82, 86–89
Cookies, 81
Cool, 138
Corn, 77
Cottages, 104
Couches, 107
Crawling, 45
Crossword puzzles, 31, 51, 72, 109, 124, 148,
    169, 189, 205, 221
Crumbs, 81
Cry, 198
Cultivate, 21–22
Cupboards, 101, 109
Curtain, 106
Cutting, 159–160, 169
Cycle, 61

Dec, 69
Deck, 172, 174
Depot, 184
Dirt, 132
Dish, 103, 109
Dog, 16, 26–30
Door, 106
Drapes, 106
Dress, 117–118
Drill, 164, 169
Driver, 181–182
Drum, 202–205
Duo, 68, 72

Ears, 35
Earth, 126–134, 180
  background reading, 127
  geological formations, 129–134
  metaphorical idioms, 150
  minerals, 149
  notes for eliciting ideas, 126–128
Eating, 85–86, 87–89
Eggs, 83
Eliciting ideas, 17–18, 34–36, 55–56, 76,
  94–95, 112, 126–128, 152–153, 173–174,
  194, 210–211
Embroidery, 121, 124
End-of-chapter activities, 32, 52, 73, 91–92,
  110, 125, 149–150, 170, 190–191, 206–207,
  222
Engineer, 181–182
Eos, 215, 221
Eponyms (names), 212–221
  background reading, 208–210
  from mythology, 212–217
  from places, 219–220
  from real people, 218
  notes for eliciting ideas, 210–211
Equipment, 151–164, 169
Eyes, 4

Fables, 91–92, 193, 206–207
Farming, 21–24
Feet, 33, 42–43
Fiddles, 203
Fight, 48, 51
Finding related words, 14–15
  historical relationships, 14–15
  pragmatics, 15
  spelling, 14
  semantics, 14
Fingers, 39–40
Fire, 145–149
  crossword puzzle, 149
fire-related words, 145–148
Fish, 26, 30–31
Flames, 128, 145–146, 148
Floods, 144
Floors, 105
Flutes, 203–205
Fog, 143
Food, 74–92
  background reading, 74–76
  baked, 80–81, 86
  cooked, 82, 86
  eggs, 76, 83
  fables, 91–92
  features, 76
  foreign, 90
  fruits, 77–79
  meat, 84
  menus, 90
  metaphor sources, 85, 89–90
  metaphor targets, 89–90
  milk, 83–84
  notes for eliciting ideas, 76
  proverbs, 91–92
  sandwiches, 74–76, 87–88
  vegetables, 77–79
Flowers, 23–25
Fray, 122, 124
Freeze, 138

Fruits, 77–79
Fruitful, 23–25

Gambling, 177
Games, 171–173, 175–179, 189
Gardens, 21–22
Generative approach, 1
Geological formations, 129–134
  connected, 133–134
  loose, 131–133
  metaphorical sources, 129–130
Gowns, 117–118
Greek gods, 208–217, 221
Ground, 131–132
Gwynne, Fred, 7–8

Hair, 35
Ham, 84, 87–88
Hammers, 152, 154–155, 169
Hands, 1–2, 34, 38–41
Harmony, 202, 205
Harvests, 22
Hats, 115–116
Hatchets, 153
Hazards, 171–172
Heads, 37
Heels, 42–43
Helmsman, 181–182
Hills, 133
Hits, 48, 51
Hold, 161–162
Homonyms, 8
Hoods, 115–116
Hooks, 161–162
Hostile actions, 48–49, 51
Hot, 138
Houses, 104–107
Human bodies, 33–53
  actions, 45–53
    hostile, 48–49
  survival, 50
  analogies, 44
  background reading, 33–34
  body parts, 33–43
  crossword puzzle, 51
  hands, 34, 38–41
  heads, 37
  legs, 42–43
  metaphorical idioms, 53
  notes for eliciting ideas, 34
Hum, 199
Human voice, 198–200
Hunters, 167
Hydro, 142

Ice, 138

Jackets, 118
Jet, 185–186
Jobs, 165–168
  expanded meanings, 166–168
  sources of surnames, 165, 170
Jour, 184
Jumping, 47

Kettles, 103
Keys, 157, 169
Kick, 48

Kitchens, 105–106
Knees, 42–43
Knots, 25, 121–122
Knuckles, 39–40

Laborers, 167–168
Leaves, 25
Legs, 42–44
Letters, 55–59
Lexical extensions, explanation, 4
Lights, 139
Lines, 62–63
Linguistics, 4–5
Loops, 60
Lyres, 204

Manus, 1–2
Meat, 84, 87–89
Mend, 123, 124
Metaphor, explanation, 3–8
Milk, 83–84
Miller, 167
Minerals, 149
Mists, 143
Mono, 67
Moon, 135
Morphemes, 2–5
Morphology, 2–5
Mountains, 133
Mouths, 36
Mushrooms, 25
Music, 192, 198–206
  bands and orchestras, 201
  crossword puzzle, 205
  instrument shapes, 206
Mythology, 208–217, 222
  background reading, 208–210
  crossword puzzle, 221
  eponyms, 212–218
  in *Harry Potter* books, 222
  notes for eliciting ideas, 210–211

Nails, 157, 162–163
Names, 165, 208–221
  eponyms, 208–221
  surnames, 165
Narcissus, 209, 213
Needles, 120, 124
Norse gods, 210–211
Numbers, 64–72
  approximate, 70
  cardinal, 64–65
  crossword puzzle, 72
  foreign number words, 67–68
  ordinal, 65–66
  unusual number words, 71–72

Orchestra, 201–205

Packs (packages), 97, 99, 109
Palms, 34, 40
Pan (bread), 100, 109
Parmesan cheese, 219
Parrish, Peggy, 7
Pasteur, Louis, 218
Patches, 123, 124
Paths, 183–184
Peaks, 134

Pedagogical principles, 9–15
    importance of socialization, 11
    importance of talking, 10
lists of related words, 12
    making connections, 10
    multisensory experiences, 11
    a need for time, 9
Phon, 201, 205
Picks, 151
Pigs, 27–30
Pilots, 172, 181–182
Pins, 119–120, 124
Pipes, 203–204
Place names, 219–220
Plants, 16–25
    actions, 23–25
    background reading, 16
    farming, 21–22
    metaphorical idioms, 32
    notes for eliciting ideas, 17–18
    shapes, 25
    sticks, 19–20
    straws, 17–20
Play, 179, 189
Playing cards, 177
Plows, 21–22
Pools, 144
Porches, 105–106
Ports, 172
Port wine, 219
Potatoes, 78
Pots, 100
Primary grade teachers, 15
Prime, 67–68, 72
Process approach, 1
Prunes, 21–22
Puns, 5–8
Pyr, 147, 148

Quad, 69

Racing, 176
Rags, 117–118
Rain, 143
Rats, 27
Real-world relationships, 2
Reap, 22
Rect, 62
Related words, finding:
    historical relationships, 14–15
    pragmatics, 15
    spelling, 14
    semantics, 14
Rings, 60
Rivets, 161–162
Rivus, 184
Roads, 183
Robes, 117–118
Roman gods, 208–217, 221
Roofs, 105
Rooms, 105–106
Roots, 23–25
Ropes, 161
Round, 60
Rugs, 107
Running, 46–47, 184

Saddles, 153
Sand, 132

Sandwiches, 74, 87–88
Saws, 151, 158
Scissors, 159–160, 169
Scoops, 103
Screams, 198
Screws, 164
Scribes, 166
Scythes, 159
Seams, 122, 124
Sewing, 119–125
Shacks, 104
Shapes, 54–61
    metaphorical idioms, 73
Shards, 159
Shears, 159–160, 169
Shelters, 104–108
    animal, 108
    human, 104–107
Ships, 172, 185–186
Shout, 199
Shovels, 164
Sky, 135–136
Sickles, 159
Simile, explanation, 4–5
Sing, 198–199
Skeletons, 9
Sky, 126, 135–139
Soil, 132
Sonare, 192–193, *see also* Sounds
Sounds, 192–205
    background reading, 192–194
    bells, 192, 193, 195–196
    human voice, 198–200
    notes for eliciting ideas, 194
    whistles, 197
Soup, 82
Source-based approach, 1–5
Spades, 164
Speak, 200
Spikes, 153, 162–163
Sports and games, 171–172, 175–179, 189
    background reading, 171–172
    crossword puzzle, 189
    metaphorical idioms, 173
    metaphorical sources, 175–179
    notes for eliciting ideas, 173–175
Spring, 144
Sprouts, 23
Stagecoaches, 174
Stars, 136
Stella, 136
Steps, 45–46
Stew, 82
Sticks, 19–20, 162–163
Stitches, 120, 124
Stones, 126. 133
Straws, 17–20
Streams, 144
Strikes, 49, 51
String, 161
Stumps, 23–24
Surnames, 165, 218
Swimming, 176

Tables, 107
Tacks, 162–163
Talk, 199
Target shooting, 177
Taxis, 173

Teaching primary-grade children, 15
Teeth, 33
Tele, 187–188
Thread, 112, 121, 124, 161
Thumbs, 39–40
Ties, 161
Tin snips, 159
Toast, 80–81, 87–89
Toes, 42–44
Tones, 200
Tongues, 12
Tools and equipment, 151–170
    background reading, 151–152
    crossword puzzle, 169
    cutters, 159–160
    diggers, 163–164
    fasteners 161–162
    hammers, 152, 154–155
    metaphorical receivers, 154–155, 170
    metaphorical sources, 154–155, 156–158
    notes for eliciting ideas, 152–153
Tracks, 170, 184
Trails, 184
Trains, 172, 185–186
Travel, 171–174, 180–186
    background reading, 171–173
    drivers, 181–182
    conveyances, 185
    notes for eliciting ideas, 173–174
    reading suggestions, 190–191
    roadways, 183–184
    tele, 187–188
Trees, 23–25
Tri, 68, 72
Turnpikes, 183

Uni, 67
Unravel, 123,124

Valleys, 134
Vapor, 142
Vegetables, 77–78, 87–89
Veils, 116

Walking, 46
Walls, 105
Wallflowers, 23–24
Warm, 138
Water
    literal to metaphorical, 140–144
    metaphorical idioms, 150
    water travel, 180
    watered stock, 4, 141
    waves, 127, 141
Ways, 183–184
Weather, 137–138
Weeds, 21–22
Whirl, 142
Whistles, 193, 197
Wind, 137
Windfall, 23–25
Windows, 106
Workshop leaders, 13–15
Wrenches, 158, 169
Wright, 168

Zippers, 112, 119, 124